Essentials of Strategic Management

J. David Hunger
Iowa State University

Thomas L. Wheelen
University of South Florida

▲ ADDISON-WESLEY

An imprint of Addison Wesley Longman, Inc.

Reading, Massachusetts • Menlo Park, California • New York • Harlow, England
Don Mills, Ontario • Sydney • Mexico City • Madrid • Amsterdam

Executive Editor: Michael Payne
Senior Project Editor: Mary Clare McEwing
Managing Editor: James Rigney
Senior Production Supervisor: Loren Hilgenhurst Stevens
Production Services: Nancy Benjamin
Copy Editor: Margaret Hill
Prepress Buying Manager: Sarah McCracken
Art Editor: Susan London-Payne
Text Design: Richard Hollant, Winston Ford Design
Cover Design Supervisor: Meredith Nightingale
Cover Design: Leslie Haimes/Meredith Nightingale
Cover Illustration: Leslie Haimes
Marketing Manager: Mark Thomas Childs
Manufacturing Manager: Hugh J. Crawford
Compositor: Compset, Inc.

Library of Congress Cataloging-in-Publication Data

Hunger, J. David, 1941–
    Essentials of strategic management / J. David Hunger. Thomas L.
Wheelen.
        p.   cm.
    Includes bibliographical references and index.
    ISBN 0-201-42186-0 (pbk.)
    1. Strategic planning.   2. Case method.   I. Wheelen, Thomas L.
II. Title.
HD30.28.H867   1996
658.4'012—dc20   96-18513
                                                                CIP

ISBN 0-201-42186-0
  345678910—MA—999897

DEDICATED TO

Kathy, Richard, Tom

Betty, Kari, Suzi, Lori, Merry, and
Smokey

People are asking us, "Why are textbooks so large and expensive?" Too many of today's textbooks are like 1950s-style automobiles: overweight and loaded down with bells, whistles, and tailfins. Students have complained that the books are now so bulky that they can't easily carry them to classes—so they leave them at home. The costs of the books have been escalating to the point that even used books are now being priced out of many students' reach—so they share them with others or don't even buy them at all!

We wrote this book to provide you with a short, concise explanation of the most important concepts and techniques in strategic management. There is no fluff in this book. *Essentials of Strategic Management* is significantly shorter than our other books, but we have not "dumbed it down" or made it "cutesy." It is a rigorous explanation of many topics and concerns in strategic management. We condensed the content of the field into ten carefully crafted chapters. The key concepts and techniques are here. We cite only enough examples to help you understand the material and we restrict our use of boxed examples to one per chapter. Although the content is based on rigorous research studies, we don't report every study and we don't provide endless footnotes. For those who want more research detail and illustrative examples, please see our other textbook, *Strategic Management*, 5th edition. For a combination of text *and* cases, please see our *Strategic Management and Business Policy*, 5th edition. If you would like to use cases to accompany this *Essentials of Strategic Management*, please consider our *Cases in Strategic Management*, 4th edition.

Features

Essentials of Strategic Management contains the following features:

- *A strategic decision-making model* based on the underlying processes of environmental scanning, strategy formulation, strategy implementation, and evaluation and control is presented in **Chapter 1** and provides an integrating framework for the book.
- Michael Porter's approach to *industry analysis* and *competitive strategy* (plus competitive tactics!) is highlighted in **Chapters 3 and 6**.
- The *resource-based view of the firm* serves in **Chapter 4** as a foundation for organizational analysis.
- *Functional analysis* and *functional strategies* receive major attention in **Chapters 4 and 6**. Sections on research and development and R&D strategies emphasize the importance of technology to strategy and product-market decisions.
- *Strategy implementation* deals not only with organization design and structure, but also with *executive leadership* and succession, *reengineering, total quality management, MBO,* and *action planning* in **Chapters 7 and 8**.
- **Chapter 9** on *evaluation and control* explains the importance of measurement and incentives to organizational performance. *Benchmarking* and *economic value-added measures* are highlighted.

- *International* considerations are included in all chapters and are highlighted in special sections in Chapters **3, 5, 7, and 8.**
- *Environmental scanning and forecasting* is given emphasis equal to industry analysis in **Chapter 3.**
- Suggested *EFAS, IFAS, and SFAS matrixes* in **Chapters 3, 4, and 5** enable the reader to better identify and evaluate strategic factors.
- *Top management* and the *board of directors* are examined in detail in their roles as strategic managers in **Chapter 2.**
- *Social responsibility* is discussed in **Chapter 2** in terms of its importance to strategic decision making.
- Suggestions for in-depth *case analysis* provide a complete listing of financial ratios, recommendations for oral and written analysis, and ideas for further research in **Chapter 10.** The *strategic audit* is proposed as an aid to case analysis. This chapter is most useful for those who wish to supplement this book with cases.
- A boxed *Spotlight on Maytag Corporation* in **every chapter** illustrates chapter concepts and integrates the material.
- **Each chapter** begins and ends with a *brief situation vignette* of an actual company that helps illustrate the material.
- **Each chapter** ends with a list of *key terms* (which are also boldfaced within the text) and a set of discussion questions.

Instructors Manual

An instructors manual has been carefully constructed to accompany this book. It includes a series of multiple choice questions and answers to discussion questions plus a set of additional discussion/essay questions to use in exams.

Acknowledgments

We are grateful to the people who reviewed this book for their constructive criticism and suggestions. Their thought and effort have resulted in a book that is superior to the original manuscript. Our thanks go to Mary Clare McEwing and Michael Payne of Addison-Wesley Publishing Company for their help in the development of this book. Without their support and encouragement, this book would never have been written. We are very grateful to Nancy Benjamin for her patience, expertise, and even disposition during the copyediting and production process. We also thank Mei Xue and Lori Hunger for their help in preparing the index.

In addition, we express our appreciation to Dr. Ben Allen, Dean, and Dr. Jim Werbel, Management Department Chair, of Iowa State University for their support of this endeavor. Both of us acknowledge our debt to Dr. William Shenkir and Dr. Frank Kaulback, former Deans of the McIntire School of Commerce of the University of Virginia, for the provision of a work climate that was most supportive of our work in strategic management.

Finally, to the many strategy/policy instructors and students who have moaned to us about the increasing size and cost of textbooks: We have tried to respond to your concerns as best we could by providing a comprehensive yet usable text that is half the size and cost of other books on the market. Instead of the usual five-course meal (complete with heartburn), we are offering you "lean cuisine." This book should taste good with fewer empty calories. Enjoy!

J.D.H.   Ames, Iowa
T.L.W.   Tampa, Florida

1

Basic Concepts of
Strategic Management

During the 1950s and 1960s, no bicycle manufacturer was as successful in the United States as Schwinn Bicycle Company. Schwinn bikes dominated the world of paper routes and after-school street races. "We used to ride Schwinns anywhere and everywhere," remembered one ex-rider wistfully. "We rode them with kids from the neighborhood to school and to baseball practice, and when they got old, we'd repaint them."

Founded in 1895 by the German immigrant Ignaz Schwinn, the firm led the U.S. bicycle market for many years. In the 1960s, one out of every four bikes sold in the United States was a Schwinn. Toward the end of the 1980s, however, everything seemed to fall apart. Sales dropped from 1 million bikes in 1987 to 500,000 in 1991. Market share declined from 10% in 1983 to less than 4% in 1992. "Schwinn used to be the only bike I'd look at," offered one biking enthusiast. "[Now] I don't even know where a Schwinn bike store is."

Between 1989 and 1992, the company lost around $50 million. Top management looked for an outside partner to save the company, but President Edward Schwinn, great-grandson of the founder, was reluctant to give up control. By 1992, the Schwinn Bicycle Company filed for Chapter 11 bankruptcy. The end was in sight for one of the most renowned brand names in the United States.

What went wrong? How could such a successful company fall on such hard times? "Schwinn never spent the money on research and development or planned for the long-term. . . . And they never took their competition seriously," explained one custom bicycle dealer. "Except for their name, they really have nothing to sell."[1] Once, when asked about the company's competition, Schwinn's management was reported to have responded, "We don't have competition. We're Schwinn."[2]

These comments suggest why the managers of today's business corporations must manage firms strategically. They cannot make decisions based on long-standing rules, historical policies, or simple extrapolations of current trends. Instead, they must look to the future as they plan organizationwide objectives, initiate strategy, and set policies. They must rise above their training and experience in such functional and operational areas as accounting, marketing, production, or finance, and grasp the overall picture. They must be willing to ask **three key strategic questions:**

1. *Where is the organization now? (Not where do we hope it is!)*
2. *If no changes are made, where will the organization be in one year? two years? five years? ten years? Are the answers acceptable?*
3. *If the answers are not acceptable, what specific actions should management undertake? What risks and payoffs are involved?*

In the 1960s and 1970s, Schwinn sold quality bicycles to a market composed mostly of school-age children. Preferring to sell its products through dealers, the company allowed Huffy and Murray to take over the low-end, mass-merchandise market (in which over 70% of today's bikes are now sold). Management seemed unaware of changing consumer tastes and did not take aggressive new rivals seriously. Newcomers Trek USA and Specialized Bicycle Components attracted biking enthusiasts with lighter, sleeker models in the early 1980s. Considering mountain bikes to be just a temporary fad, management continued to crank out Schwinn's durable, but bulky, standbys. Trying to reduce costs, Schwinn began making its bikes overseas using cheaper foreign labor. This shift led to quality problems that began to erode the brand's image. By the end of the 1980s, management's inability to manage the company strategically resulted in a crisis. Schwinn's management had failed to realize that environmental changes had altered the rules for success. A poor job of environmental scanning had resulted in poor strategic planning; poor strategic planning had led to ineffective strategic management.

1.1 The Study of Strategic Management

Strategic management is that set of managerial decisions and actions that determines the long-run performance of a corporation. It includes environmental scanning (both external and internal), strategy formulation (strategic or long-range planning), strategy implementation, and evaluation and control. The study of strategic management therefore emphasizes the monitoring and evaluating of external opportunities and threats in light of a corporation's strengths and weaknesses. Originally called business policy, strategic management incorporates such topics as long-range planning and strategy. **Business policy,** in contrast, has a general management orientation and tends primarily to look inward with its concern for properly integrating the corporation's many functional activities. *Strategic management, as a field of study, incorporates the integrative concerns of business policy with a heavier environmental and strategic emphasis.* Therefore, *strategic* *management* has tended to replace *business policy* as the preferred name of the field of study.

How Has Strategic Management Evolved?

Many of the concepts and techniques dealing with long-range (now called strategic) planning and strategic management have been developed and used successfully by business corporations such as General Electric and the Boston Consulting Group. Nevertheless, not all organizations use these tools or even attempt to manage strategically. Many are able to succeed for a while with unstated objectives and intuitive strategies. American Hospital Supply Corporation (AHS) was one such organization until Karl Bays became chief executive and introduced strategic planning to a sales-dominated management. Previously, the company's idea of long-range planning was "Maybe in December we should look at next year's budget," recalled a former AHS executive.[3]

From his extensive work in this field, Bruce Henderson of the Boston Consulting Group concluded that intuitive strategies cannot be continued successfully if (1) the corporation becomes large, (2) the layers of management increase, or (3) the environment changes substantially. The increasing risks of error, costly mistakes, and even economic ruin are causing today's professional managers to take strategic management seriously in order to keep their company competitive in an increasingly volatile environment. As top managers attempt to better deal with their changing world, strategic management within a firm generally evolves through four sequential phases:

> *Phase 1. Basic financial planning:* Seeking better operational control by trying to meet budgets.
>
> *Phase 2. Forecast-based planning:* Seeking more effective planning for growth by trying to predict the future beyond the next year.
>
> *Phase 3. Externally oriented planning (strategic planning):* Seeking increased responsiveness to markets and competition by trying to think strategically.
>
> *Phase 4. Strategic management:* Seeking a competitive advantage and a successful future by managing all resources.[4]

Phase 4 in the evolution of strategic management includes a consideration of strategy implementation and evaluation and control, in addition to Phase 3's emphasis on strategic planning.

General Electric, one of the pioneers of strategic planning, led the transition from strategic planning to strategic management during the 1980s. By the 1990s, most corporations around the world had also begun the conversion to strategic management.

What Is the Impact of Strategic Management on Performance?

Research has revealed that organizations that engage in strategic management generally outperform those that do not. The attainment of an appropriate match or "fit" between an organization's environment and its strategy, structure, and processes has positive effects on the organization's performance. For example, a study of the impact of deregulation on U.S. railroads found that railroads that changed their strategy as their environment changed outperformed those that did not change their strategies.[5]

Nevertheless, to be effective, strategic management need not always be a formal process. Studies of the planning practices of actual organizations suggest that the real value of strategic planning may be more in the future orientation of the planning process itself than in any resulting written strategic plan. Small companies, in particular, may plan informally and irregularly. The president and a handful of top managers might get together casually to resolve strategic issues and plan their next steps.

In large, multidivisional corporations, however, strategic planning can become complex and time consuming. It often takes slightly more than 12 months for a large company to move from situation assessment to a final decision agreement. Because a strategic decision affects a relatively large number of people, a large firm needs a formalized, more sophisticated system to ensure that strategic planning leads to successful performance. Otherwise, top management becomes isolated from developments in the divisions and lower level managers lose sight of the corporate mission.

1.2 ▶ Initiation of Strategy: Triggering Events

After much research, Henry Mintzberg discovered that strategy formulation is typically not a regular, continuous process: "It is most often an irregular, discontinuous process, proceeding in fits and starts. There are periods of stability in strategy development, but also there are periods of flux, of groping, of piecemeal change, and of global change."[6] This view of strategy formulation as an irregular process reflects the human tendency to continue on a particular course of action until something goes wrong or a person is forced to question his or her actions. This period of "strategic drift" may simply be a result of the organization's inertia, or it may reflect management's belief that the current strategy is still appropriate and needs only some fine-tuning. Most large organizations tend to follow a particular strategic orientation for about 15 to 20 years before they make a significant change in direction. After this rather long period of fine-tuning an existing strategy, some sort of shock to the system is needed to motivate management to seriously reassess the corporation's situation.

A **triggering event** is something that stimulates a change in strategy. Some of the possible triggering events are:

- **New CEO.** By asking a series of embarrassing questions, the new CEO cuts through the veil of complacency and forces people to question the very reason for the corporation's existence.
- **Intervention by an external institution.** The firm's bank suddenly refuses to agree to a new loan or suddenly calls for payment in full on an old one.

- **Threat of a change in ownership.** Another firm may initiate a takeover by buying the company's common stock.
- **Management's recognition of a performance gap.** A performance gap exists when performance does not meet expectations. Sales and profits either are no longer increasing or may even be falling.

Maytag Corporation is an example of one company in which a triggering event forced management to radically rethink what it was doing. See the *Company Spotlight on Maytag Corporation* feature to see how specific questions from the CEO stimulated a change in strategy.

COMPANY SPOTLIGHT

MAYTAG Corporation

Strategic Management Process

Maytag Corporation is a successful full-line manufacturer of major home appliances. Beginning with its very successful high-quality washers and dryers, it branched out through acquisitions into cooking appliances (Magic Chef, Hardwick, and Jenn-Air), refrigerators (Admiral), and vacuum cleaners (Hoover). Until 1978, however, the corporation (then known simply as Maytag Company) was strictly a laundry appliances manufacturer. Its only experience with any sort of strategic planning was in preparing the next year's budget!

In 1978, Daniel Krumm, Maytag's CEO, asked Leonard Hadley (at that time the company's Assistant Controller in charge of preparing the annual budget) and two other managers (from manufacturing and marketing) to serve as a strategic planning task force. Krumm posed to these three people the question: *"If we keep doing what we're now doing, what will the Maytag Company look like in five years?"* The question was a challenge to answer, especially considering that the company had never done financial modeling and none of the three knew much about strategic planning. Hadley worked with a programmer in his MIS section to develop "what if" scenarios. The task force presented its conclusion to the board of directors: A large part of Maytag's profits (the company at that time had the best profit margin in the industry) was coming from products and services with no future: repair parts, portable washers and dryers, and wringer washing machines.

This report triggered Maytag's interest in strategic change. After engaging in a series of acquisitions to broaden its product line, the corporation was poised to become a global power in the major home appliance industry. Its 1988 purchase of Hoover gave Maytag not only a firm with worldwide strength in floor-care appliances, but also Hoover's strong laundry, cooking, and refrigeration appliance business in the United Kingdom and Australia. The trend toward the unification of Europe and rapid economic development of the Far East meant that Maytag could no longer survive simply as a specialty appliance manufacturer serving only North America.

1.3 Basic Model of Strategic Management

Strategic management consists of four basic elements: (1) **environmental scanning,** (2) **strategy formulation,** (3) **strategy implementation,** and (4) **evaluation and control.** Figure 1.1 shows how these four elements interact. Management scans both the external environment for opportunities and threats and the internal environment for strengths and weaknesses. The factors that are most important to the corporation's future are called **strategic factors** and are summarized by the acronym SWOT, or Strengths, Weaknesses, Opportunities, and Threats.

What Is Environmental Scanning?

Environmental scanning is the monitoring, evaluating, and disseminating of information from the external and internal environments to key people within the corporation. The **external environment** consists of variables (**O**pportunities and **T**hreats) that are outside the organization and not typically within the short-run control of top management. These variables form the context within which the corporation exists. They may be general forces and trends within the overall *societal* environment or specific factors that operate within an organization's specific *task* environment—often called its *industry*. (*These external variables are defined and discussed in more detail in Chapter 3.*)

The **internal environment** of a corporation consists of variables (**S**trengths and **W**eaknesses) that are within the organization itself and are not usually within the short-run control of top management. These variables form the context in which work is done. They include the corporation's *structure, culture, and resources.* (*These internal variables are defined and discussed in more detail in Chapter 4.*)

What Is Strategy Formulation?

Strategy formulation is the development of long-range plans for the effective management of environmental opportunities and threats, in light of corporate strengths and weaknesses. It includes defining the corporate *mission*, specifying achievable *objectives*, developing *strategies*, and setting *policy* guidelines.

FIGURE 1.1   **Basic Elements of the Strategic Management Process**

What Is a Mission?

A organization's **mission** is its purpose, or the reason for its existence. It tells what it is providing to society—either a service like housecleaning or a product like automobiles. A well-conceived mission statement defines the fundamental, unique purpose that sets a company apart from other firms of its type and identifies the scope of the company's operations in terms of products (including services) offered and markets served. It puts into words not only what the company is now, but what it wants to become—management's *strategic vision* of the firm's future. It promotes a sense of shared expectations in employees and communicates a public image to important stakeholder groups in the company's task environment. *It tells who we are and what we do.*

One example of a mission statement is that by Maytag Corporation:

> To improve the quality of home life by designing, building, marketing, and servicing the best appliances in the world.

A mission may be defined narrowly or broadly. One example of a **broad mission statement** is that used by a number of corporations: *Serve the best interests of shareowners, customers, and employees.* A broadly defined mission statement such as this keeps the company from restricting itself to one field or product line, but it fails to clearly identify either what it makes or which product/market it plans to emphasize. Because this broad statement is so general, a **narrow mission statement**, such as Maytag's statement emphasizing its appliances, is more useful. A narrow mission very clearly states the organization's primary business, but it may limit the scope of the firm's activities in terms of product or service offered, the technology used, and the market served.

What Are Objectives?

Objectives are the end results of planned activity. They state *what* is to be accomplished by *when* and should be *quantified* if possible. The achievement of corporate objectives should result in the fulfillment of the corporation's mission. Maytag Corporation, for example, could have established the following objectives:

1. To increase profitability.
2. To be a major competitor in Europe and Asia by the end of the decade.
3. To grow the North American appliance business and become the third largest appliance manufacturer (in unit sales) in North America by the end of the decade.

The term *goal* is often confused with *objective*. In contrast to an objective, a **goal** is an open-ended statement of what one wishes to accomplish with no quantification of what is to be achieved and no timeframe for completion. For example, Maytag Corporation's first statement of "increased profitability" is really a goal because it does not state how much profit it wishes to make the next year.

Some of the areas in which a corporation might establish its goals and objectives are:

- Profitability (net profits)
- Efficiency (low costs, etc.)
- Growth (increase in total assets, sales, etc.)
- Stockholder wealth (dividends plus stock price appreciation)
- Utilization of resources (ROE or ROI)
- Reputation (being considered a "top" firm)
- Contributions to employees (employment security, wages)
- Contributions to society (taxes paid, participation in charities, providing a needed product or service)
- Market leadership (market share)
- Technological leadership (innovations, creativity)
- Survival (avoiding bankruptcy)
- Personal needs of top management (using the firm for personal purposes, such as providing jobs for relatives)

What Are Strategies?

A **strategy** of a corporation forms a comprehensive master plan stating how the corporation will achieve its mission and objectives. It maximizes competitive advantage and minimizes competitive disadvantage. For example, Maytag Corporation planned to achieve its objectives through the following corporate-level growth strategies:

1. Expand in those major home appliance product lines and geographic areas, such as Europe and Asia, where the corporation is not yet well represented, through external acquisitions or joint ventures. (Tied to objective 2.)
2. Improve the efficiency and quality of acquired companies and use one business unit's expertise in one area to introduce quality products to a business unit in another area. (Tied to objectives 1 and 3.)

Just as many firms often have no formally stated objectives, many CEOs have unstated, incremental, or intuitive strategies that have never been articulated or analyzed. Often the only way to spot the implicit strategies of a corporation is to look not at what management says, but at what it does. Implicit strategies can be derived from corporation policies, programs approved (and disapproved), and authorized budgets. Programs and divisions favored by budget increases and staffed by managers who are considered to be on the fast promotion track reveal where the corporation is putting its money and its energy.

What Are Policies?

A **policy** is a *broad guideline* for decision making that serves to link the formulation of strategy with its implementation. Maytag Corporation uses a number of policies to make sure that employees throughout the firm make decisions and take actions that support the corporation's mission, objectives, and strategies. Some of these policies are the following:

1. No cost reduction proposal will be approved if it reduces product quality in any way.
2. Every product, from the least expensive to the highest priced, should be superior to the competition in overall quality and performance.
3. The corporation must not emphasize market share at the expense of profitability.
4. Business units must be managed for synergies, while simultaneously allowing the specialized expertise among those units to flourish.

Policies like these provide clear guidance to managers throughout the organization. *(Strategy formulation is discussed in greater detail in Chapters 5 and 6.)*

What Is Strategy Implementation?

Strategy implementation is the process by which strategies and policies are put into action through the development of *programs*, *budgets*, and *procedures*. This process might involve changes within the overall culture, structure, and/or management system of the entire organization. Except when such drastic corporate-wide changes are needed, however, middle and lower level managers typically implement strategy, with review by top management. Sometimes referred to as operational planning, strategy implementation often involves day-to-day decisions in resource allocation.

What Are Programs?

A **program** is a statement of the activities or steps needed to accomplish a single-use plan. It makes the strategy action oriented. It may involve restructuring the corporation, changing the company's internal culture, or beginning a new research effort. To implement its strategies, Maytag Corporation might develop the following programs (each program would require a series of steps):

1. Work with Bosch-Siemens to develop joint marketing and supplier agreements to reduce costs and to increase sales of Hoover major home appliances in Europe.
2. Initiate a program to analyze and develop the Asian market—growing probably through current distributors and licensees and possibly through a joint venture partner.
3. Develop new major home appliances for continental Europe.
4. Develop television advertising for Jenn-Air and Magic Chef to ensure distribution of these brands in all "power dealers."
5. Develop plans to eventually consolidate into two large, modern, dedicated plants the manufacturer of washing machines and clothes dryers currently being done separately by each of the U.S. business units.

What Are Budgets Used For?

A **budget** is a statement of a corporation's programs in dollar terms. Used in planning and control, it lists the detailed cost of each program. Many corporations demand a certain percentage return on investment, often called a *hurdle rate*, before management will approve a new program. This is done to ensure that the new program will significantly add to the corporation's profit performance and thus build stockholder value. The budget thus not only serves as a detailed plan of the new strategy in action, it also specifies through pro-forma financial statements the expected impact on the firm's future financial situation. For example, Maytag Corporation might establish a budget of $500,000 to develop a new advertising campaign for the Jenn-Air and Magic Chef brands (program 4 in the preceding list).

What Are Procedures?

Procedures, sometimes termed Standard Operating Procedures (SOP), are a system of sequential steps or techniques that describe in detail how a particular task or job is to be done. They typically detail the various activities that must be carried out for completion of the corporation's program. Some of the procedures that Maytag Corporation might generate are as follows:

1. Develop procedures for joint purchasing and the possible joint marketing of Bosch-Siemens with Hoover major home appliances in Europe.
2. Coordinate the marketing, manufacturing, and purchasing activities of the business units through corporate-wide planning committees chaired by representatives from the corporate planning staff.
3. Research and development activities for each major product line are to take place in the business unit where they are housed but in coordination with experts specialized in that area from other parts of the corporation. For example, because Hoover is the corporation expert in front-loading washers, other units wishing to produce a front-loader should call on Hoover for assistance in developing it.
4. Consolidate all advertising under one agency but, for each brand category, establish internal advertising directors who will interact with each other to ensure that the advertising and promotions among the various brands achieve their objectives but do not clash.

(Strategy implementation is discussed in more detail in Chapters 7 and 8.)

What Is Evaluation and Control?

Evaluation and control is the process by which corporate activities and performance results are monitored so that actual performance can be compared with desired performance. Managers at all levels use the resulting information to take corrective action and resolve problems. Although evaluation and control is the final major element of strategic management, it also can pinpoint weaknesses in previously implemented strategic plans and thus stimulate the entire process to begin again.

For evaluation and control to be effective, managers must obtain clear, prompt, and unbiased information from the people below them in the corporation's hierarchy. Using this information, managers compare what is actually happening with what was originally planned in the formulation stage.

For example, Maytag Corporation might monitor and evaluate its success in achieving its objectives as follows:

1. Require the heads of all business units to provide monthly status reports on sales and costs by product line plus any trends in expenses to the CEO and VP of Finance.
2. Require the heads of all business units to provide annual reports giving operating revenues, costs, and expenses as well as identifiable assets in dollars, plus property additions and deletions to the VP of Finance.
3. Require the heads of all business units to provide quarterly assessments of competitive activity and overall trends affecting each of their product lines to the VP of Marketing.
4. Require the heads of all business units to inform the CEO and VP of Finance before they proceed on any financially risky plan.

The evaluation and control of performance completes the strategic management model. Based on performance results, management may need to adjust its strategy formulation, implementation, or both. *(Evaluation and control is discussed in more detail in Chapter 9.)*

1.4   Strategic Decision Making

The distinguishing characteristic of strategic management is its emphasis on strategic decision making. As organizations grow larger and more complex with more uncertain environments, decisions become increasingly complicated and difficult to make. This book proposes a strategic decision making framework that can help people make these types of decisions.

What Makes a Decision Strategic?

Unlike many other decisions, **strategic decisions** deal with the long-run future of the entire organization and have three characteristics:

1. **Rare:** Strategic decisions are unusual and typically have no precedent to follow.
2. **Consequential:** Strategic decisions commit substantial resources and demand a great deal of commitment.
3. **Directive:** Strategic decisions set precedents for lesser decisions and future actions throughout the organization.[7]

What Are Mintzberg's Modes of Strategic Decision Making?

Some strategic decisions are made in a flash by one person (often an entrepreneur or a powerful chief executive officer) who has a brilliant insight and is quickly able to convince others to follow this idea. Other strategic decisions seem to develop out of a series of small incremental choices that over time push the organization more in one direction than another. According to Henry Mintzberg, the most typical approaches or modes of strategic decision making are entrepreneurial, adaptive, and planning:

- **Entrepreneurial mode.** In this mode of strategic decision making, the strategy is made by one powerful individual. The focus is on opportunities, and problems are secondary. Strategy is guided by the founder's own vision of direction and is exemplified by large, bold decisions. The dominant goal is growth of the corporation. Bill Gates, founder and Chairman of Microsoft Corporation, embodies this mode of strategic decision making. The company reflects his vision of the personal computer industry. Although Microsoft's clear mission—competitiveness, tenacity, and technological self-confidence which emanate from Gates—are certainly advantages of the entrepreneurial mode, its tendency to introduce products before they are ready is a significant disadvantage.
- **Adaptive mode.** Sometimes referred to as "muddling through," this decision-making mode is characterized by reactive solutions to existing problems, rather than a proactive search for new opportunities. Much bargaining goes on concerning priorities of objectives. Strategy is fragmented and is developed to move the corporation forward in incremental steps. This mode is typical of most universities, many large hospitals, a large number of governmental agencies, and a surprising number of large corporations.
- **Planning mode.** This mode of strategic decision making involves the systematic gathering of appropriate information for situation analysis, the generation of feasible alternative strategies, and the rational selection of the most appropriate strategy. This mode includes both the *proactive* search for new opportunities and the *reactive* solution of existing problems. Maytag Corporation uses the planning mode. After realizing how the major home appliance industry was changing in the U.S. and throughout the world, Maytag's top management deliberately chose to transform the company from a domestic high-quality niche producer of laundry appliances to a full-line global competitor.[8]

In some instances, a corporation might follow a fourth approach called **logical incrementalism,** which is a synthesis of the planning, adaptive, and to a lesser extent the entrepreneurial modes of strategic decision making. As described by J. B. Quinn, top management might have a reasonably clear idea of the corporation's mission and objectives, but, in its development of strategies, it chooses to use "an interactive process in which the organization probes the future, experiments and learns from a series of partial (incremental) commitments rather than through global formulations of total strategies."[9] This approach appears to be useful when the environment is changing rapidly and when it is important to build consensus and develop needed resources before committing the entire corporation to a specific strategy.

How Can Managers Make Better Strategic Decisions?

Good arguments can be made for using either the entrepreneurial or adaptive modes (or logical incrementalism) in certain situations. This book proposes, however, that in most situations the planning mode, which includes the basic elements of the strategic management process, is a more rational and thus better way of making strategic decisions. The planning mode is more analytical and less political than are the other modes. This approach has been used successfully by corporations like Warner-Lambert, Dayton Hudson, Avon Products, Bechtel Group, Inc., and Taisei Corporation. To improve the making of strategic decisions, we therefore propose the following eight-step **strategic decision making process** (which is also illustrated in Figure 1.2):

1. **Evaluate current performance results** in terms of (a) return on investment, profitability, and so forth, and (b) the current mission, objectives, strategies, and policies.
2. **Examine and evaluate strategic managers**, specifically the board of directors and top management.
3. **Scan the external environment** to locate strategic factors that pose Opportunities and Threats.
4. **Scan the internal corporate environment** to determine strategic factors that are Strengths and Weaknesses.
5. **Analyze strategic (SWOT) factors** to (a) pinpoint problem areas, and (b) review and revise the corporate mission and objectives as necessary.
6. **Generate, evaluate, and select the best alternative strategy** in light of the analysis conducted in Step 5.
7. **Implement** selected strategies via programs, budgets, and procedures.
8. **Evaluate** implemented strategies via feedback systems, and the control of activities to ensure their minimum deviation from plans.

1.5 Hierarchy of Strategy

A **hierarchy of strategy** is the grouping of strategy categories by level in the organization. The typical large, multidivisional business firm has three levels of strategy beginning at the top of the organization: corporate, business, and functional.

Corporate strategy describes a company's overall direction in terms of its general attitude toward growth and the management of its various businesses and product lines to achieve a balanced portfolio of products and services. Beyond this, it is (a) the pattern of decisions regarding the types of businesses in which a firm should be involved, (b) the flow of financial and other resources to and from its divisions, and (c) the relationship of the corporation to key groups in its environment. Corporate strategy may be one of *stability*, *growth*, or *retrenchment*. *(These strategies are defined and discussed in Chapter 5.)*

Business strategy, also called **competitive strategy**, usually occurs at the divisional level and emphasizes improvement of the competitive position of a

FIGURE
1.2

Strategic Decision-Making Process

3(a)

Scan
External
Environment:
• Societal
• Task

3(b)

Select
Strategic
Factors:
• Opportun-
  ities
• Threats

1(a)

Evaluate
Current
Performance
Results

1(b)

Examine and
Evaluate the
Current:
• Mission
• Objectives
• Strategies
• Policies

2

Review
Strategic
Managers:
• Board of
  Directors
• Top Man-
  agement

5(a)

Analyze
Strategic
Factors
(SWOT)
in Light of
Current
Situation

4(a)

Scan
Internal
Environment:
• Structure
• Culture
• Resources

4(b)

Select
Strategic
Factors:
• Strengths
• Weak-
  nesses

**Strategy
Formulation:
Steps 1 — 6**

Source: T. L. Wheelen and J. D. Hunger, "Strategic Decision-Making Process." Copyright © 1994 by Wheelen and Hunger Associates. Reprinted by permission.

corporation's products or services in the specific industry or market segment served by that division. A division's business/competitive strategy probably would stress the increasing of its profit margin in the production and sales of its products and services. Business/competitive strategies also should integrate various functional activities so that divisional objectives are achieved. Business/competitive strategy may be one of *overall cost leadership* or *differentiation*. *(These strategies are defined and discussed in Chapter 6.)*

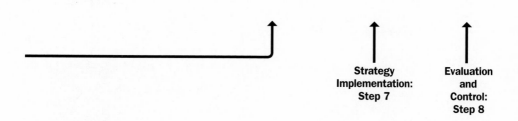

Functional strategy is concerned primarily with maximizing resource productivity. Within the constraints of the corporate and business strategies around them, functional departments develop strategies in which their various activities and competencies are pulled together for the improvement of performance. Examples of R&D functional strategies are *technological followership* (imitate the products of other companies) and *technological leadership* (pioneer an innovation). *(These strategies are defined and discussed in Chapter 6.)*

The three levels of strategy—corporate, business, and functional—form a hierarchy of strategy within a large corporation. They interact closely and must be well integrated if the total corporation is to be successful. The model presented earlier in Figure 1.1 reflects the strategic management process at each level within an organization. As depicted in Figure 1.3, each level of strategy forms the strategic environment of the next level in the corporation. A division's external environment, for example, includes not only those task and societal variables of special importance to the division, but also the mission, objectives, strategies, and policies of corporate headquarters. Similarly both corporate and divisional constraints form a large part of the external environment of a functional department. Therefore, the strategic plan for each lower level is constrained by the strategic plan(s) of the next higher level(s).

F. A. Maljers, Chairman of the Board of Unilever, points out how this hierarchy of strategy must be integrated if the corporation is to be managed successfully:

> If a global company is to function successfully, strategies at different levels need to interrelate. The strategy at corporate level must build upon the strategies at lower levels in the hierarchy. However, at the same time, all parts of the business have to work to accommodate the overriding corporate goals.[10]

FIGURE 1.3   Hierarchy of Strategy*

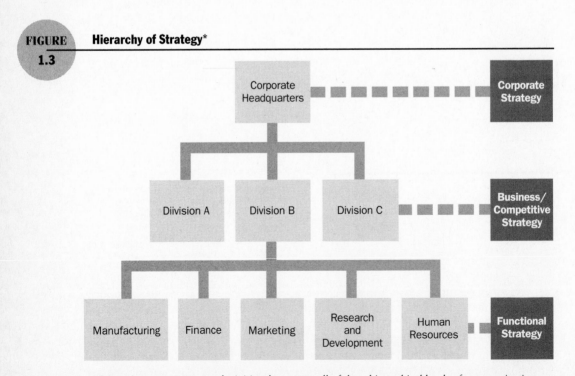

*Strategic management may be initiated at any or all of these hierarchical levels of an organization.

In Conclusion . . .

Schwinn is back! In January 1993, a group of investors acquired Schwinn for $43 million. They immediately invested $7 million more into a new downsized bicycle and moved the company from Chicago to Boulder, Colorado. Schwinn's new slogan was "Established 1895. Re-established 1994." To attract bike enthusiasts, Schwinn doubled its advertising budget to $10 million and sponsored a three-member professional mountain-bike team that placed in the top 15 among 74 racers at the World Cup in Vail, Colorado, in the summer of 1993. "We're telling the world we've reestablished Schwinn," announced Ralph Murray, President and CEO.[11]

Discussion Questions

1. Why has strategic management become so important to today's corporations?
2. How does strategic management typically evolve in a corporation?
3. What information is needed for the proper formulation of strategy?
4. Why are strategic decisions different from other kinds of decisions?
5. When is the planning mode of strategic decision making superior to the entrepreneurial and adaptive modes?

Key Terms

strategic management
business policy
triggering event
strategic factors
SWOT
environmental scanning
external environment
internal environment
strategy formulation
mission
goals and objectives
strategy
policy
strategy implementation

program
budget
procedures
evaluation and control
strategic decisions
entrepreneurial mode
adaptive mode
planning mode
logical incrementalism
strategic decision-making process
hierarchy of strategy
corporate strategy
business/competitive strategy
functional strategy

2

Strategic Decision Makers and Social Responsibility

At one time, the Eastman Kodak Company had been one of the most respected companies in the United States and perhaps the world. It was known for its excellent product quality and reliability. From 1983 to 1993, the company fell, however, from the top 10% to the bottom 18% of admired companies. Industry analysts portrayed the firm as bloated, slow-moving, myopic, and incapable of dealing effectively with its falling share of the photographic film market. Top management made strategic decisions based on protecting current products instead of looking to future ones. For example, even though Kodak had been one of the first companies to develop a camcorder, management decided not to introduce it because it was costly and might detract from the current sales of its amateur film products. Profits were consistently below expectations. The company incurred billions of dollars in repeated "one-time" charges as it undertook incremental efforts to streamline and improve its performance.

Kodak's board of directors was extremely concerned with the inability of Chief Executive Officer Kay Whitmore to turn the company around. Whitmore had joined Kodak in 1957 as an engineer and epitomized the company's cautious home-grown management. On August 6, 1993, Kodak's board of directors, led by a group of outside directors, fired Whitmore. Instead of looking internally for a replacement, the board offered the CEO position to George Fisher, then Chairman and CEO of Motorola, Inc. Motorola had long been regarded as a well-managed company, known for its dedication to hard work and quality. The board expected Fisher to deliver fast and deep cost cuts. Just four months later, however, Fisher stated that cost-cutting alone would not be the answer. He proposed to commit the entire company to imaging opportunities and to divest non-core businesses.[1]

This example illustrates the impact of top management and the board of directors on a firm's performance. Kodak's top managers had traditionally been promoted from within. They became so dedicated to the company's past in chemical imaging that they were unable to perceive a future in electronic imaging. As strategic managers, top management had failed to adjust to a changing environment. Although slow to react, the board of directors finally moved to bring in some new blood. Would this be enough to save Kodak and return it to its past position of industry dominance?

Strategic decision makers are the people in a corporation who are directly involved in the strategic management process. They are the strategic managers who (with some assistance from staff) scan the internal and external environments; formulate and implement objectives, strategies, and policies; and evaluate and control the results. The board of directors and top management are directly responsible for this process. The chief executive officer (CEO), the chief operations officer (COO) or president, the executive vice-president(s), and the vice-presidents in charge of operating divisions and functional areas typically form the top management group. Traditionally boards of directors have engaged in strategic management only to the extent that they passively approved proposals from top management and hired and fired their CEOs. Their role, however, is changing dramatically. The strategic management process, therefore, is also changing.

2.1   Corporate Board of Directors

Over the past decade, stockholders and various interest groups have seriously questioned the role of the board of directors in corporations. They are concerned that outside board members often lack sufficient knowledge, involvement, and enthusiasm to adequately provide guidance to top management. For example, when officials of the California Public Employees' Retirement System—a key stockholder group—criticized IBM's board of directors for not doing more to prevent the company's recent nosedive in earnings, the four outside members of the board's executive committee admitted that they did not know enough about the company's business to properly evaluate management. Like IBM's top management, they had missed the trend away from mainframe computers to personal computers. Board members actually admitted in the meeting that none of them felt comfortable using a personal computer. According to one director, "Not one of us has a PC in our home or office."[2]

The general public has not only become more aware and more critical of many boards' apparent lack of responsibility for corporate activities, it has begun to push government to demand accountability. As a result, the board as a rubber stamp of the CEO or as a bastion of the "old boy" selection system is being replaced by more active, more professional boards.

What Are the Responsibilities of the Board?

Laws and standards defining the responsibilities of boards of directors vary from country to country. For example, board members in Ontario, Canada, face more than 100 provincial and federal laws governing director liability. The United States, however, has no clear national standards or federal laws. Specific requirements of directors vary, depending on the state in which the corporate charter is issued. There is, nevertheless, a developing worldwide consensus concerning the major responsibilities of a board. Interviews with 200 directors from eight countries (Canada, Finland, France, Germany, the Netherlands, Switzerland, the United Kingdom, and Venezuela) revealed strong agreement on the following five **board of director responsibilities** listed in order of importance:

1. Setting corporate strategy, overall direction, mission or vision.
2. Succession—hiring and firing the CEO and top management.
3. Controlling, monitoring, or supervising top management.
4. Reviewing and approving the use of resources.
5. Caring for stockholder interests.[3]

Directors in the United States must make certain, in addition to the duties just listed, that the corporation is managed in accordance with the laws of the state in which it is incorporated. They must also ensure management's adherence to laws and regulations such as those dealing with the issuance of securities, insider trading, and other conflict-of-interest situations. They must also be aware of the needs and demands of constituent groups so that they can achieve a judicious balance among the interests of these diverse groups while ensuring the continued functioning of the corporation.

In a legal sense, the board is required to direct the affairs of the corporation but not to manage them. It is charged by law to act with *due care,* sometimes called *due diligence*. If a director or the board as a whole fails to act with due care and, as a result, the corporation is in some way harmed, the careless director or directors can be held personally liable for the harm done.

What Is the Role of the Board in Strategic Management?

How does a board of directors fulfill its many responsibilities? The **role of the board in strategic management** is to carry out three basic tasks:

- **Monitor:** By acting through its committees, a board can keep abreast of developments both inside and outside the corporation. It can thus bring to management's attention developments it might have overlooked. At a minimum, a board should carry out this task.
- **Evaluate and influence:** A board can examine management's proposals, decisions, and actions; agree or disagree with them; give advice and offer suggestions; and outline alternatives. More active boards do this in addition to monitoring management's activities.
- **Initiate and determine:** A board can delineate a corporation's mission and specify strategic options to its management. Only the most active boards take on this task in addition to the previous two.

Is There a Board of Directors Continuum?

A board of directors is involved in strategic management to the extent that it carries out the three tasks of monitoring, evaluating and influencing, and initiating and determining. The **board of directors continuum** shown in Figure 2.1 shows the possible degree of involvement (from low to high) in the strategic management process. Boards can range from phantom boards with no real involvement to catalyst boards with a very high degree of involvement. Research does suggest that active board involvement in strategic management is positively related to corporate financial performance.

Highly involved boards tend to be very active. They take their tasks of monitoring, evaluating and influencing, and initiating and determining very seriously; they advise when necessary and keep management alert. As depicted in Figure 2.1, their heavy involvement in the strategic management process places them in the active participation or even catalyst position. At Control Data Corporation, for example, the board of directors spends the day before the official board meeting studying a business sector, such as computer peripherals, or an issue, such as efforts to improve quality. Other corporations with actively participating boards are Mead Corporation, Rolm and Haas, Whirlpool Corporation, Westinghouse, Dayton-Hudson, and General Motors.

As a board becomes less involved in the affairs of the corporation, it moves farther to the left on the continuum (see Figure 2.1). On the far left are passive phantom or rubber stamp boards that typically never initiate or determine strategy unless a crisis occurs. In these situations, the CEO also serves as Chairman of the Board and works to keep board members under his or her control by giving them the "mushroom treatment"—*throw manure on them and keep them in the dark!*

FIGURE 2.1   Board of Directors Continuum

← DEGREE OF INVOLVEMENT IN STRATEGIC MANAGEMENT →

Low
(Passive)

High
(Active)

Phantom	Rubber Stamp	Minimal Review	Nominal Participation	Active Participation	Catalyst
Never knows what to do, if anything; no degree of involvement.	Permits officers to make all decisions. It votes as the officers recommend on action issues.	Formally reviews selected issues that officers bring to its attention.	Involved to a limited degree in the performance or review of selected key decisions, indicators, or programs of management.	Approves, questions, and makes final de-cisions on mis-sion, strategy, policies, and objectives. Has active board committees. Performs fiscal and manage-ment audits.	Takes the leading role in establishing and modifying the mission, objectives, strategy, and policies. It has a very active strategy committee.

Source: T. L. Wheelen and J. D. Hunger, "Board of Directors Continuum." Copyright © 1994 by Wheelen and Hunger Associates. Reprinted by permission.

Generally, the smaller the corporation, the less active is its board of directors. The board tends to be dominated by directors who are also owner-managers of the company. Other directors are usually friends or family members. As the corporation grows and goes public, however, the boards become more active in terms of roles and responsibilities.

Most large, publicly owned corporations probably have boards that operate at some point between nominal and active participation. Few corporations have catalyst boards, except for those with major problems (that is, pending bankruptcies, mergers, or acquisitions). One study of boards ranging from hospitals to Fortune 500 firms found that:

- 30% of the boards actively worked with management to develop strategic direction (**active/catalyst**).
- 30% worked to revise as well as ratify management's proposals (**minimal/ nominal participation**).
- 40% merely ratified management's strategic proposals (**phantom/rubber stamp**).[4]

Who Are Members of a Board of Directors?

The boards of most publicly owned corporations are composed of both inside and outside directors. **Inside directors** (sometimes called management directors) are typically officers or executives employed by the corporation. **Outside directors** may be executives of other firms but are not employees of the board's corporation.

Although there is no clear evidence that a high proportion of outsiders on a board results in improved corporate performance, there is a trend in the United States to increase the number of outsiders on boards. Outsiders now account for 74–75% of the board members in large U.S. corporations and around 40% in small U.S. companies. People who favor such a high proportion of outsiders state that outside directors are less biased and more likely to evaluate management's performance objectively than are inside directors. This is the main reason why the New York Stock Exchange requires that all companies listed on the exchange have an audit committee composed entirely of independent, outside members. In contrast, those who prefer inside over outside directors contend that outside directors are less effective than are insiders because the outsiders are less likely to have the necessary interest, availability, or competency. Directors sometimes serve on so many boards that they spread their time and interest too thin to actively fulfill their responsibilities.

The majority of outside directors are active or retired CEOs and COOs of other corporations. Others are academicians, attorneys, consultants, former government officials, major stockholders, and bankers. A 1992 survey of 327 large U.S. corporations by Korn/Ferry International found that 60% of the boards had at least one woman director—up from 11% twenty years earlier. Minority representation increased from 9% in 1973 to 46% of board membership in 1992. Outside directors serving on the boards of large U.S. corporations earned on average $34,276.[5] Directors serving on the boards of small companies usually received less than $10,000 annually.

The vast majority of inside directors are chief executive officers, chief operating officers, and presidents or vice-presidents of key operating divisions or functional units. Few if any inside directors receive any extra compensation for assuming this extra duty. Very rarely does a U.S. board include any lower level operating employees.

Codetermination: Should Employees Serve On Boards?

Codetermination, the inclusion of a corporation's workers on its board, began only recently in the United States. Corporations such as Chrysler, Northwest Airlines, and Wheeling-Pittsburgh Steel have added representatives from employee associations to their boards as part of union agreements. Critics raise the issue of conflict of interest. Can a member of the board, who is privy to confidential managerial information, function, for example, as a union leader whose primary duty is to fight for the best benefits for the union members?

Although the movement to place employees on the boards of directors of U.S. companies shows little likelihood of increasing, the European experience reveals an increasing acceptance of worker participation on corporate boards. The Federal Republic of Germany pioneered the practice. Most other western European countries have either passed similar codetermination legislation or use worker councils to work closely with management.

Why Are Interlocking Directorates Useful?

CEOs often nominate chief executives (as well as board members) from other firms to membership on their own boards in order to create an interlocking directorate. A *direct* **interlocking directorate** occurs when two firms share a director or when an executive of one firm sits on the board of a second firm. An *indirect* interlock occurs when two corporations have directors who also serve on the board of a third firm, such as a bank.

Although the Clayton Act and the Banking Act of 1933 prohibit interlocking directorates by U.S. companies competing in the same industry, interlocking continues to occur in almost all corporations, especially large ones. Interlocking occurs because large firms have a significant impact on other corporations; and these other corporations, in turn, have some control over the firm's inputs and marketplace. Interlocking directorates are also a useful method for gaining both inside information about an uncertain environment and objective expertise about potential strategies and tactics. Family-owned corporations, however, are less likely to have interlocking directorates than are corporations with highly dispersed stock ownership, probably because family-owned corporations do not like to dilute their corporate control by adding outsiders to boardroom discussions. Nevertheless, there is some evidence to indicate that well-interlocked corporations are better able to survive in a highly competitive environment.[6]

How Are People Nominated and Elected to Boards?

Traditionally the CEO of the corporation decided whom to invite to board membership and merely asked the stockholders for approval. Allowing the CEO free rein in nominating directors may be dangerous, however. The CEO might select only board members who, in the CEO's opinion, will not disturb the company's policies and functioning. Moreover, directors selected by the CEO often feel that they should go along with any proposals the CEO makes. Thus board members find themselves accountable to the very management they are charged to oversee. Because this is likely to happen, there is an increasing tendency for a special board committee to nominate new outside board members for election by the stockholders. Approximately 60–70% of large U.S. corporations now use nominating committees to identify potential directors.

Virtually every corporation whose directors serve terms of more than one year divides the board into classes and staggers elections so that only a portion of the board stands for election each year. Arguments in favor of this practice are that it provides continuity by reducing the chance of an abrupt turnover in membership and that it reduces the likelihood of electing people unfriendly to management (who might be interested in a hostile takeover) through cumulative voting.

How Are Boards Organized?

The corporation's charter and its bylaws, in compliance with state laws, determine board size. Although some states require a minimum number of board members, most corporations have quite a bit of discretion in determination of board size. The average large, publicly held firm has about twelve directors. The average small or medium size privately held company has approximately seven to eight members.

Approximately 76% of the top executives of large, U.S. publicly held corporations hold the dual designation of chairman and CEO. This practice is being increasingly criticized because of the potential for conflict of interest. The CEO is supposed to concentrate on strategy, planning, external relations, and responsibility to the board. The chairman's responsibility is to ensure that the board and its committees perform their functions as stated in its charter. Further, the chairman schedules board meetings and presides over the annual stockholders' meeting. Critics of combining the two offices in one person ask how the board can properly oversee top management if the chairman is also top management. For this reason, the chairman and CEO roles are separated by law in Germany, the Netherlands, and Finland. A similar law is being considered in Britain and Australia. Recent research does suggest that firms that separate the two positions outperform financially those firms that combine the offices.[7]

The most effective boards accomplish much of their work through committees. Although the committees do not have legal duties, unless detailed in the bylaws, most committees are granted full power to act with the authority of the board between board meetings. Typical standing committees are the executive, audit, compensation, finance, and nominating committees. The executive committee is formed from local directors who can meet between board meetings to attend to matters that must be settled quickly. This committee acts as an extension of the board and, consequently, may have almost unrestricted authority in certain areas.

What Are the Trends in Boards of Directors?

The board of directors is likely to play a more active role in the strategic management of the corporation in the future. The change, however, will probably be more evolutionary than radical or revolutionary. Different boards are at different levels of maturity and will not be changing in the same direction or at the same rate. Some of today's trends that are likely to continue include:

- Institutional investors, such as pension funds, mutual funds, and insurance companies, are increasing their pressure on top management to improve corporate performance.
- Stockholders are demanding that directors and top managers own more than token amounts of stock in the corporation.
- Outside or nonmanagement directors are increasing in numbers and power in publicly held corporations as CEOs loosen their grip on boards.
- Society, in the form of special interest groups, increasingly expects boards of directors to balance the economic goal of profitability with the social needs of society.

2.2 Top Management

The CEO of the corporation usually performs the top management function in coordination with the COO or president, executive vice-president, and vice-presidents of divisions and functional areas. Hence, an understanding of top management is especially important to the study of strategic management.

What Are the Responsibilities of Top Management?

Top management, and especially the CEO, is responsible to the board of directors for the overall management of the corporation. Its task is to get things accomplished through and with others, in order to meet the corporate objectives. Top management's job is thus multidimensional and is oriented toward the welfare of the total organization. Specific top management tasks vary from firm to firm and are developed from an analysis of the mission, objectives, strategies, and key activities of the corporation. The chief executive officer, in particular, must successfully handle three responsibilities crucial to effective strategic management: (1) *fulfill key roles*, (2) *provide executive leadership and a strategic vision*, and (3) *manage the strategic planning process*.

What Key Roles Do CEOs Need to Fulfill?

Key roles are those activities that must be fulfilled for successful CEO performance. From five weeks of in-depth observation of five chief executives, Henry Mintzberg concluded that a top manager's job contains ten interrelated roles. The importance of each role and the amount of time demanded by each probably vary from one job to another, but they need to be fulfilled if the CEO is to be successful. These roles are as follows:

- **Figurehead:** Acts as legal and symbolic head and performs obligatory social, ceremonial, or legal duties (hosts retirement dinners; signs contracts for the corporation; represents firm at civic affairs).
- **Leader:** Motivates, develops, and guides subordinates (introduces Total Quality Management; acts as a role model; provides a vision for the company's future).
- **Liaison:** Maintains a network of contacts and information sources with key people in the task environment (meets with stockholder groups; is active in industry trade association; plays golf with other CEOs).
- **Monitor:** Seeks and obtains information needed for understanding the corporation and its environment (reads business periodicals; subscribes to data services; reviews key indicators of firm's performance).
- **Disseminator:** Transmits information to the rest of the top management team and other key people in the corporation (chairs staff meetings; communicates strategic plan; makes policy announcements).
- **Spokesperson:** Transmits information to key groups and people in the task environment (writers letter to stockholders; talks to Chamber of Commerce; participates in advertising campaign).
- **Entrepreneur:** Searches the corporation and its environment for projects to improve products, processes, procedures, and structures (reorganizes the company; originates a study of new product development; initiates search for joint venture partners).
- **Disturbance Handler:** Takes corrective action in times of trouble or crisis (personally talks with key creditors or union representatives; establishes investigative committees; replaces disruptive employees).
- **Resource Allocator:** Allocates corporate resources by making and/or approving decisions (reviews budgets; plans personnel loads; sets objectives).
- **Negotiator:** Represents the corporation in negotiating important agreements (resolves disputes between divisions; negotiates with key customers, suppliers, and creditors; reviews contracts).[8]

Should Executive Leadership Promote a Strategic Vision?

Executive leadership is the directing of activities toward the accomplishment of corporate objectives. Executive leadership is important because it sets the tone for the entire corporation. A **strategic vision** is a description of what the company is capable of becoming. It is often communicated in the mission statement. People in an organization want to have a sense of mission, but only top management is in the position to specify and communicate this strategic vision to the general workforce. Top management's enthusiasm (or lack of it) about the corporation tends to be contagious. The importance of executive leadership is illustrated by John Welch, Jr., the successful Chairman and CEO of General Electric Company (GE).

According to Welch: "Good business leaders create a vision, articulate the vision, passionately own the vision, and relentlessly drive it to completion."[9]

Chief executive officers with a clear strategic vision are often perceived as dynamic and charismatic leaders. For instance, the positive attitudes characterizing many well-known industrial leaders—such as Bill Gates at Microsoft, Mary Kay Ash at Mary Kay Cosmetics, Ted Turner at CNN, Herb Kelleher at Southwest Airlines, and Andy Grove at Intel—have energized their respective corporations. They are able to command respect and to influence strategy formulation and implementation because they tend to have three key characteristics:

1. The CEO *articulates a strategic vision* for the corporation. The CEO envisions the company not as it currently is, but as it can become. Because the CEO's vision puts activities and conflicts in a new perspective, it gives renewed meaning to everyone's work activities and enables employees to see beyond the details of their own jobs to the functioning of the total corporation.
2. The CEO *presents a role* for others to identify with and to follow. The CEO sets an example in terms of behavior and dress. The CEO's attitudes and values concerning the corporation's purpose and activities are clear cut and constantly communicated in words and deeds.
3. The CEO *communicates high performance standards* but also *shows confidence in the followers' abilities* to meet these standards. No leader ever improved performance by setting easily attainable goals that provided no challenge. The CEO must be willing to follow through by coaching people.

How Does Top Management Manage the Strategic Planning Process?

Top management must initiate and manage the strategic planning process. To do so, it must take a very long-range view. Top management, for example, should allocate the largest proportion of planning time to looking five or more years ahead. A department manager, however, should devote the largest proportion of planning time to looking a year or two into the future. Even though a first-line supervisor may sometimes look ahead a year or so, he or she will need to spend most planning time on activities taking place within the next few weeks or months.

To accomplish its tasks, top management must use information provided by three key corporate groups: a strategic planning staff, divisional or SBU managers, and managers of functional departments. A **strategic planning staff** typically consists of a few people, headed by a senior vice-president or director of corporate planning. To generate the data top management needs to make its strategic decisions, this staff monitors both internal and external environments. It also suggests to top management possible changes in the corporate mission, objectives, strategies, and policies. Nearly all large corporations have a planning staff. As strategic planning responsibilities are being shifted to line managers, staff planners are being increasingly used as consultants who respond to requests for assistance.

Divisional (or **SBU**) **managers**, with the assistance of the strategic planning staff and with input from their product managers, perform the strategic planning function for each division. These divisional managers typically initiate proposals for top management's consideration and/or respond to requests for such proposals by corporate headquarters. They may also carry out strategies and policies decided on at the corporate level for organizationwide implementation. These division managers typically work with the heads of various functional units within the division to develop the appropriate functional strategies for implementing planned business-level strategies.

Managers of functional departments (marketing, engineering, R&D managers, etc.) report directly either to divisional managers in a multidivisional corporation or to top management if the corporation has no divisions. Although these managers may develop specific functional strategies, they generally do so within the framework of divisional or corporate strategies. They also respond to initiatives from above that ask for input or require them to develop strategies for implementing divisional plans.

What Are the Characteristics of Top Management Tasks?

Two **characteristics of top management tasks** differentiate them from other managerial tasks. First, *very few of them are continuous*. Rarely does a manager work on these tasks all day. The responsibilities, however, are always present, even though the tasks themselves are sporadic. And when the tasks do arise, they are crucial, for example, the selection of a person to head a new division. This characteristic, however, can create a problem. Because their activities are not continuous, people in top management often have unplanned free time. They tend therefore to get caught up in the day-to-day work in manufacturing, marketing, accounting, engineering, or in other operations of the corporation. They may find themselves constantly solving crises that could probably be handled better by lower level managers.

The second characteristic of top management tasks is that *they require a wide range of capabilities and temperaments*. Some tasks require the capacity to analyze and carefully weigh alternative courses of action. Some require an awareness of and an interest in people, whereas others call for the ability to pursue abstract ideas, concepts, and calculations. This can also create a problem. Top managers may perceive only those aspects and responsibilities of the top management function that are compatible with their abilities, experience, and temperaments. And, if the board of directors fails to state explicitly what it considers to be the key responsibilities and activities of top management, the top managers are free to define the job themselves. Therefore, important tasks can be overlooked until a crisis occurs.

2.3 Social Responsibilities of Strategic Decision Makers

Should strategic decision makers be responsible only to stockholders or do they have broader responsibilities? The concept of **social responsibility** proposes that a private corporation has responsibilities to society that extend beyond making a profit. Strategic decisions often affect more than just the corporation. A decision to retrench by closing some plants and discontinuing product lines, for example, affects not only the firm's workforce but also communities where the plants are located and those customers having no other source of the discontinued product. This brings into consideration the question of the appropriateness of certain missions, objectives, and strategies of business corporations. Some businesspeople believe profit maximization is the primary goal of their firm, whereas concerned interest groups argue that other goals should have a priority, such as the hiring of minorities and women or the safety of their neighborhoods. Strategic managers must be able to deal with these conflicting interests to formulate a viable strategic plan.

What Are the Responsibilities of a Business Firm?

What are the responsibilities of a business firm and how many of them must strategic managers fulfill? Milton Friedman and Archie Carroll offer two contrasting views of the responsibilities of business firms to society.

What Is Friedman's Traditional View of Business Responsibility?

Milton Friedman, in urging a return to a *laissez-faire* worldwide economy with a minimum of government regulation, argues against the concept of social responsibility. If a businessperson acts "responsibly" by cutting the price of the firm's product to prevent inflation, or by making expenditures to reduce pollution, or by hiring the hard-core unemployed, that person, according to Friedman, is spending the stockholders' money for a general social interest. Even if the businessperson has stockholder permission or encouragement to do so, he or she is still acting from motives other than economic and may, in the long run, cause harm to the very society the firm is trying to help. By taking on the burden of these social costs, the business becomes less efficient—either prices go up to pay for the increased costs or investment in new activities and research is postponed. These results negatively affect—perhaps fatally—the long-term efficiency of a business. Friedman thus referred to the social responsibility of business as a "fundamentally subversive doctrine" and stated that "there is one and only one social responsibility of business—to use its resources and engage in activities designed to increase its profits so long as it stays within the rules of the game, which is to say, engages in open and free competition without deception or fraud."[10]

What Are Carroll's Four Responsibilities of Business?

Archie Carroll proposes that the managers of business organizations have **four responsibilities**: economic, legal, ethical, and discretionary.[11] These responsibilities are displayed in Figure 2.2 and are defined as follows:

- **Economic responsibilities** are to produce goods and services of value to society so that the firm may repay its creditors and stockholders.

FIGURE
2.2
Responsibilities of Business

Social Responsibilities

Economic	Legal	Ethical	Discretionary
(Must Do)	(Have to Do)	(Should Do)	(Might Do)

Source: Adapted from A. B. Carroll, "A Three Dimensional Conceptual Model of Corporate Performance," *Academy of Management Review* (October 1979), p. 499. Reprinted with permission.

- **Legal responsibilities** are defined by governments in laws that management is expected to obey.
- **Ethical responsibilities** are to follow the generally held beliefs about how one should act in a society. For example, society generally expects firms to work with the employees and the community in planning for layoffs, even though there may be no law requiring this. The affected people can get very upset if an organization's management fails to act according to generally prevailing ethical values.
- **Discretionary responsibilities** are the purely voluntary obligations a corporation assumes, for example, philanthropic contributions, training the hard-core unemployed, and providing day-care centers. The difference between ethical and discretionary responsibilities is that few people expect an organization to fulfill discretionary responsibilities, whereas many expect an organization to fulfill ethical ones.

Carroll lists these four responsibilities in order of priority. A business firm must first make a profit to satisfy its economic responsibilities. To continue in existence, it must follow the laws, thus fulfilling its legal responsibilities. To this point Carroll and Friedman are in agreement. Carroll, however, goes further by arguing that business managers have responsibilities beyond economic and legal.

Once the two basic responsibilities are satisfied, according to Carroll, the firm should look to fulfilling its social responsibilities. *The term "social responsibility," therefore, includes both ethical and discretionary, but not economic and legal responsibilities.* A firm can fulfill its ethical responsibilities by doing those things that society tends to value but has not yet put into law. Once ethical responsibilities are satisfied, a firm can focus on discretionary responsibilities—purely voluntary actions that society has not yet decided are important. One example of a discretionary responsibility is Volkswagen's pilot project to design cars for disassembly and recycling.

The discretionary responsibilities of today may become the ethical responsibilities of tomorrow. The provision of day-care facilities is, for example, moving rapidly from a discretionary to an ethical responsibility. Carroll suggests that to the extent that business corporations fail to acknowledge discretionary or ethical responsibilities, society, through government, will act, making them legal responsibilities. This may be done by government, moreover, without regard to an organization's economic responsibilities. As a result, the organization may have greater difficulty in earning a profit than it would have had in assuming voluntarily some ethical and discretionary responsibilities.

Both Friedman and Carroll argue their positions based on the impact of socially responsible actions on a firm's profits. Friedman says that socially responsible actions hurt a firm's efficiency. Carroll proposes that a lack of social responsibility results in an increase in government regulations, thus reducing a firm's efficiency. Research has failed, unfortunately, to consistently support either position. There is no clear relationship between social responsibility and financial performance.[12]

Who Are Corporate Stakeholders?

The concept that business must be socially responsible sounds appealing until one asks, "Responsible to whom?" A corporation's task environment includes a large number of groups with interest in a business organization's activities. These groups are referred to as **stakeholders** because they affect or are affected by the achievement of the firm's objectives. Should a corporation be responsible only to some of these groups, or does business have an equal responsibility to all of them?

In any one strategic decision, the interests of one stakeholder group can conflict with another. For example, a business firm's decision to use only recycled materials in its manufacturing process may have a positive effect on environmental groups but a negative effect on stockholder dividends. See the *Company Spotlight on Maytag Corporation* for another example involving the firm's decision to move dishwasher production from Iowa to a lower wage location. On the one hand, stockholders were generally pleased with the decision because it would lower costs. On the other hand, however, Iowa officials and the local union were very unhappy at what they called "community cannibalism." Which group's interests should have priority?

Given the wide range of interests and concerns present in any organization's task environment, one or more groups, at any one time, probably will be dissatisfied with an organization's activities—even if management is trying to be socially responsible. Strategic managers must therefore realize that before making a strategic decision, they should consider how each alternative will affect important stakeholder groups. What seems at first to be the best decision because it appears to be the most profitable may actually result in the worst set of consequences to the corporation. A decision now to continue legal but unsafe conditions to avoid the cost of repair may keep costs low temporarily, but it could result in a very expensive lawsuit in the future.

Throughout its history, Maytag Corporation has tried to act responsibly in light of the various concerns of its many stakeholder groups. Even though the corporation has kept its headquarters in Newton, Iowa, the recent acquisitions of Magic Chef and Hoover have meant that Maytag Corporation had to view things differently from Maytag Company. The company previously made only Maytag-brand major appliances in Newton, Iowa. The corporation now makes Maytag, Admiral, Magic Chef, Jenn-Air, Hardwick, Norge, and Hoover brand appliances and Dixie-Narco vending machines, throughout North America and the world. Maytag Corporation's top management (many of whom came from Maytag Company) now has to consider not only their responsibilities to the stakeholders of Maytag Company, but also their responsibilities to the various stakeholders of Magic Chef, Jenn-Air, Hoover, Admiral, and Dixie-Narco, and to stakeholders of the corporation as a whole. This has not been an easy matter.

Maytag's reputation as a good corporate citizen was tarnished in some people's eyes when it announced the decision to move dishwasher manufacturing from Newton to Jackson, Tennessee. Chairman and CEO Daniel Krumm announced that the plant would consolidate the manufacturing of all the brands marketed by the corporation into one large, highly efficient plant.

Lonnie White, President of United Auto Workers Local 997 (the bargaining unit representing Maytag Company unionized employees in Newton, Iowa) responded with dismay to top management's decision. "Where is their commitment to the community and the state of Iowa?" asked White. "They can add a facility here in Newton to do the same thing that they're doing in Jackson, Tennessee." Pointing out that Maytag owned plenty of unused land in Newton, White contended that management could have only three reasons for moving dishwasher production to Tennessee: (1) to escape the union shop, (2) to reduce wage costs, and (3) to cut benefits. "The Newton dishwasher line is only running one shift. Other lines run two shifts," said White in response to the statement that the line was near capacity. He indicated that the union was not so much concerned with itself as it was with the impact on local communities and the need to avoid "community cannibalism." Referring to the perceived change in the relationship between labor and management after Maytag became a large corporation, White ruefully concluded: "We're no longer dealing with Mother Maytag. Now we're dealing with a corporation."

In Conclusion . . .

Strategic managers can have a huge impact on the entire corporation through their values and their vision. For example, when Kay Anderson founded the Medical Graphics Corporation in 1978 in St. Paul, Minnesota, she acted out of a desire to achieve more than just profits. Concerned with improving medical diagnostics since her father died suddenly of a heart attack when she was 13 years old, Kay had a personal mission to help save lives. She used Medical Graphics to help achieve that mission. After Kay had done everything from building the equipment, to writing software, to visiting hospitals to demonstrate and sell her products, the corporation's sales climbed to almost $10 million annually. In her words: "I was on a crusade to save lives by inventing and perfecting a technology that would aid the early detection and diagnosis of heart and lung disease. . . . It was a crusade and I was its driving force." In all her actions as CEO, Kay showed that the real mission of the corporation was to prevent heart and lung disease in people like her father. To her surprise, her employees also identified with this mission and were energized by it. "It turned out that all of us were in it for something more than money," concluded Kay.[13]

Discussion Questions

1. Does a corporation really need a board of directors?
2. What recommendations would you make to improve the effectiveness of today's boards of directors?
3. What makes an effective top management? What types of skills and experiences should a person have to become a CEO?
4. Do you agree with economist Milton Friedman that social responsibility is a "fundamentally subversive doctrine" that will only hurt a business corporation's long-term efficiency?
5. Should a company be concerned if some of its suppliers in developing countries are abusing their workers, employing child labor, and paying near starvation wages?

Key Terms

strategic decision makers
board of director responsibilities
role of the board
board of directors continuum
inside directors
outside directors
codetermination
interlocking directorate
CEO key roles
executive leadership

strategic vision
strategic planning staff
characteristics of top management
   tasks
social responsibility
economic responsibilities
legal responsibilities
ethical responsibilities
discretionary responsibilities
stakeholders

3

Environmental Scanning
and Industry Analysis

The decades of the 1960s and 1970s were exciting days for Tupperware, the company that originated airtight, easy-to-use, plastic food-storage containers. Housewives gathered ten at a time in each others' homes to socialize and play games at Tupperware parties. New products were demonstrated and sold at these parties by a local Tupperware lady. The party concept as a marketing and distribution device was a huge success—company sales nearly doubled every five years.

During this same time period, however, the company's environment changed—with serious implications for Tupperware. By 1980, divorces had become more common and more women were working full-time. More customers were single, childless, and working outside the home. As a result, Tupperware parties began to lose their popularity. From 1984 to 1992, Tupperware's North American sales slipped from 59% to a little over 40% of the market. (In contrast, Rubbermaid's market share increased from a little over 5% to close to 40% of units sold during this same time period.) The number of dealers dropped from 32,000 to 24,000. By 1992, most American women either had no idea how to find Tupperware or no desire to go to a Tupperware party. About 40% of the company's sales were from people who skipped the parties but sent orders along with friends who attended. Nevertheless, still hoping that these environmental changes were only temporary, management refused to change its marketing system. Tupperware's president actually predicted that during the 1990s the party concept would return to popularity because women and families would be spending more time at home. Unfortunately Rubbermaid and other competitors, who had switched to marketing their containers in grocery and discount stores, continued to grow at the expense of Tupperware.[1]

The preceding example shows how quickly a pioneering company can become an also-ran because of its failure to adapt to environmental change or, even worse, its failure to create change. To be successful over time, an organization needs to be in tune with its external environment. There must be a *strategic fit* between what the environment wants and what the corporation has to offer, as well as between what the corporation needs and what the environment can provide. Current predictions are that the environment for all organizations will become even more uncertain as the world enters the twenty-first century. **Environmental uncertainty** is the degree of *complexity* plus the degree of *change* existing in an organization's external environment. Environmental uncertainty is a threat to strategic managers because it hampers their ability to develop long-range plans and to make strategic decisions to keep the corporation in equilibrium with its external environment.

3.1 Environmental Scanning

Before an organization can begin strategy formulation, it must scan the external environment to identify possible opportunities and threats and its internal environment for strengths and weaknesses. **Environmental scanning** is the monitoring, evaluating, and disseminating of information from the external and internal environments to key people within the corporation. It is a tool that a corporation uses to avoid strategic surprise and to ensure long-term health. Research has found a positive relationship between environmental scanning and profits.[2]

What External Environmental Variables Should Be Scanned?

In undertaking environmental scanning, strategic managers must first be aware of the many variables within a corporation's societal and task environments. The **societal environment** includes general forces that do not directly touch on the short-run activities of the organization but that can, and often do, influence its long-run decisions. These forces, shown in Figure 3.1, are as follows:

- **Economic forces** that regulate the exchange of materials, money, energy, and information
- **Technological forces** that generate problem-solving inventions
- **Political–legal forces** that allocate power and provide constraining and protecting laws and regulations
- **Sociocultural forces** that regulate the values, mores, and customs of society

The **task environment** includes those elements or groups that directly affect the corporation and, in turn, are affected by it. These groups include governments, local communities, suppliers, competitors, customers, creditors, employees/labor unions, special-interest groups, and trade associations. A corporation's task environment is typically the industry within which it operates. The term **industry analysis** refers to an in-depth examination of key factors within a corporation's task environment. Both the societal and task environments must be monitored so that strategic factors that are likely to have a strong impact on corporate success or failure can be detected.

FIGURE
3.1

Environmental Variables

What Should Be Scanned in the Societal Environment?

The societal environment contains many possible strategic factors. The number of factors becomes enormous when one realizes that, generally speaking, each country in the world can be represented by its own unique set of societal forces—some of which are very similar to neighboring countries and some of which are very different. For example, even though Austria and the Czech Republic share borders in Central Europe, the Czech Republic's recent history as a communist-bloc country means that in 1990 it had none of the commercial infrastructure to support the transition from a centrally planned to a free market economy. Consequently, starting a business in Austria was significantly easier than in the Czech Republic where the old lethargic, state-controlled companies were neither able to quickly produce needed supplies nor able to distribute products effectively. Nevertheless, excellent school systems in both countries have produced well-educated and cultured consumers and employees.

How Should Societal Trends Be Monitored?   As noted in Table 3.1, large corporations categorize the societal environment in any one geographic region into four

TABLE 3.1	Some Important Variables in the Societal Environment			
	Economic	**Technological**	**Political–Legal**	**Sociocultural**
	GDP trends	Total government spending for R&D	Antitrust regulations	Lifestyle changes
	Interest rates	Total industry spending for R&D	Environmental protection laws	Career expectations
	Money supply	Focus of technological efforts	Tax laws	Consumer activism
	Inflation rates		Special incentives	Rate of family formation
	Unemployment levels	Patent protection	Foreign trade regulations	Growth rate of population
	Wage/price controls	New products	Attitudes toward foreign companies	Age distribution of population
	Devaluation/revaluation	New developments in technology transfer from lab to marketplace	Laws on hiring and promotion	Regional shifts in population
	Energy availability and cost		Stability of government	Life expectancies
	Disposable and discretionary income	Productivity improvements through automation		Birth rates

areas and focus their scanning in each area on trends with corporatewide relevance. Obviously, trends in any one area may be very important to the firms in one industry but of lesser importance to firms in other industries. Trends in the *political–legal* part of the societal environment have a significant impact on business firms. For example, periods of strict enforcement of U.S. antitrust laws directly affect corporate growth strategy. As large companies find it more difficult to acquire another firm in the same or in a related industry, they are typically driven to diversify into unrelated industries.

Demographic trends are part of the *sociocultural* aspect of the societal environment. The demographic bulge in the U.S. population caused by the "baby boom" in the 1950s strongly affected the ski resort industry, among others. Instead of emphasizing steep down-hill slopes and the singles bar aspect of the ski lodge as was successfully done in the 1960s and 1970s, resorts have switched in the 1990s to offering ski classes for children and more gentle "family slopes." According to Howard Harris, president of Eagle Direct, a Denver marketing firm with ski-area clients, "Your hot-dog skier of 20 years ago is now craving white wine and chateaubriand and has two kids he's introducing to skiing. The resorts are trying to hang onto that skier longer."[3] Even now, companies are preparing for the inevitable aging of this demographic group. As the 1990s wear on, health care and financial planning are moving to center stage. Can retirement homes and adult diapers be far behind?

In the United States, six sociocultural trends are helping to define what North America will look like at the beginning of the next century:

1. **Increasing environmental awareness:** Recycling and conservation are becoming more than slogans. Busch Gardens, for example, eliminated the use of disposable styrofoam trays in favor of washing and reusing plastic trays.

2. **Growth of the seniors market:** As their number increases, people over age 55 will become an even more important market. Already, some companies are segmenting the senior population into Young Matures, Older Matures, and the Elderly—each having a different set of attitudes and interests.

3. **New baby boomlet:** With a new interest in babies, a decline in the percentage increase of women entering the workforce, and younger women showing more interest in starting families earlier than their older sisters, the signs point to a new baby boomlet. The actual number of births thus far in the decade have been significantly greater than Census Bureau projections.

4. **Decline of the mass market:** Niche markets are beginning to define the marketers' environment. People want products that are adapted more to their personal needs. For example, Estée Lauder's All Skin and Maybelline's Shades of You lines of cosmetic products are specifically made for African-American women.[4]

5. **Pace and location of life:** Instant communication via fax machines, car telephones, and overnight mail enhances efficiency but increases the pressure on people. The merging of the personal computer with the communication and entertainment industry through telephone lines, satellite dishes, and cable television means an increasing number of choices for consumers. It also means that people can leave overcrowded urban areas for small towns and "telecommute" to work via personal computers and modems.

6. **Changing household:** According to the U.S. Census Bureau, the number of people living alone will grow from 13% in 1960 to 26% in 2000. Only 20% of U.S. homes will have one child under 18, compared with 44% in 1960. Although the baby boomlet trend may alter this estimate, a household clearly will no longer be the same as it was once portrayed in the "Brady Bunch," or even the "Cosby Show" programs of the 1970s and 1980s.[5]

What Are International Societal Considerations?   For each country or group of countries in which a company operates, management must face a whole new societal environment having different economic, technological, political–legal, and sociocultural variables. International societal environments vary so widely that a corporation's internal environment and strategic management process must be very flexible. Cultural trends in Germany, for example, have resulted in the inclusion of worker representatives in corporate strategic planning. Differences in societal environments strongly affect the ways in which a multinational corporation (MNC) conducts its marketing, financial, manufacturing, and other functional activities. For example, the existence of regional associations like the European Union (EU) and the North American Free Trade Agreement (NAFTA) has a significant impact on the competitive "rules of the game" for both those MNCs operating within and those MNCs that want to enter these areas. To account for the many differences among societal environments from one country to another, Table 3.1 would need to be changed to include such variables as GDP trends, climate, and regional associations under Economic; plus natural resource availability, transportation network, and patent protection under Technological; plus form of government, regulations on foreign ownership, and terrorist activity under Political–legal; plus language, social institutions, and attitudes toward foreigners under Sociocultural.

Before a company plans its strategy for a particular international location, it must scan the particular country environment(s) in question for opportunities and threats and compare them to its own organizational strengths and weaknesses. For example, if a company wants to operate successfully in a global industry such as automobiles, tires, electronics, or watches, it must be prepared to establish a significant presence in the three developed areas of the world known collectively as the *Triad*. Coined by Kenichi Ohmae, Triad refers to the three markets of Japan, North America, and Western Europe, which now form a single market with common needs.[6] Focusing on the Triad is essential for an MNC pursuing success in a global industry, according to Ohmae, because close to 90% of all high–value-added, high-technology manufactured goods are produced and consumed in North America, Western Europe, and Japan. Ideally a company should have a significant presence in each of these regions so that it can produce and market its products simultaneously in all three areas. Otherwise, it will lose competitive advantage to Triad-oriented MNCs. No longer can an MNC develop and market a new product in one part of the world before it exports it to other developed countries.

What Should Be Scanned in the Task Environment?

As shown in Figure 3.2, a corporation's scanning of the environment should include analyses of all the relevant elements in the task environment. These analyses take the form of individual reports written by various people in different parts of the firm. At

FIGURE 3.2   Scanning the External Environment

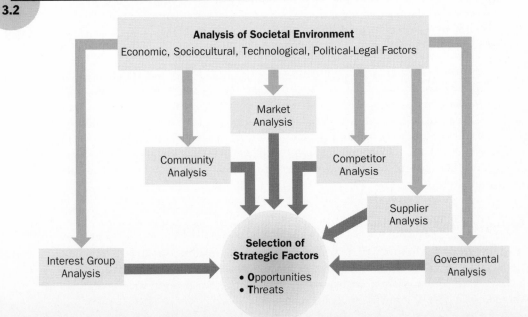

Procter & Gamble (P&G), for example, each quarter, people from each of the brand management teams work with key people from the sales and market research departments to research and write a "competitive activity report" on each of the product categories in which P&G competes. People in purchasing write similar reports concerning new developments in the industries that supply P&G. These and other reports are then summarized and transmitted up the corporate hierarchy for top management to use in strategic decision making. If a new development is reported regarding a particular product category, top management may then send memos to people throughout the organization to watch for and report on developments in related product areas. The many reports resulting from these scanning efforts, when boiled down to their essentials, act as a detailed list of external strategic factors.

How Can Managers Identify External Strategic Factors?

Few firms successfully monitor all important external factors. The personal values of a corporation's top managers as well as the success of current strategies are likely to bias both their perception of what is important to monitor in the external environment and their interpretations of what they perceive. Therefore, companies often respond differently to the same environmental changes because of differences in the ability of their strategic managers to recognize and understand strategic issues and factors. If one of these firms needs to change its strategy, it might not be gathering the appropriate external information to change strategies successfully.

One way to identify and analyze developments in the external environment is to use the **issues priority matrix** (provided in Figure 3.3) as follows:

1. Identify a number of likely trends emerging in the societal and task environments. These are strategic environmental issues—those important trends that, if they happen, will determine what the industry or the world will look like.
2. Assess the probability of these trends actually occurring from low to high.
3. Attempt to ascertain the likely impact (from low to high) of each of these trends on the corporation.

A corporation's **external strategic factors** are those key environmental trends that are judged to have both a *medium to high probability of occurrence* and a *medium to high probability of impact on the corporation*. The issues priority matrix can then be used to help managers decide which environmental trends should be merely scanned (low priority) and which should be monitored as strategic factors (high priority). Those environmental trends judged to be a corporation's strategic factors are then categorized as *opportunities* and *threats* and are included in strategy formulation.

3.2   Industry Analysis: Analyzing the Task Environment

An **industry** is a group of firms producing a similar product or service, such as financial services or soft drinks. An examination of the important stakeholder groups, such as suppliers and customers, in a particular corporation's task environment is a part of industry analysis.

FIGURE
3.3

Issues Priority Matrix

Probable Impact on Corporation

Source: Adapted from L. L. Lederman, "Foresight Activities in the U.S.A.: Time for a Re-Assessment?" *Long-Range Planning* (June 1984), p. 46. Copyright ©1984 by Pergamon Press, Ltd. Reprinted by permission.

What Is Michael Porter's Approach to Industry Analysis?

Michael Porter, an authority on competitive strategy, contends that a corporation is most concerned with the intensity of competition within its industry. Basic competitive forces, which are depicted in Figure 3.4, determine the intensity level. "The collective strength of these forces," he contends, "determines the ultimate profit potential in the industry, where profit potential is measured in terms of long-run return on invested capital."[7] The stronger each of these forces is, the more companies are limited in their ability to raise prices and earn greater profits. Although Porter mentions only five forces, a sixth—other stakeholders—is added here to reflect the power that governments, local communities, and other groups from the task environment wield over industry activities.

Using the model in Figure 3.4, a strong force can be regarded as a threat because it is likely to reduce profits. In contrast, a weak force can be viewed as an opportunity because it may allow the company to earn greater profits. In the short run, these forces act as constraints on a company's activities. In the long run, however, it may be possible for a company, through its choice of strategy, to change the strength of one or more of the forces to the company's advantage.

**FIGURE
3.4**   **Forces Driving Industry Competition**

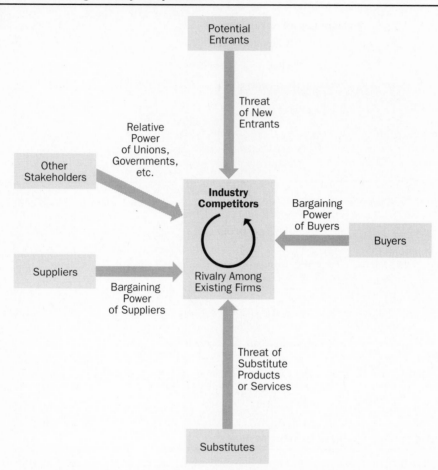

Source: Adapted/reprinted with permission of The Free Press, an imprint of Simon & Schuster, from *Competitive Strategy: Techniques for Analyzing Industries and Competitors* by Michael E. Porter. Copyright © 1980 by The Free Press.

In carefully scanning its industry, the corporation must assess the importance to its success of each of the following six forces: threat of new entrants, rivalry among existing firms, threat of substitute products, bargaining power of buyers, bargaining power of suppliers, and relative power of other stakeholders.[8]

What Is the Threat of New Entrants?

New entrants to an industry typically bring to it new capacity, a desire to gain market share, and substantial resources. They are, therefore, threats to an established corporation. The threat of entry depends on the presence of entry barriers and the reaction that can be expected from existing competitors. An **entry barrier** is an obstruction that makes it difficult for a company to enter an industry. For example, no new domestic automobile companies have been successfully established in the United States since the 1930s because of the high capital requirements to build production facilities and to develop a dealer distribution network. Some barriers to entry are:

- **Economies of Scale:** Scale economies in the production and sale of mainframe computers, for example, gave IBM a significant cost advantage over any new rival.
- **Product Differentiation:** Corporations like Procter & Gamble and General Mills, which manufacture products like Tide and Cheerios, create high entry barriers through their high levels of advertising and promotion.
- **Capital Requirements:** The need to invest huge financial resources in manufacturing facilities in order to produce computer microprocessors creates a significant barrier to entry to any competitor for Intel.
- **Switching Costs:** Once a software program like Lotus 1-2-3 or WordPerfect becomes established in an office, office managers are very reluctant to switch to a new program because of the high training costs.
- **Access to Distribution Channels:** Small entrepreneurs often have difficulty obtaining supermarket shelf space for their goods because large retailers charge for space on their shelves and give priority to the established firms who can pay for the advertising needed to generate high customer demand.
- **Cost Disadvantages Independent of Size:** Microsoft's development of the first widely adopted operating system (MS-DOS) for the IBM-type personal computer gave it a significant advantage over potential competitors. Its introduction of Windows helped to cement that advantage.
- **Government Policy:** Governments can limit entry into an industry through licensing requirements by limiting access to raw materials, such as off-shore oil drilling sites.

What Is Rivalry Among Existing Firms?

In most industries, corporations are mutually dependent. A competitive move by one firm can be expected to have a noticeable effect on its competitors and thus may cause retaliation or counterefforts. For example, the entry by mail order companies such as Dell and Gateway into a PC industry previously dominated by IBM, Apple, and Compaq increased the level of competitive activity to such an extent that any price reduction or new product introduction is now quickly followed by similar moves from other PC makers. According to Porter, intense rivalry is related to the presence of several factors:

- **Number of Competitors:** When competitors are few and roughly equal in size, such as in the U.S. auto and major home appliance industries, they watch each other carefully to make sure that any move by another firm is matched by an equal countermove.

- **Rate of Industry Growth:** Any slowing in passenger traffic tends to set off price wars in the airline industry because the only path to growth is to take sales away from a competitor.
- **Product or Service Characteristics:** Many people choose a videotape rental store based on the store's location, variety of selection, and pricing, based on the assumption that videotapes are a *commodity*—a product whose characteristics are the same regardless of who sells it.
- **Amount of Fixed Costs:** Because airlines must fly their planes on a schedule regardless of the number of paying passengers for any one flight, cheap standby fares are used whenever a plane has empty seats.
- **Capacity:** If the only way a company can increase its manufacturing capacity is to add it in a large increment by building a new plant, it will run that new plant at full capacity to keep its unit costs as low as possible, thus making so many products that the selling price falls throughout the industry.
- **Height of Exit Barriers:** Exit barriers keep a company from leaving an industry. The brewing industry, for example, has a low percentage of companies that leave the industry because breweries are specialized assets with few uses except for making beer.
- **Diversity of Rivals:** Rivals that have very different ideas of how to compete are likely to cross paths often and unknowingly challenge each other's position.

What Is the Threat of Substitute Products or Services?

Substitute products are those products that appear to be different but can satisfy the same need as another product. According to Porter, "Substitutes limit the potential returns of an industry by placing a ceiling on the prices firms in the industry can profitably charge."[9] To the extent that switching costs are low, substitutes may have a strong effect on an industry. Tea can be considered a substitute for coffee. If the price of coffee goes up high enough, coffee drinkers will slowly begin switching to tea. The price of tea thus puts a price ceiling on the price of coffee. Sometimes a difficult task, the identification of possible substitute products or services means searching for products or services that can perform the same function, even though they may not appear to be easily substitutable.

What Is the Bargaining Power of Buyers?

Buyers affect an industry through their ability to force down prices, bargain for higher quality or more services, and play competitors against each other. A buyer or a group of buyers is powerful if some of the following conditions hold true:

- A buyer purchases a large proportion of the seller's product or service (e.g., oil filters for an automaker).
- A buyer has the potential to integrate backward by producing the product itself (e.g., paper for a newspaper chain).
- Alternative suppliers are plentiful because the product is standard or undifferentiated (e.g., gas stations).
- Changing suppliers costs very little (e.g., office supplies).

- The purchased product represents a high percentage of a buyer's costs, thus providing an incentive to shop around for a lower price (e.g., gasoline purchased by convenience stores).
- A buyer earns low profits and is thus very sensitive to costs and service differences (e.g., grocery stores).
- The purchased product is unimportant to the final quality or price of a buyer's products or services and thus can be easily substituted without affecting the final product adversely (e.g., electric wire in lamps).

What Is the Bargaining Power of Suppliers?

Suppliers can affect an industry through their ability to raise prices or reduce the quality of purchased goods and services. A supplier or supplier group is powerful if some of the following conditions apply:

- The supplier industry is dominated by a few companies, but sells to many (e.g., petroleum industry).
- Its product or service is unique and/or it has built up switching costs (e.g., word processing software).
- Substitutes are not readily available (e.g., electricity).
- Suppliers are able to integrate forward and compete directly with their present customers (e.g., a microprocessor producer like Intel).
- A purchasing industry buys only a small portion of the supplier group's goods and services and is thus unimportant to the supplier (e.g., sales of lawn mower tires are less important to the tire industry than are sales of auto tires).

What Is the Relative Power of Other Stakeholders?

A sixth force should be added to Porter's list to include a variety of other stakeholder groups from the task environment. Some of these groups are governments, local communities, creditors (if not included with suppliers), trade associations, special-interest groups, and stockholders. The importance of these stakeholders varies by industry. For example, environmental groups in Maine, Michigan, Oregon, and Iowa successfully fought to pass bills outlawing disposable bottles and cans, and thus deposits for most drink containers are now required. This effectively raised costs across the board, with most impact on the marginal producers who could not internally absorb all of these costs.

Do Industries Evolve Over Time?

Over time most industries evolve through a series of stages from growth through maturity to eventual decline. The strength of each of the six competitive forces described in the preceding section varies according to the stage of industry evolution. The industry life cycle is useful for explaining and predicting trends among the six forces driving industry competition. For example, when an industry is new, people often buy the product regardless of price because it fulfills a unique need. The industry may be fragmented—each firm serves only its local area (e.g., Chinese restaurants). As new competitors enter the industry, prices drop as a result of competition. Companies use the experience curve (to be discussed in Chapter 4) and economies of scale to reduce costs faster than the competition. Companies integrate to reduce costs even further by acquiring their suppliers and distributors. Competitors try to differentiate their products from one another's to avoid the fierce price competition common to a maturing industry.

By the time an industry enters maturity, products tend to become more like commodities. As buyers become more sophisticated over time, they base their purchasing decisions on better information. Price becomes a dominant concern given a minimum level of quality and features. One example of this trend is the videocassette recorder industry. By the 1990s, there were few major differences among VCRs. Consumers realized that, because slight improvements cost significantly more money, paying more than the minimum for a VCR made little sense.

As an industry moves through maturity toward possible decline, the growth rate of its products' sales slows and may even begin to decrease. To the extent that exit barriers are low, firms will begin converting their facilities to alternative uses or will sell them to another firm. The industry tends to consolidate around fewer but larger competitors. For example, the U.S. major home appliance industry (described in the *Company Spotlight on Maytag Corporation* feature) changed from being a "fragmented" industry of hundreds of appliance manufacturers in the industry's early years to a mature oligopoly of five companies (including Maytag) controlling over 98% of U.S. major home appliance sales.

How Are International Industries Categorized?

World industries vary on a continuum from multidomestic to global (see Figure 3.5).[10] **Multidomestic industries** are specific to each country or group of countries. This type of international industry is a collection of essentially domestic industries, like retailing and insurance. The activities in a subsidiary of a multinational corporation (MNC) in this type of industry are essentially independent of the activities of the MNC's subsidiaries in other countries. In each country, the MNC tailors its products or services to the very specific needs of consumers in that particular country. **Global industries**, in contrast, operate worldwide, with MNCs making only small adjustments for country-specific circumstances. A global industry is one in which an MNC's activities in one country are significantly affected by its activities in other countries. MNCs produce products or services in various locations throughout the world and sell them all over the world, making only minor adjustments for specific country requirements. Examples of global industries are commercial aircraft, television sets, semiconductors, copiers, automobiles, watches, and tires. The largest industrial corporations in the world in terms of dollar sales are, for the most part, multinational corporations operating in global industries.

The factors that tend to determine whether an industry will be primarily multidomestic or primarily global are (1) the *pressure for coordination* within the multinational corporations operating in that industry and (2) the *pressure for local*

COMPANY SPOTLIGHT

MAYTAG
Corporation

**Evolution of
the U.S. Major
Home Appliance
Industry**

In 1945, there were approximately 300 U.S. major home appliance manufacturers in the United States. By 1995, however, the "big five" of Whirlpool, General Electric, AB Electrolux (*no* relation to Electrolux Corporation, a U.S. company selling Electrolux brand vacuum cleaners), Maytag, and Raytheon controlled over 98% of the U.S. market. The consolidation of the industry over the period was a result of fierce domestic competition. Emphasis on quality and durability coupled with strong price competition drove the surviving firms to increased efficiencies and a strong concern for customer satisfaction.

Prior to World War II, most appliance manufacturers produced a limited line of appliances deriving from one successful product. General Electric made refrigerators, Maytag focused on washing machines, Hotpoint produced electric ranges. Each offered variations of its basic product, but not until 1945 did firms begin to offer full lines of various appliances. By 1955, the major appliance industry began experiencing overcapacity, leading to mergers and acquisitions and a proliferation of national and private brands. Product reliability improved even though real prices (adjusted for inflation) declined about 10%.

Acknowledging that the U.S. major home appliance industry had reached maturity (future U.S. unit sales were expected to grow only 1–2% annually on average for the foreseeable future), U.S. appliance makers decided to expand into Europe (where unit sales were expected to grow 5% annually). With Whirlpool's acquisition of the appliance business of Philips (the Netherlands), GE's joint venture with GEC (United Kingdom), AB Electrolux's (Sweden) purchase of White in the United States, and Maytag's acquisition of Hoover (vacuum cleaners worldwide plus major home appliances in the U.K.), the level of competition increased dramatically in both Europe and North America during the 1990s. In addition, rapid economic growth in Asia as well as in Mexico and South America had tremendous implications for the emerging global appliance industry. Environmental scanning and industry analysis had to be international in scope if a firm was to succeed in the twenty-first century.

responsiveness on the part of individual country markets. To the extent that the pressure for coordination is strong and the pressure for local responsiveness is weak for multinational corporations within a particular industry, that industry will tend to become global. In contrast, when the pressure for local responsiveness is strong and the pressure for coordination is weak for multinational corporations in an industry, that industry will tend to be multidomestic. Between these two extremes lie a number of industries with varying characteristics of both multidomestic and global industries.

FIGURE
3.5

Continuum of International Industries

Multidomestic ◄——————————————————————————————————► *Global*

Industry in which companies tailor their products to the specific needs of consumers in a particular country.	Industry in which companies manufacture and sell the same products, with only minor adjustments made for individual countries around the world.
• Retailing	• Automobiles
• Insurance	• Tires
• Banking	• Television sets

What Is a Strategic Group?

A **strategic group** is a set of business units or firms that "pursue similar strategies with similar resources."[11] Categorizing firms in any one industry into a set of strategic groups is very useful to strategic managers as a way of better understanding the competitive environment. Because a corporation's structure and culture tend to reflect the kinds of strategies it follows, companies or business units belonging to a particular strategic group within the same industry tend to be strong rivals and tend to be more similar to each other than to competitors in other strategic groups within the same industry. For example, although McDonald's and Olive Garden are a part of the same restaurant industry, they have different missions, objectives, and strategies and thus belong to different strategic groups. They generally have very little in common and pay little attention to each other when planning competitive actions. Burger King and Hardee's, however, have a great deal in common with McDonald's in terms of their similar strategy of producing a high volume of low-priced meals targeted for sale to the average family. Consequently they are strong rivals and are organized to operate in a similar fashion.

Strategic groups in a particular industry can be *mapped* by plotting the market positions of industry competitors on a two-dimensional graph using two strategic variables as the vertical and horizontal axes. See Figure 3.6. *First*, select two broad characteristics, such as price and menu, that differentiate the companies in an industry from one another. *Second*, plot the firms using these two characteristics as the dimensions. *Third*, draw a circle around those companies that are closest to one another as one strategic group, varying the size of the circle in proportion to the group's share of total industry sales. Name each strategic group in the restaurant industry with an identifying title, such as quick fast food or buffet style service.

Other dimensions, such as quality and degree of vertical integration, can also be used in additional graphs of the restaurant industry to show how the various firms in the industry compete. Keep in mind, however, that the two dimensions should not be highly correlated; otherwise, the circles on the map will simply lie along the diagonal, providing very little new information other than the obvious.

FIGURE 3.6

Mapping Strategic Groups in the U.S. Restaurant Chain Industry

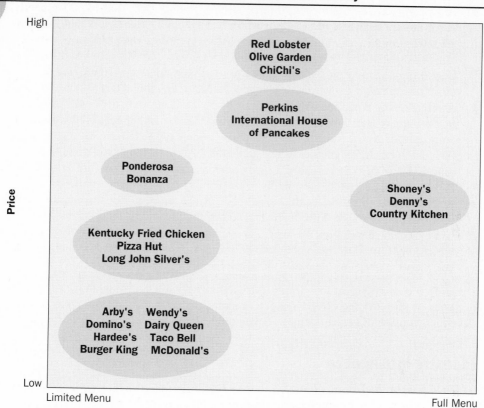

High

Red Lobster
Olive Garden
ChiChi's

Perkins
International House
of Pancakes

Ponderosa
Bonanza

Shoney's
Denny's
Country Kitchen

Kentucky Fried Chicken
Pizza Hut
Long John Silver's

Arby's   Wendy's
Domino's   Dairy Queen
Hardee's   Taco Bell
Burger King McDonald's

Price

Low

Limited Menu

Full Menu

Product-Line Breadth

What Are Strategic Types?

In analyzing the level of competitive intensity within a particular industry or strategic group, it is useful to characterize the various competitors for predictive purposes. A **strategic type** is a category of firms based on a common strategic orientation and a combination of structure, culture, and processes consistent with that strategy. According to Miles and Snow, competing firms within a single industry can be categorized on the basis of their general strategic orientation into one of four basic types.[12] This distinction helps explain why companies facing similar situations behave differently and why they continue to do so over a long period of time. These general types have the following characteristics:

- **Defenders** are companies with a limited product line that focus on improving the efficiency of their existing operations. This cost orientation makes them unlikely to innovate in new areas. An example is the Adolph Coors Company, which for many years emphasized production efficiency in its one Colorado brewery and virtually ignored marketing.

- **Prospectors** are companies with fairly broad product lines that focus on product innovation and market opportunities. This sales orientation makes them somewhat inefficient. They tend to emphasize creativity over efficiency. An example is the Miller Brewing Company, which successfully promoted "light" beer and generated aggressive, innovative advertising campaigns, but had to close a brand-new brewery when management overestimated market demand.

- **Analyzers** are corporations that operate in at least two different product-market areas, one stable and one variable. In the stable areas, efficiency is emphasized; in the variable areas, innovation is emphasized. An example is Anheuser-Busch, which can take a defender orientation to protect its massive market share in U.S. beer and a prospector orientation to generate sales in its snack foods and amusement parks.

- **Reactors** are corporations that lack a consistent strategy-structure-culture relationship. Their (often ineffective) responses to environmental pressures tend to be piecemeal strategic changes. An example is the Pabst Brewing Company, which, because of numerous takeover attempts, has been unable to generate a consistent strategy to keep its sales from dropping.

Dividing the competition into these four categories enables the strategic manager not only to monitor the effectiveness of certain strategic orientations, but also to develop scenarios of future industry developments (discussed later in this chapter).

3.3 Industry Intelligence

Much external environmental scanning is done on an informal and individual basis. Information is obtained from a variety of sources, such as customers, suppliers, bankers, consultants, publications, personal observations, subordinates, superiors, and peers. For example, R&D scientists and engineers can learn about new products and competitors' ideas at professional meetings; someone from the purchasing department, speaking with supplier-representatives' personnel, may also uncover valuable bits of information about a competitor. A study of product innovation in the scientific instrument and machine tool industries found that customers initiated 80% of all product innovations with their inquiries and complaints.[13] In these industries, the sales force and service departments must be especially vigilant.

Industry intelligence, however, is a formal program of gathering information on a company's competitors. Less than 5% of U.S. corporations have fully developed intelligence programs. In contrast, all Japanese corporations involved in international business and over half of German and Swedish companies have active intelligence programs.[14] This situation is changing, however. At General Mills, for example, all employees of the company have been trained to recognize and tap sources of competitive information. Janitors no longer simply place orders with suppliers of cleaning materials, they also ask about relevant practices at competing firms!

Most corporations rely on outside organizations to provide them with environmental data. Firms such as A. C. Nielsen Co. provide subscribers with bimonthly data on brand share, retail prices, percentages of stores stocking an item, and percentages of stock-out stores. Management can use these data to spot regional and national trends as well as to assess market share. "Information brokers" such as FIND/SVP and Finsbury Data Services sell information on market conditions, government regulations, competitors, and new products. Typically the largest corporations spend from $25,000 to $30,000 per year for information services. Many business corporations have established their own in-house libraries and computerized information systems to deal with the growing mass of available information.

Some companies, however, choose to use industrial espionage or other intelligence-gathering techniques to get their information straight from their competitors. For example, Avon Products hired private investigators to retrieve documents (some of them shredded) that Mary Kay Corporation had thrown away in a public Dumpster. Even Procter & Gamble, which defends itself like a fortress from information leaks, is vulnerable. A competitor was able to learn the precise launch date of a concentrated laundry detergent in Europe when one of its people visited the factory where machines were being made. Simply asking a few questions about what a certain machine did, for whom it was being built, and when it would be delivered was all that was necessary.

3.4 Forecasting

Once a company has collected data about its current environmental situation, it must analyze present trends to learn if they will continue. The strategic planning horizon for many large corporations is from five to ten years in the future. A long-term planning horizon is especially necessary for large, capital-intensive corporations such as automobile or heavy-machinery manufacturers. In these corporations, moving from an accepted proposal to a finished product requires many years. Most corporations must base their future plans on a forecast, a set of assumptions about what that future will look like. These assumptions can be derived from an entrepreneur's vision, from a head-in-the-sand hope that the future will be similar to the present, or from the opinions of experts.

Why Are Assumptions Dangerous?

A forecast is nothing more than a leap of faith into the future. Environmental scanning provides reasonably hard data on the present situation, but intuition and luck are needed to accurately predict the future. Faulty underlying assumptions are the most frequent cause of forecasting errors. Nevertheless, many managers who formulate and implement strategic plans have little or no realization that their success is based on a series of assumptions. Many long-range plans are simply based on projections of the current situation. Tupperware is an example of what can happen when corporate strategy rests on the very questionable assumption that the future will simply be an extension of the present. Management not only assumed in the 1960s and 1970s that Tupperware parties would continue to be an excellent distribution channel, but its faith in this assumption blinded it to information about America's changing lifestyles and their likely impact on sales. Even in the 1990s, when Tupperware executives realized that their extrapolated sales forecasts were no longer justified, instead of working to improve their forecasting techniques, they merely changed their assumptions.

What Forecasting Techniques Are Available?

Various techniques are used to forecast future situations, and each has its proponents and critics. A study of nearly 500 of the world's largest corporations revealed trend extrapolation to be the most widely practiced form of forecasting—over 70% use this technique either occasionally or frequently.[15] Simply stated, **extrapolation** is the extension of present trends into the future. It rests on the assumption that the world is reasonably consistent and changes slowly in the short run. Approaches of this type include time-series methods, which attempt to carry a series of historical events forward into the future. The basic problem with extrapolation is that a historical trend is based on a series of patterns or relationships among so many different variables that a change in any one can drastically alter the future direction of the trend. As a rule of thumb, the further into the past one can find relevant data supporting the trend, the more confidence one can have in the prediction.

Brainstorming and statistical modeling also are popular forecasting techniques. **Brainstorming** is a nonquantitative approach requiring simply the presence of people with some knowledge of the situation to be predicted. The basic ground rule is to propose ideas without first mentally screening them. No criticism is allowed. Ideas tend to build on previous ideas until a consensus is reached. This is a good technique to use with operating managers who have more faith in "gut feel" than in quantitative "number-crunching" techniques. **Statistical modeling** is a quantitative technique that attempts to discover causal or at least explanatory factors that link two or more time series together. Examples of statistical modeling are regression analysis and other econometric methods. Although very useful in the grasping of historic trends, statistical modeling, like trend extrapolation, is based on historical data. As the patterns of relationships change, the accuracy of the forecast deteriorates. Other forecasting techniques, such as cross-impact analysis (CIA) and trend-impact analysis (TIA), have not established themselves successfully as regularly employed tools.

Scenario writing appears to be the most widely used forecasting technique after trend extrapolation. Originated by Royal Dutch Shell, scenarios are focused descriptions of different likely futures presented in a narrative fashion. The scenario thus may be merely a written description of some future state, in terms of key variables and issues, or it may be generated in combination with other forecasting techniques.

An **industry scenario** is a forecasted description of a particular industry's likely future. It is a scenario that is developed by analyzing the probable impact of future societal forces on key groups in a particular industry. The process may operate as follows:[16]

1. Examine possible shifts in the societal variables.
2. Identify uncertainties in each of the six forces of the task environment (e.g., potential entrants, competitors, likely substitutes, buyers, suppliers, and other key stakeholders).
3. Make a range of plausible assumptions about future trends.
4. Combine assumptions about individual trends into internally consistent scenarios.
5. Analyze the industry situation that would prevail under each scenario.
6. Determine the sources of competitive advantage under each scenario.
7. Predict competitors' behavior under each scenario.
8. Select those scenarios that are either most likely to occur or are most likely to have a strong impact on the future of the company. Use these in strategy formulation.

3.5   Synthesis of External Factors—EFAS

Once strategic managers have scanned the societal and task environments and identified a number of likely external factors for their particular corporation, they may want to refine their analysis of these factors using a form such as that given in Table 3.2. The **EFAS (External Factors Analysis Summary) Matrix** is one way to organize the external factors into the generally accepted categories of opportunities and threats as well as to analyze how well a particular company's management (rating) is responding to these specific factors in light of the perceived importance (weight) of these factors to the company. To generate an EFAS Matrix, complete the following steps for the company being analyzed:

- *Column 1* **External Factors:** List the eight to ten most important opportunities and threats facing the company.
- *Column 2* **Weight:** Assign a weight for each to each factor from **1.00** (*Most Important*) to 0.00 (*Not Important*) based on that factor's probable impact on a particular company's current strategic position. The higher the weight, the more important this factor is to the current and future success of the company. **(All weights must sum to 1.00 regardless of the number of strategic factors.)**
- *Column 3* **Rating:** Assign a rating to each factor from 5 (*Outstanding*) to 1 (*Poor*) based on that particular company's current response to that particular factor. Each rating is a judgment regarding how well the company is currently dealing with each external factor.

5	4	3	2	1
Outstanding	Above Average	Average	Below Average	Poor

- *Column 4* **Weighted Score:** Multiply the **weight** in Column 2 for each factor times its **rating** in Column 3 to obtain that factor's **weighted score.** This results in a weighted score for each factor ranging from **5.00** (*Outstanding*) **to 1.00** (*Poor*) with 3.00 as the average.
- *Column 5* **Comments:** Note why a particular factor was selected and how its weight and rating were estimated.

TABLE 3.2 **External Strategic Factor Analysis Summary (EFAS): Maytag as Example**

External Strategic Factors	Weight	Rating	Weighted Score	Comments
	1	2	3	4	5
Opportunities				
• Economic integration of European Community	.20	4	.80	Acquisition of Hoover
• Demographics favor quality appliances	.10	5	.50	Maytag quality
• Economic development of Asia	.05	1	.05	Low Maytag presence
• Opening of Eastern Europe	.05	2	.10	Will take time
• Trend to "Super Stores"	.10	2	.20	Maytag weak in this channel
Threats				
• Increasing government regulations	.10	4	.40	Well positioned
• Strong U.S. competition	.10	4	.40	Well positioned
• Whirlpool and Electrolux strong globally	.15	3	.45	Hoover weak globally
• New product advances	.05	1	.05	Questionable
• Japanese appliance companies	.10	2	.20	Only Asian presence is Australia
Total	**1.00**		**3.15**	

Notes:

1. List opportunities and threats (5–10 each) in column 1.

2. Weight each factor from 1.0 (Most Important) to 0.0 (Not Important) in Column 2 based on that factor's probable impact on the company's strategic position. **The total weights must sum to 1.00.**

3. Rate each factor from 5 (Outstanding) to 1 (Poor) in Column 3 based on the company's response to that factor.

4. Multiply each factor's weight times its rating to obtain each factor's weighted score in Column 4.

5. Use Column 5 (comments) for rationale used for each factor.

6. Add the weighted scores to obtain the total weighted score for the company in Column 4. This tells how well the company is responding to the strategic factors in its external environment.

Finally, *add the weighted scores for all the external factors in Column 4* to determine the total weighted score for that particular company. The **total weighted score** indicates how well a particular company is responding to current and expected factors in its external environment. The score can be used to compare that firm to other firms in its industry.

As an example of this procedure, Table 3.2 includes a number of external factors for Maytag Corporation with corresponding weights, ratings, and weighted scores provided.

In Conclusion . . .

When Wal-Mart comes to town, it is not always appreciated. In fact, it is sometimes referred to as the "Merchant of Death." Wal-Mart earned that reputation when small town merchants were unable to compete with the newcomer's wide selection and low prices and went out of business. When Fred Nelson, owner of Nelson Mill & Agri-Center in Viroqua, Wisconsin, learned that Wal-Mart was planning to come to town, he did something about it. He took six employees on a spying mission to visit the discounter 140 miles away in Anamosa, Iowa. After checking prices and service at the Wal-Mart, Nelson talked with the manager of the farm store next door to learn how he responded to the new neighbor. Nelson learned that he couldn't match Wal-Mart's prices because it buys in such large quantities, but he could focus on available niches. Returning home to Viroqua, Nelson reduced his inventories of toys and housewares and eliminated health and beauty aids entirely. He focused on clothing, tools, and giftwares and stocked better quality brands and a broader range than Wal-Mart. He expanded his repair and parts-ordering services, liberalized his returns policy, and extended his hours. He stressed his service to his main clientele—local farmers. He expanded his farm supply department and priced basics like WD-40 at Wal-Mart levels. Thanks to his environmental scanning efforts, Fred Nelson's new strategy has resulted in stable profits and annual sales in excess of $8 million—up from $6.8 million before Wal-Mart came to town.[17]

Discussion Questions

1. Discuss how a development in a corporation's societal environment can affect the corporation through its task environment.

2. According to Porter, what determines the level of competitive intensity in an industry?

3. According to Porter's discussion of industry analysis, is Pepsi Cola a substitute for Coca-Cola?

4. How can a strategic decision maker identify strategic factors in the corporation's external environment?

5. Compare and contrast trend extrapolation with the writing of scenarios as forecasting techniques.

Key Terms

environmental uncertainty
environmental scanning
societal environment
task environment
issues priority matrix
industry analysis
external strategic factors
industry
entry barriers
substitute products
multidomestic industry

global industry
strategic group
strategic type
industry intelligence
extrapolation
brainstorming
statistical modeling
scenario writing
industry scenario
EFAS Matrix

4

Internal Scanning: Organizational Analysis

A man stands before his mirror and, as he does many times a week, prepares to shave. After applying shaving cream, he deliberately shaves only one side of his face. He then changes razors to do the other side. He runs his fingers over his cheeks to check the closeness of the shave. "That's the only way to really compare shaves," he comments. This is a typical morning for Alfred Zeien, chairman and chief executive officer of Gillette Company, who routinely tests both his company's razors against those of his competition.

Gillette is a company obsessed with shaving and with making the best razors. It routinely spends large amounts of money on research and development. At any given time, Gillette is working on as many as 20 experimental razors. Why does this company spend so much time and money on a product so simple and as mundane as a razor? The answer lies in Gillette's dedication to being not only the best in its field, but also in designing razors that are difficult for its competitors to copy. In the days of the double-edge razor, others could make blades that fit Gillette's, as well as their own, razors relatively easily. Trac II and the Sensor razor changed things—it took some time for rivals to imitate these products. The Sensor design, in particular, was very difficult to copy, partially because the manufacturing equipment needed to produce it was so expensive and complicated. This gave Gillette the competitive advantage it needed to dominate the marketplace.[1]

4.1 Resource-based View of the Firm

Scanning and analyzing the external environment for opportunities and threats is not enough to provide an organization a competitive advantage. Strategic managers must also look within the corporation itself to identify **internal strategic** factors—those critical strengths and weaknesses that are likely to determine if the firm will be able to take advantage of opportunities while avoiding threats. This internal scanning is often referred to as **organizational analysis** and is concerned with identifying and developing an organization's resources.

How Do Resources Determine Competitive Advantage?

Proposing that a company's sustained competitive advantage is primarily determined by its resource endowments, Grant proposes a five-step, resource-based approach to strategy analysis:

1. Identify and classify the firm's resources in terms of strengths and weaknesses.
2. Combine the firm's strengths into specific capabilities. **Corporate capabilities** are the things that a corporation can do exceedingly well. These are often referred to as a firm's *distinctive* or *core competencies*.
3. Appraise the profit potential of these resources and capabilities in terms of their potential for sustainable competitive advantage and the ability to harvest the profits resulting from the use of these resources and capabilities.
4. Select the strategy that best exploits the firm's resources and capabilities relative to external opportunities.
5. Identify resource gaps and invest in upgrading weaknesses.[2]

As indicated in Step 2, when an organization's resources are combined, they form a number of capabilities. In the example provided earlier, Gillette has two identifiable resources: (1) the technology itself, and (2) the capability for developing and using new technological resources.

What Determines the Sustainability of an Advantage?

The following four characteristics of resources and capabilities are important determinants of the sustainability of a firm's competitive advantage:

- **Durability:** The rate at which a firm's underlying resources and capabilities depreciate or become obsolete. For example, Intel's skills in using CISC technology to design and manufacture 486 and pentium microprocessors for personal computers won't be of much use when the industry moves to RISC technology.
- **Transparency:** The speed with which competitors can understand the relationship of resources and capabilities supporting a successful firm's strategy. For example, because companies in the U.S. major home appliance industry use very similar manufacturing processes, any new product feature offered by one company is usually copied by competitors the next year.
- **Transferability:** The ability of competitors to gather the resources and capabilities necessary to support a competitive challenge. For example, it may be very difficult to duplicate another firm's key resource of Rocky Mountain spring water, especially if the imitator is located in Alabama.
- **Replicability:** The ability of competitors to use duplicated resources and capabilities to imitate a firm's success. For example, although competitors have tried to imitate Procter & Gamble's success with brand management by hiring

brand managers away from P&G, they have often failed to duplicate P&G's success. The competitors failed to identify less visible P&G coordination mechanisms or to realize that P&G's brand management style conflicted with their own corporate culture.

An organization's resources and capabilities can be placed on a continuum based on the extent to which they can be duplicated (that is, are transparent, transferable, and replicable) by another firm. This continuum is depicted in Figure 4.1. At one extreme are *slow-cycle resources,* which are durable and enduring because they are shielded by patents, geography, strong brand names, and the like. These resources and capabilities provide a sustainable competitive advantage. Gillette's Sensor razor is a good example of a product built around slow-cycle resources. The other extreme includes *fast-cycle resources,* which face the highest imitation pressures because they are based on a concept or technology that can be easily duplicated, such as Sony's Walkman. To the extent that a company has fast-cycle resources, the primary way it can compete successfully is through increased speed from lab to marketplace. Otherwise, it has no real sustainable competitive advantage.

4.2 ⟩ Scanning the Internal Environment

Strategic managers should identify those variables within their company that may be important strengths or weaknesses. A variable is a strength if it provides a company with a competitive advantage. It is something the firm does or has the potential to do particularly well relative to the abilities of existing or potential competitors. A variable is a weakness if it is something the corporation does poorly or doesn't have

FIGURE 4.1   Continuum of Resource Sustainability

Source: Suggested by J. R. Williams, "How Sustainable Is Your Competitive Advantage?" *California Management Review* (Spring 1992), p. 33.

the capacity to do although its competitors have that capacity. Evaluate the importance of these variables to ascertain if they are **internal strategic factors**—the particular strengths and weaknesses that will help determine the future of the company. This can be done by comparing measures of these variables with measures of (1) the company's past performance, (2) the company's key competitors, and (3) the industry as a whole. To the extent that a variable (such as a firm's financial situation) is significantly different from the firm's past, its key competitors, or the industry average, that variable is likely to be a strategic factor and should be considered in strategic decisions.

One of the simplest ways to scan and analyze the internal environment of an organization is to examine its functional resources. Functional resources include not only the financial, physical, and human resources in each area, but also the ability of the people in each area to formulate and implement, under corporate guidance, the necessary functional objectives, strategies, and policies. Thus the resources include both the knowledge of analytical concepts and procedural techniques common to each area and the ability of the people in each area to use them effectively. If used properly, these resources serve as strengths to support strategic decisions.

What Are the Typical Organizational Structures?

Although an almost infinite variety of structural forms are possible, certain basic types predominate in modern complex organizations. Figure 4.2 illustrates three basic structures: *simple, functional,* and *divisional.* The conglomerate structure is a variant of divisional structure and is thus not depicted as a fourth structure. Generally speaking, each structure tends to support some corporate strategies over others.

- **Simple structure** has no functional or product categories and is appropriate for a small, entrepreneur-dominated company with one or two product lines that operates in a reasonably small, easily identifiable market niche. Employees tend to be generalists and jacks-of-all-trades.
- **Functional structure** is appropriate for a medium-sized firm with several product lines in one industry. Employees tend to be specialists in the business functions important to that industry, such as manufacturing, marketing, finance, and human resources.
- **Divisional structure** is appropriate for a large corporation with many product lines in several related industries. Employees tend to be functional specialists organized according to product or market distinctions. General Motors, for example, groups its various auto lines into the separate divisions of Chevrolet, Pontiac, Oldsmobile, Buick, and Cadillac. Management attempts to find some synergy among divisional activities through the use of committees and horizontal linkages.
- **Conglomerate structure** is appropriate for a large corporation with many product lines in several unrelated industries. A variant of the divisional structure, the conglomerate structure (sometimes called a holding company) is typically an assemblage of legally independent firms (subsidiaries) operating under

FIGURE
4.2
Basic Structures of Corporations

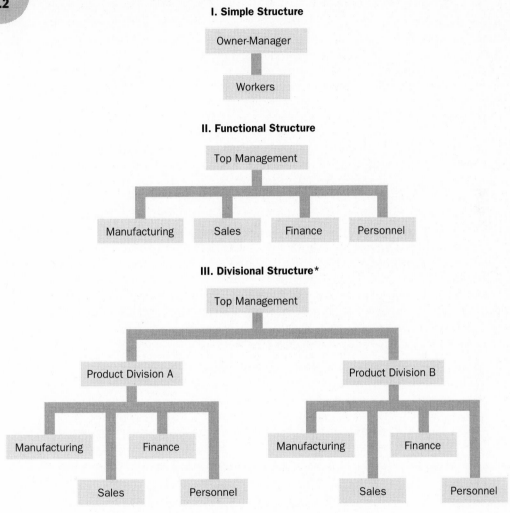

*Conglomerate structure is a variant of the divisional structure.

one corporate umbrella but controlled thorough the subsidiaries' boards of directors. The unrelated nature of the subsidiaries prevents any attempt at gaining synergy among them.

If the current basic structure of a corporation does not easily support a strategy under consideration, top management must decide if the proposed strategy is feasible or if the structure should be changed to a more advanced structure such as the Strategic Business Unit (SBU), matrix, or network (*to be discussed in Chapter 7*).

What Is Corporate Culture?

Corporate culture is the collection of beliefs, expectations, and values learned and shared by a corporation's members and transmitted from one generation of employees to another. The term *corporate culture* generally reflects the values of the founder(s) and the mission of the firm. It gives a company a sense of identity: "This is who we are. This is what we do. This is what we stand for." The culture includes the dominant orientation of the company, such as research and development at Hewlett-Packard, customer service at Nordstrom's, or product quality at Maytag.

Corporate culture has two distinct attributes.[3] The first of these, **intensity** (or depth) is the degree to which members of a unit accept the norms, values, or other culture content associated with the unit. Organizations with strong norms promoting a particular value, such as quality at Maytag, have intensive cultures, whereas new firms (or those in transition) have weaker, less intensive cultures. Employees of a company with an intensive culture tend to exhibit consistency in behavior, that is, they tend to act similarly over time. The second attribute, **integration** (or breadth) is the extent to which units throughout an organization share a common culture. Organizations with a pervasive dominant culture may be hierarchically controlled and power oriented, such as a military unit, and have highly integrated cultures. All employees tend to hold the same cultural values and norms. In contrast, a company that is structured into diverse units by functions or divisions usually exhibits some strong subcultures (e.g., R&D versus manufacturing) and an overall weaker corporate culture.

Corporate culture fulfills several important functions in an organization:

1. Culture conveys a sense of identity for employees.
2. Culture helps generate employees' commitment to something greater than themselves.
3. Culture adds to the stability of the organization as a social system.
4. Culture serves as a frame of reference for employees to use to make sense out of organizational activities and to use as a guide for appropriate behavior.[4]

Corporate culture shapes the behavior of people in the corporation. Because these cultures have a powerful influence on the behavior of managers at all levels, they can strongly affect a corporation's ability to shift its strategic direction. A strong culture should not only promote survival, but should also create the basis for a superior competitive position. To the extent that the critical capability is embedded in an organization's culture, it will be very hard for a competitor to duplicate it. The *Company Spotlight on Maytag Corporation* feature explains how corporate culture affects Maytag's strategic managers.

A change in mission, objectives, strategies, or policies is not likely to be successful if it goes against the firm's accepted culture. Foot-dragging and even sabotage may result, as employees fight to resist a radical change in corporate philosophy. Like structure, if an organization's culture is compatible with a new strategy, it is an internal strength. But if the corporate culture is not compatible with the proposed strategy, it is a serious weakness.

COMPANY SPOTLIGHT

MAYTAG Corporation

Culture as a Key Strength

In the 1990s, the Maytag Corporation still reflected the strong ideas of Maytag Company founder F. L. Maytag. The corporate headquarters were housed on the second floor of a relatively small and modest building. Built in 1961, the Newton, Iowa, building also housed Maytag Company administrative offices on the first floor. Responding to a comment from outside observers that the corporation had "Spartan" offices, Leonard Hadley, then-Chief Operating Officer, looked around at his rather small, windowless office and said, "See for yourself. We want to keep corporate staff to a minimum." Hadley felt that the headquarters' location, coupled with the fact that most of the corporate officers had originally been with the Maytag Company, resulted in an overall top management concern for product quality and financial conservatism.

When asked to discuss specific resources that gave the corporation a competitive edge, past-Chairman and CEO Daniel Krumm pointed to the firm's roots and focused on dedication to quality above corporate perquisites:

That, of course, has been Maytag's hallmark for as long as any of us can remember. We believe quality and reliability are, ultimately, what the consumer wants. That has been a challenge to us as we have acquired companies that may have had a different emphasis, but we have made significant recent strides in improving the quality of all our products.

What Are the Strategic Marketing Issues?

The marketing manager is the company's primary link to the customer and the competition. The manager must therefore be especially concerned with the firm's market position and marketing mix.

What Are Market Position and Segmentation?

Market position deals with the question, "Who are our customers?" It refers to the selection of specific areas for marketing concentration and can be expressed in terms of market, product, and geographical locations. Through market research, corporations are able to practice **market segmentation** with various products or services so that managers can discover what niches to seek, which new types of products to develop, and how to ensure that a company's many products do not directly compete with one another.

What Is Marketing Mix?

The **marketing mix** refers to the particular combination of key variables under the corporation's control that it can use to affect demand and to gain competitive advantage. These variables are *product*, *place*, *promotion*, and *price*. Within each of these four variables are several subvariables, listed in Table 4.1, that should be analyzed in terms of their effects on divisional and corporate performance.

What Is the Product Life Cycle?

One of the most useful concepts in marketing insofar as strategic management is concerned is that of the product life cycle. As depicted in Figure 4.3, the **product life cycle** is a graph showing time plotted against the dollar sales of a product as it moves from introduction through growth and maturity to decline. This concept enables a marketing manager to examine the marketing mix of a particular product or group of products in terms of its position in its life cycle.

What Are the Strategic Financial Issues?

The financial manager must ascertain the best sources of funds, uses of funds, and control of funds. Cash must be raised from internal or external sources and allocated for different uses. The flow of funds in the operations of the organization must be monitored. To the extent that a corporation is involved in international activities, currency fluctuations must be dealt with to ensure that profits aren't wiped out by the rise or fall of the dollar versus the yen, Deutsche mark, and other currencies. Benefits, in the form of returns, repayments, or products and services, must be given to the sources of outside financing. All these tasks must be handled in a way that complements and supports overall corporate strategy.

What Is Financial Leverage?

The mix of externally generated short-term and long-term funds in relation to the amount and timing of internally generated funds should be appropriate to the cor-

---

TABLE 4.1   **Marketing Mix Variables**

Product	Place	Promotion	Price
Quality	Channels	Advertising	List price
Features	Coverage	Personal selling	Discounts
Options	Locations	Sales promotion	Allowances
Style	Inventory	Publicity	Payment periods
Brand name	Transport		Credit terms
Packaging			
Sizes			
Services			
Warranties			
Returns			

Source: Philip Kotler, *Marketing Management: Analysis, Planning, and Control,* 4th ed. (Englewood Cliffs, N.J.: Prentice-Hall, 1980), p. 89. Copyright © 1980. Reprinted by permission of Prentice-Hall, Inc.

FIGURE
4.3

The Product Life Cycle

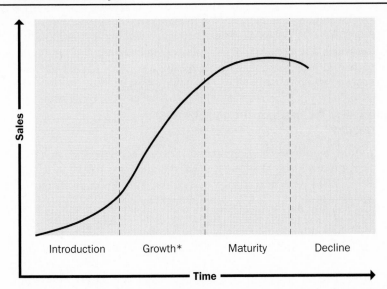

*The right end of the Growth stage is often called Competitive Turbulence because of price and distribution competition that shakes out the weaker competitors. For further information, see C. R. Wasson, *Dynamic Competitive Strategy and Product Life Cycles*, 3rd ed. (Austin, Tex.: Austin Press, 1978).

porate objectives, strategies, and policies. The concept of **financial leverage** (the ratio of total debt to total assets) helps describe the use of debt to increase the earnings available to common stockholders. Financing company activities by selling bonds or notes instead of through issuing stock boosts earnings per share: the interest paid on the debt reduces taxable income, but fewer stockholders share the profits. The debt, however, does raise the firm's break-even point above what it would have been if the firm had financed from internally generated funds only. High leverage may therefore be perceived as a corporate strength in times of prosperity and ever-increasing sales or as a weakness in times of a recession and falling sales because leverage magnifies the effect of an increase or decrease in dollar sales on earnings per share.

What Is Capital Budgeting?

Capital budgeting is the analyzing and ranking of possible investments in fixed assets such as land, buildings, and equipment in terms of the additional outlays and additional receipts that will result from each investment. A good finance department will be able to prepare such capital budgets and to rank them on the basis of some accepted criteria or *hurdle rate* (for example, years to pay back investment, rate of return, or time to break-even point) for the purpose of strategic decision making.

What Are the Strategic Research and Development (R&D) Issues?

The R&D manager is responsible for suggesting and implementing a company's technological strategy in light of its corporate objectives and policies. The manager's job therefore involves (1) choosing among alternative new technologies to use within the corporation, (2) developing methods of embodying the new technology in new products and processes, and (3) deploying resources so that the new technology can be successfully implemented.

What Are R&D Intensity, Technological Competence, and Technology Transfer?

The company must make available the resources necessary for effective research and development. A company's **R&D intensity** (its spending on R&D as a percentage of sales revenue) is a principal means of gaining market share in global competition. The amount spent on R&D often varies by industry. For example, the computer software and drug industries spend an average of 13.2% and 11.5%, respectively, of their sales dollar for R&D. A good rule of thumb for R&D spending is that a corporation should spend at a "normal" rate for that particular industry.

Simply spending money on R&D or new projects does not mean, however, that the money will produce useful results. A company's R&D unit should be evaluated for **technological competence** in both the development and the use of innovative technology. Not only should the corporation make a consistent research effort (as measured by reasonably constant corporate expenditures that result in usable innovations), it should also be proficient in managing research personnel and integrating their innovations into its day-to-day operations. If a company is not proficient in **technology transfer**, the process of taking a new technology from the laboratory to the marketplace, it will not gain much advantage from new technological advances. For example, Xerox Corporation has been criticized because it failed to take advantage of various innovations (such as the mouse and the graphical user interface for personal computers) developed originally in its sophisticated Palo Alto Research Center.

What Is the R&D Mix?

Scientists conduct **Basic R&D** in well-equipped laboratories, focusing on theoretical problem areas. The best indicators of a company's capability in this area are its patents and research publications. **Product R&D** concentrates on marketing and is concerned with product or product-packaging improvements. The best measurements of ability in this area are the number of successful new products introduced and the percentage of total sales and profits coming from products introduced within the past five years. **Engineering** or **process R&D** is concerned with engineering, concentrating on improving quality control, design specifications, and production equipment. A company's capability in this area can be measured by consistent reductions in unit manufacturing costs and product defects. Most corporations have a mix of basic, product, and process R&D, which varies by industry, company, and product line. The balance of these types of research is known as the **R&D mix** and should be appropriate to the strategy being considered and to each product's life cycle. For example, it is generally accepted that product R&D normally dominates the early stages of a product's life cycle (when the product's optimal form and features are still being debated), whereas process R&D becomes especially important in the later stages (when the product's design is solidified and the emphasis is on reducing costs and improving quality).

What Is the Impact of Technological Discontinuity on Strategy?

The R&D manager must determine when to abandon present technology and when to develop or adopt new technology. Richard Foster of McKinsey and Company states that the displacement of one technology by another (**technological discontinuity**) is a frequent and strategically important phenomenon. Such a discontinuity occurs when a new technology cannot simply be used to enhance the current technology but actually substitutes for that technology to yield better performance. For each technology within a given field or industry, according to Foster, the plotting of product performance against research effort/expenditures on a graph results in an S-shaped curve. He describes the process depicted in Figure 4.4 as follows:

> Early in the development of the technology a knowledge base is being built and progress requires a relatively large amount of effort. Later, progress comes more easily. And then, as the limits of that technology are approached, progress becomes slow and expensive. That is when R&D dollars should be allocated to technology with more potential. That is also—not so incidentally—when a competitor who has bet on a new technology can sweep away your business or topple an entire industry.[5]

The presence of a technological discontinuity in the world's steel industry during the 1960s explains why the large capital expenditures by U.S. steel companies failed to keep them competitive with the Japanese firms, which adopted the new technologies. As Foster points out, "History has shown that as one technology nears the end of its S curve, competitive leadership in a market generally changes hands."[6]

What Are the Strategic Operations Issues?

The primary task of the operations (manufacturing or service) manager is to develop and operate a system that will produce the required number of products or services, with a certain quality, at a given cost, within an allotted time. Many of the key concepts and techniques popularly used in manufacturing can be applied to service businesses. In general terms, manufacturing can be intermittent or continuous. In **intermittent systems** (job shops), the item is normally processed sequentially, but the work and sequence of the process vary. At each location, the tasks determine the details of processing and the time required for them. In contrast, **continuous systems** are those laid out as lines on which products can be continuously assembled or processed. An example is an automobile assembly line.

FIGURE
4.4

Technological Discontinuity

What the S-Curves Reveal

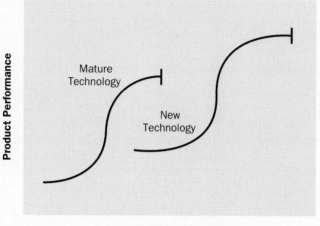

Research Effort/Expenditure

In the corporate planning process, it is generally assumed that incremental progress in technology will occur. But past developments in a given technology cannot be extrapolated into the future, because every technology has its limits. The key to competitiveness is to determine when to shift resources to a technology with more potential.

Source: P. Pascarella, "Are You Investing in the Wrong Technology?" *Industry Week* (July 25, 1983), p. 38. Copyright © 1983 Penton/IPC. All rights reserved. Reprinted by permission.

The type of manufacturing system that a corporation uses determines divisional or corporate strategy. It makes no sense, for example, to plan to increase sales by saturating the market with low-priced products if the company's manufacturing process was designed as an intermittent job shop system that produces one-time-only products to a customer's specifications. Conversely, a plan to produce several specialty products might not be economically feasible if the manufacturing process was designed to be a mass-producing, continuous system using low-skilled labor or special-purpose robots.

What Is Operating Leverage?

Continuous systems are popular because they allow a company to take advantage of manufacturing operating leverage. **Operating leverage** is the impact of a given change in sales volume on net operating income. For example, a highly labor-intensive firm has little automated machinery and thus a small amount of fixed costs. It has a fairly low break-even point, but its variable cost line has a relatively steep slope. Because most of the costs associated with the product are variable (many employees earn piece-rate wages), its variable costs are higher than those of automated firms. Its advantage over other firms is that it can operate at low levels and still be profitable. Once its sales reach break-even, however, the huge variable costs as a percentage of total costs keep the profit per unit relatively low. Its low operating leverage thus prevents the firm from gathering the huge profits possible from a high volume of sales. In terms of strategy, this firm should look for a niche in the marketplace for which it can produce and sell a reasonably small quantity of goods.

In contrast, a capital-intensive firm has a lot of money in fixed investments, such as automated processes and highly sophisticated machinery. Its relatively small but highly skilled labor force earns salaries rather than piece-rate wages. Consequently this firm has a high amount of fixed costs. It also has a relatively high break-even point, but its variable cost line rises slowly. Its advantage is that once it reaches break-even, its profits rise faster than do those of less automated firms. In terms of strategy, this firm needs to find a high-demand niche in the marketplace for which it can produce and sell a large quantity of goods. Its high operating leverage makes it an extremely profitable and competitive firm once it reaches its high break-even point. Changes in the level of sales have a magnified (leveraged) impact on profits. However, this type of firm is likely to suffer huge losses during a recession. During an economic downturn, the firm with less automation, and thus less leverage, is more likely to survive comfortably because a drop in sales primarily affects variable costs. It is often easier to lay off labor than to sell off specialized plants and machines.

What Is the Experience Curve?

A conceptual framework that many large corporations have used successfully is the experience curve (originally called the learning curve). The **experience curve** suggests that unit production costs decline by some fixed percentage (commonly 20–30%) each time the total accumulated volume of production (in units) doubles. The actual percentage varies by industry and is based on many variables: the amount of time it takes a person to learn a new task, scale economies, product and process improvements, and lower raw materials costs, among others. For example, in an industry with an 85% experience curve, a corporation might expect a 15% reduction in costs for every doubling of volume. The total costs per unit can be expected to drop from $100 when the total production is 10 units to $85 ($100 × 85%) when production increases to 20 units and to $72.25 ($85 × 85%) when it reaches 40 units. Achieving these results often means investing in R&D and fixed assets, resulting in higher operating leverage and less flexibility. Nevertheless, the manufacturing strategy is to build capacity ahead of demand in order to achieve the lower unit costs that develop from the experience curve. On the basis of some future point on the experience curve, price the product or service very low to preempt competition and increase market demand. The resulting high number of units sold and high market share should result in high profits, based on the low unit costs.

Management commonly uses the experience curve to estimate the production costs of (1) a product never before made with the present techniques and processes or (2) current products produced by newly introduced techniques or processes. The concept was first applied in the airframe industry and can be applied in the service industry as well. Although many firms have used experience curves extensively, an unquestioning acceptance of the industry norm (such as 80% for the airframe industry or 70% for integrated circuits) is risky. The experience curve of the industry as a whole might not hold true for a particular company for a variety of reasons.

What Is Flexible Manufacturing?

Recently the use of large mass-production facilities to take advantage of experience-curve economies has been criticized. The use of Computer-Assisted Design and Computer-Assisted Manufacturing (CAD/CAM) and robot technology means that learning times are shorter and products can be economically manufactured in small, customized batches. **Economies of scope** (in which common parts of the manufacturing activities of various products are combined to gain economies even though small numbers of each product are made) replace **economies of scale** (in which unit costs are reduced by making large numbers of the same product) in flexible manufacturing. **Flexible manufacturing** permits the low-volume output of custom-tailored products at relatively low unit costs through economies of scope. It is thus possible to have the cost advantages of continuous systems with the customer-oriented advantages of intermittent systems.

What Are the Strategic Human Resource Issues?

The primary task of the manager of human resources is to improve the match between individuals and jobs. A good HRM department should know how to use attitude surveys and other feedback devices to assess employees' satisfaction with their jobs and with the corporation as a whole. HRM managers should also use job analysis to obtain job description information about what each job needs to accomplish in terms of quality and quantity. Up-to-date job descriptions are essential not only for proper employee selection, appraisal, training, and development; wage and salary administration; and labor negotiations, but also for summarizing the corporatewide human resources in terms of employee-skill categories. Just as a company must know the number, type, and quality of its manufacturing facilities, it must also know the kinds of people it employs and the skills they possess. The best strategies are meaningless if employees do not have the skills to carry them out or if jobs cannot be designed to accommodate the available workers. Hewlett-Packard, for example, uses employee profiles to ensure that it has the right mix of talents for implementing its planned strategies.

How Should Teams Be Used?

Strategic managers are beginning to realize that they must be more flexible in their utilization of employees in order for human resources to be a strength. Human resource managers therefore need to be knowledgeable about work options such as part-time work, job sharing, flextime, extended leaves, contract work, and especially in the proper use of teams. About one in five U.S. companies is successfully using autonomous or self-directed work teams in which a group of people work together without a supervisor to plan, coordinate, and evaluate their own work.[7] Productivity and quality increased to such an extent at Northern Telecom that the company was able to reduce the number of quality inspectors by 40%.[8]

As a way to move a product more quickly through its development stage, companies like Motorola, Chrysler, NCR, Boeing, and General Electric have begun using cross-functional work teams. Instead of developing products in a series of steps—beginning with a request from sales, which leads to design, then to engineering and on to purchasing, and finally to manufacturing (often resulting in customer rejection of a costly product)—companies are tearing down the traditional walls separating departments so that people from each discipline can get involved in projects early on. In a process called *concurrent engineering*, the once-isolated specialists now work side by side and compare notes constantly in an effort to design cost-effective products with features customers want.

How Important Are Union Relations?

If the corporation is unionized, a good human resource manager should be able to work closely with the union. Although union membership in the United States has dropped to 11.9% of private-sector workers (16.1% if government workers are included) in 1992 from 23.3% in 1977, unions still represent close to 24% of workers in manufacturing in the United States. Outside the United States, however, the average proportion of unionized workers among 17 major industrialized nations actually increased from 48% in 1970 to 53% in 1987.[9] These developments have significant implications for the management of multinational corporations. To save jobs, U.S. unions are increasingly willing to support employee involvement programs designed to increase worker participation in decision making.

What Is the Quality of Work Life?

Human resource departments have found that to reduce employee dissatisfaction and unionization efforts (or, conversely, to improve employee satisfaction and existing union relations), they must consider the quality of work life in the design of jobs. Partially a reaction to the traditionally heavy emphasis on technical and economic factors in job design, **Quality of Work Life** emphasizes improving the human dimension of work. The knowledgeable human resource manager should therefore be able to improve the corporation's quality of work life by (1) introducing participative problem solving, (2) restructuring work, (3) introducing innovative reward systems, and (4) improving the work environment. These improvements should lead to a more participative corporate culture and thus higher productivity and quality products.

An organization's human resources are especially important in today's world of global communication and transportation systems. Competitors around the world copy advances in technology almost immediately. Because people are not as willing to move to other companies in other countries, the only long-term resource advantage remaining to corporations operating in the industrialized nations may lie in the area of skilled human resources.

What Are the Strategic Information Systems Issues?

The primary task of the manager of information systems (IS) is to design and manage the flow of information in an organization in ways that improve productivity and decision making. Information must be collected, stored, and synthesized in such a manner that it can answer important operating and strategic questions. The importance of this function is growing.

A corporation's information system can be a strength or a weakness in all three elements of strategic management. Not only can it aid in environmental scanning and in controlling a company's many activities, it can also be used as a strategic weapon in gaining competitive advantage. For example, American Hospital Supply (AHS), a leading manufacturer and distributor of a broad line of products for doctors, laboratories, and hospitals, developed an order-entry distribution system that directly linked the majority of its customers to AHS computers. The system was successful because it simplified ordering processes for customers, reduced costs for both AHS and the customer, and allowed AHS to provide pricing incentives to the customer. As a result, customer loyalty was high and AHS's share of the market grew.

An assessment of a corporation's strengths and weaknesses should take into account the level of development of the firm's information system. Information system development has at least four distinct phases:

Phase One: Companies use information systems to improve the efficiency of existing businesses through customer billing, data entry, and report writing. The IS helps companies save money but cannot yet be used for competitive advantage. For example, American Airlines first installed its Sabre computerized reservation system to keep better track of available seats on its flights.

Phase Two: Companies attempt to differentiate themselves from their competitors by using their installed IS to introduce new, electronically delivered products and services to *existing* customers. During this phase, for example, American Airlines connected its Sabre system to travel agents' offices. Because this made reservations easier for agents, American's ticket sales increased.

Phase Three: Companies attempt to sell new information-based products and services to *new* customers. American in this phase opened up its Sabre system to competing airlines. It not only gained revenues from processing other airlines' tickets, it further increased its own ticket sales.

Phase Four: Firms develop new, innovative information-based products and services on an ongoing basis. During this phase, American Airlines began selling information gathered from travel agents on Sabre. American used its database on fliers for its Advantage program by tracking their mileage and offering free flights for specific amounts of mileage on American flights.[10]

Synthesis of Internal Factors—IFAS

After strategic managers have scanned the internal organizational environment and identified factors for their particular corporation, they may wish to summarize their analysis of these factors using a form such as that given in Table 4.2. This **IFAS (Internal Factor Analysis Summary) Matrix** is one way to organize the internal factors into the generally accepted categories of strengths and weaknesses as

TABLE 4.2 **Internal Strategic Factor Analysis Summary (IFAS): Maytag as Example**

Internal Strategic Factors	Weight	Rating	Weighted Score	Comments
Strengths	1	2	3	4	5
• Quality Maytag culture	.15	5	.75	Quality key to success
• Experienced top management	.05	4	.20	Know appliances
• Vertical integration	.10	4	.40	Dedicated factories
• Employee relations	.05	3	.15	Good, but deteriorating
• Hoover's international orientation	.15	3	.45	Hoover name in cleaners
Weaknesses				
• Process-oriented R&D	.05	2	.10	Slow on new products
• Distribution channels	.05	2	.10	Superstores replacing small dealers
• Financial position	.15	2	.30	High debt load
• Global positioning	.20	2	.40	Hoover weak outside the United Kingdom and Australia
• Manufacturing facilities	.05	4	.20	Investing now
Total	**1.00**		**3.05**	

Notes:

1. List strengths and weaknesses (5–10 each) in Column 1.

2. Weight each factor from 1.0 (Most Important) to 0.0 (Not Important) in Column 2 based on that factor's probable impact on the company's strategic position. **The total weights must sum to 1.00.**

3. Rate each factor from 5 (Outstanding) to 1 (Poor) in Column 3 based on the company's response to that factor.

4. Multiply each factor's weight times its rating to obtain each factor's weighted score in Column 4.

5. Use Column 5 (comments) for rationale used for each factor.

6. Add the weighted scores to obtain the total weighted score for the company in Column 4. This tells how well the company is responding to the strategic factors in its internal environment.

Source: T. L. Wheelen and J. D. Hunger, "Internal Strategic Factor Analysis Summary (IFAS)." Copyright © 1991 by Wheelen and Hunger Associates. Reprinted by permission.

well as to analyze how well a particular company's management is responding to these specific factors in light of the perceived importance of these factors to the company. To use the IFAS Matrix, complete the following steps for the company being analyzed:

- *Column 1* **Internal Factors:** List the eight to ten most important strengths and weaknesses facing the company.
- *Column 2* **Weight:** Assign a weight for each to each factor from **1.00** (*Most Important*) to **0.00** (*Not Important*) based on that factor's probable impact on a particular company's current strategic position. The higher the weight, the more important this factor is to the current and future success of the company. (**All weights must sum to 1.00 regardless of the number of strategic factors.**)
- *Column 3* **Assign Rating:** Assign a rating to each factor from **5** (*Outstanding*) **to 1** (*Poor*) based on management's current response to that particular factor. Each rating is a judgment regarding how well the company's management is currently dealing with each internal factor.

- *Column 4* **Weighted Score:** Multiply the **weight** in Column 2 for each factor times its **rating** in Column 3 to obtain that factor's **weighted score**. This results in a weighted score for each factor ranging from **5.00** (*Outstanding*) **to 1.00** (*Poor*) with 3.00 as the average.
- *Column 5* **Comments:** Note why a particular factor was selected and how its weight and rating were estimated.

Finally, *add the weighted scores for all the internal factors in Column 4* to determine the total weighted score for that particular company. The **total weighted score** indicates how well a particular company is responding to current and expected factors in its internal environment. The score can be used to compare that firm to other firms in its industry.

As an example of this procedure, Table 4.2 includes a number of internal factors for Maytag Corporation with corresponding weights, ratings, and weighted scores provided. It is thus very similar to the EFAS Matrix (Table 3.2) that summarized external factors.

In Conclusion . . .

Animation has always been a distinctive competency at Walt Disney Productions. It has given the company a sustainable competitive advantage over the years because this capability is durable and hard for competitors to imitate. Thanks to its founder, this competency has become embedded in the corporate culture and has become a part of the firm's very identity. Even though the company had expanded from simple cartoons into theme parks and hotels, Walt Disney had always pointed to animation (and especially to Mickey Mouse, his personal creation) as a strategic factor for the company. One of his favorite expressions was "Remember, it all started with a mouse."

Discussion Questions

1. What is the relevance of the resource-based view of the firm to strategic management?
2. In what ways can a corporation's structure and culture be internal strengths or weaknesses?
3. What kind of internal factors help managers decide whether a firm should emphasize the production and sales of a large number of low-priced products or a small number of high-priced products?
4. What are the pros and cons of management's using the experience curve to determine strategy?
5. How might a firm's management decide whether it should continue to invest in current known technology or in new, but untested technology? What factors might encourage or discourage such a shift?

Key Terms

internal strategic factors
organizational analysis
corporate capabilities
internal strategic factors
simple structure
functional structure
divisional structure
corporate culture
market position
market segmentation
marketing mix
product life cycle
financial leverage
capital budgeting
R&D intensity
technological competence

technology transfer
basic R&D
product R&D
process R&D
R&D mix
technological discontinuity
intermittent systems
continuous systems
operating leverage
experience curve
flexible manufacturing
economies of scale
economies of scope
Quality of Work Life
IFAS Matrix

5

Strategy Formulation: Situation Analysis and Corporate Strategy

When Lewis Platt stepped into the job of CEO of Hewlett-Packard Company in 1992, he soon realized that the company was in danger of missing critical opportunities. Computers, communications, and consumer electronics were rapidly converging into one interrelated industry. Unfortunately Hewlett-Packard (HP) was not involved in the strategic alliances and acquisitions needed to take advantage of this development. A close look internally at Hewlett-Packard's strengths identified a unique mix of core technologies that no single competitor could match. HP offered a broad and well-regarded family of computers; it was a leader in test and measurement instruments; and it was strong in computer networking. Management proposed that it should blend these three technologies to create new product categories.

Following this idea, Hewlett-Packard developed a diagnostic system for Ford Motor Company's dealers that combined instruments that monitor a car's internal operations with an HP computer. HP also began developing other products that could take advantage of its core competencies—video servers, interactive TV devices, digital cable TV decoders, video printers, interactive notepads, health monitors, and a physician's workstation, among others. Soon this strategy began to pay off for the company in terms of increased sales and profits.[1]

5.1 ▶ Situational Analysis: SWOT

Strategy formulation is often referred to as strategic planning or long-range planning and is concerned with developing a corporation's mission, objectives, strategies, and policies. It begins with situation analysis: the process of finding a strategic fit between external opportunities and internal strengths while working around external threats and internal weaknesses. **SWOT** is an acronym used to describe those particular Strengths, Weaknesses, Opportunities, and Threats that are strategic factors for a specific company. SWOT analysis should result in the identification of a corporation's **distinctive** or **core competencies**—the particular capabilities and resources a firm possesses and the superior way in which they are used. An appropriate use of a firm's distinctive competence (core capabilities) should give it a sustainable competitive advantage.

As described earlier, the Hewlett-Packard illustration shows how a corporation can use situational analysis to initiate the strategy formulation process. Both Hewlett-Packard's external and internal environments were analyzed in some depth to find the company's distinctive competence that would enable it to take advantage of newly developing opportunities.

How to Generate a Strategic Factors Analysis Summary (SFAS) Matrix?

The **SFAS (Strategic Factors Analysis Summary) Matrix** summarizes a corporation's strategic factors by combining the *external* factors from the **EFAS Matrix** with the *internal* factors from the **IFAS Matrix**. The EFAS and IFAS examples given of Maytag Corporation in Tables 3.2 and 4.2 list a total of 20 internal and external factors. These are too many factors for most people to use in strategy formulation. The SFAS Matrix requires the strategic decision maker to condense these strengths, weaknesses, opportunities, and threats into fewer than 10 strategic factors. This is done by reviewing *each* of the weights for the individual factors in the EFAS and IFAS Matrixes. The highest weighted EFAS and IFAS factors should appear in the SFAS Matrix.

As shown in Figure 5.1, list the most important EFAS and IFAS items in the Key Strategic Factors column. After each factor, indicate whether it is a strength (S), weakness (W), opportunity (O), or threat (T). As with the EFAS and IFAS Matrixes presented earlier, the Weight column for all of the internal and external strategic factors must still total 1.00. *This means that the individual weights calculated earlier for EFAS and IFAS will probably have to be adjusted.* The ratings of how the company's management is responding to each strategic factor will be the same as those listed in the EFAS and IFAS Matrixes. Calculate the weighted scores as done earlier for EFAS and IFAS. Add a duration column as depicted in Figure 5.1. **S** stands for short term (*less than one year*); **I** for intermediate term (*one to three years*); and **L** for long term (*three years and beyond*). Repeat/revise your comments for each strategic factor from the previous EFAS and IFAS Matrixes. The resulting SFAS Matrix lists the firm's external and internal strategic factors in one table. The matrix includes only the most important factors and provides the basis for strategy formulation.

What Is the Value of a Propitious Niche?

One desired outcome of analyzing strategic factors is identifying a propitious niche where an organization could use its distinctive competence to take advantage of a particular opportunity. A **propitious niche** is a company's specific competitive role that is so well suited to the firm's internal and external environment that other corporations are not likely to challenge or dislodge it.[2]

TABLE
4.2
Internal Strategic Factor Analysis Summary (IFAS): Maytag as Example

Internal Strategic Factors	Weight	Rating	Weighted Score	Comments
	1	2	3	4	5
Strengths				
• Quality Maytag culture	.15	5	.75	Quality key to success
• Experienced top management	.05	4	.20	Know appliances
• Vertical integration	.10	4	.40	Dedicated factories
• Employee relations	.05	3	.15	Good, but deterio-rating
• Hoover's international orientation	.15	3	.45	Hoover name in cleaners
Weaknesses				
• Process-oriented R&D	.05	2	.10	Slow on new products
• Distribution channels	.05	2	.10	Superstores replac-ing small dealers
• Financial position	.15	2	.30	High debt load
• Global positioning	.20	2	.40	Hoover weak out-side the United Kingdom and Australia
• Manufacturing facilities	.05	4	.20	Investing now
Total	1.00		3.05	

TABLE
3.2
External Strategic Factor Analysis Summary (EFAS): Maytag as Example

External Strategic Factors	Weight	Rating	Weighted Score	Comments
	1	2	3	4	5
Opportunities				
• Economic integration of European Community	.20	4	.80	Acquisition of Hoover
• Demographics favor quality appliances	.10	5	.50	Maytag quality
• Economic development of Asia	.05	1	.05	Low Maytag presence
• Opening of Eastern Europe	.05	2	.10	Will take time
• Trend to "Super Stores"	.10	2	.20	Maytag weak in this channel
Threats				
• Increasing government regulations	.10	4	.40	Well positioned
• Strong U.S. competition	.10	4	.40	Well positioned
• Whirlpool and Electrolux strong globally	.15	3	.45	Hoover weak globally
• New product advances	.05	1	.05	Questionable
• Japanese appliance companies	.10	2	.20	Only Asian presence is Australia
Total	1.00		3.15	

FIGURE 5.1

Strategic Factor Analysis Summary (SFAS) Matrix

Key Strategic Factors (Select the most important opportunies/threats from EFAS, Table 3.2 and the most important strengths and weaknesses from IFAS, Table 4.2) [1]	Weight [2]	Rating [3]	Weighted Score [4]	SHORT	INTERMEDIATE	LONG	Comments [6]
					Duration [5]		
• Quality Maytag culture (S)	.10	5	.5			X	Quality key to success
• Hoover's international orientation (S)	.10	3	.3		X		Name recognition
• Financial position (W)	.10	2	.2		X		High debt
• Global positioning (W)	.15	2	.3			X	Only in N.A., U.K., and Australia
• Economic integration of European Community (O)	.10	4	.4			X	Acquisition of Hoover
• Demographics favor quality (O)	.10	5	.5		X		Maytag quality
• Trend to super stores (O + T)	.10	2	.2	X			Weak in this channel
• Whirlpool and Electrolux (T)	.15	3	.45	X			Dominate industry
• Japanese appliance companies (T)	.10	2	.2			X	Asian presence
Total	1.00		3.05				

Notes:

1. List each of your key strategic features developed in your IFAS and EFAS tables in Column 1.

2. Weight each factor from 1.0 (Most Important) to 0.0 (Not Important) in Column 2 based on that factor's probable impact on the company's strategic position. **The total weights must sum to 1.00.**

3. Rate each factor from 5 (Outstanding) to 1 (Poor) in Column 3 based on the company's response to that factor.

4. Multiply each factor's weight times its rating to obtain each factor's weighted score in Column 4.

5. For duration in Column 5, check appropriate column (short term—less than 1 year; intermediate—1 to 3 years; long term—over 3 years.)

6. Use Column 6 (comments) for rationale used for each factor.

Source: T. J. Wheelen and J. D. Hunger. "Strategic Factor Analysis Summary (SFAS)." Copyright © 1993 by Wheelen and Hunger Associates. Reprinted by permission.

Finding such a niche is not always easy. A firm's management must be always looking for *strategic windows*, that is, unique market opportunities at a particular time. The first one through the strategic window can occupy a propitious niche and discourage competition (if the firm has the required internal strengths). One company that has successfully found a propitious niche is Frank J. Zamboni & Company, the manufacturer of the machines that smooth the ice at skating and hockey rinks. Frank Zamboni invented the unique tractor-like machine in 1949, and no one has found a substitute for what it does. Before the machine was invented, people had to clean and scrape the ice by hand to prepare the surface for skating. Now hockey fans look forward to intermissions just to watch "the Zamboni" slowly drive up and down the ice rink turning rough, scraped ice into a smooth mirror surface—almost as if by magic. So long as the Zamboni company is able to produce the machines in the quantity and quality desired at a reasonable price, it's not worth another company's while to go after Frank Zamboni & Company's propitious niche.

A company may also discover in its situation analysis that it may need to invest heavily in its capabilities to keep them competitively strong in a changing niche. Cummins Engine took this approach when it realized that it did not have what was needed to take advantage of a developing opportunity in the diesel engine market. It invested $1 billion—more than three times the market value of its stock—in two new lines of engines in the early 1980s. Ten years later, eager customers such as Ford and Chrysler were purchasing so many of the fuel-efficient motors for their trucks that Cummins had to build a second plant to meet demand. "Competence has given us an economic opportunity," explained CEO Henry Schacht. In retrospect, the CEO pointed out that if in 1981 the company had not chosen to invest heavily, "we would be in decline if not out of business."[3]

5.2 Review of Mission and Objectives

A corporation must reexamine its current mission and objectives before it can generate and evaluate alternative strategies. Even when formulating strategy, managers tend to concentrate on the alternatives—the action possibilities—rather than on a mission to fulfill and objectives to achieve. This tendency is so attractive because it is much easier to deal with alternative courses of action that exist right here and now than to really think about what the corporation wants to accomplish in the future. In the end, managers often choose strategies that set their objectives for them, rather than having their choices incorporate clear objectives and a mission statement.

Problems in performance can derive from an inappropriate statement of mission, which may be too narrow or too broad. If the mission does not provide a common thread (a unifying theme) for a corporation's businesses, managers may be unclear about where the company is heading. Objectives and strategies might be in conflict with each other. Divisions might be competing against one another rather than against outside competition—to the detriment of the corporation as a whole.

A company's objectives can also be inappropriately stated. They can either focus too much on short-term operational goals or be so general that they provide little real guidance. A gap may exist between planned and achieved objectives. When such a gap occurs, either the strategies have to be changed to improve performance or the objectives need to be adjusted downward to be more realistic. Consequently objectives should be constantly reviewed to ensure their usefulness. This is what happened at Toyota Motor Corporation when top management realized that its "Global 10" objective of aiming for 10% of the global vehicle market by the end of the century was no longer feasible. Emphasis was then shifted from market share to profits. According to senior managing director Iwao Isomura, "This notion of more production and more market share is not an important principle of the company any more."[4]

5.3 Corporate Strategy

Corporate strategy specifies (1) the firm's orientation toward growth and (2) the industries or markets in which it competes. It also includes decisions regarding the flow of financial and other resources to and from a company's product lines and business units. These decisions are crucial to the corporation's future and typically involve top management and the board of directors. All corporations—from the smallest company offering one product in only one industry to the largest conglomerate operating in many industries with many products—must at one time or another consider the questions embedded within corporate strategy:

- Should we expand, cut back, or continue our operations unchanged?
- Should we concentrate our activities within our current industry or should we diversify into other industries?
- If we want to grow and expand, should we do so through internal development or through external acquisitions, mergers, or joint ventures?

The answers to these questions should be based on an analysis of the strategic factors within the firm's internal and external (especially economic) environments.

What Are the Types of Corporate Strategy?

Corporate strategy is composed of three general orientations (sometimes called grand strategies):

- **Growth strategies** expand the company's activities.
- **Stability strategies** make no change to the company's current activities.
- **Retrenchment strategies** reduce the company's level of activities.

Once the general orientation (such as growth) is chosen, a company's strategic managers can select from several more specific corporate strategies, such as concentration within one product line/industry or diversification into other products/industries. (See Figure 5.2.) These strategies are useful both to corporations operating in only one industry with one product line and to those operating in many industries with many product lines.

When Are Growth Strategies Appropriate?

By far the most widely pursued corporate strategies of business firms are those designed to achieve growth in sales, assets, profits, or some combination of these.

FIGURE
5.2

Corporate Strategies

- Growth
    - Concentration
        - Vertical Integration
        - Horizontal Integration
    - Diversification
        - Concentric
        - Conglomerate

- **Stability**
    - Pause
    - Proceed with Caution
    - No Change
    - Profit

- **Retrenchment**
    - Turnaround
    - Captive Company
    - Selling Out/Divestiture
    - Bankruptcy
    - Liquidation

Those companies that do business in dynamic environments must grow to survive. Continuing growth means increasing sales and a chance to take advantage of the experience curve to reduce the per-unit cost of products sold, thereby increasing profits. This cost reduction becomes extremely important if a corporation's industry is growing quickly and competitors are engaging in price wars in attempts to increase their shares of the market. Firms that have not reached "critical mass" (that is, gained the necessary economy of large-scale production) will face large losses unless they can find and fill a small, but profitable, niche where special product or service features can offset higher prices. That is why Motorola, Inc., continued to spend large sums on the product development of cellular phones, pagers, and two-way radios, despite a serious drop in profits in 1990. According to Motorola's Chairman George Fisher, "What's at stake here is leadership." Even though the industry was changing quickly, the company was working to avoid the erosion of its market share by jumping into new wireless markets as fast as possible. Continuing as the market leader in this industry would almost guarantee Motorola enormous future returns.

Growth is, however, a very seductive strategy for two key reasons:

- A growing firm can cover up mistakes and inefficiencies more easily than can a stable one. A growing flow of revenue into a highly leveraged corporation can create a large amount of *organization slack* (unused resources) that can be used to quickly resolve problems and conflicts between departments and divisions. There is also a big cushion for a turnaround in case a strategic error is made. Large firms also have more clout than do small firms and are more likely to obtain support from their unions and local communities in case of impending bankruptcy.

- A growing firm can offer more opportunities for advancement, promotion, and interesting jobs. Growth itself is exciting and ego-enhancing for CEOs. The marketplace and potential investors tend to view a growing corporation as a "winner" or "on the move." Executive compensation tends to increase as an organization expands. Large firms are also more difficult to acquire than are smaller ones; thus, an executive's job is more secure.

There are two basic growth strategies: **concentration** on the current product line(s) in one industry and **diversification** into other product lines in other industries.

Why Use Concentration Strategies? If a company's current product lines have real growth potential, concentration of resources on those product lines makes sense as a strategy for growth. There are two basic concentration strategies: vertical and horizontal integration.

What Is Vertical Integration? Growth can be achieved via **vertical integration** by taking over a function previously provided by a supplier (*backward integration*) or by a distributor (*forward integration*). This is a logical strategy for a corporation or business unit with a strong competitive position in a highly attractive industry. To keep and even improve its competitive position through backward integration, the company may act to minimize resource acquisition costs and inefficient operations as well as to gain more control over quality and product distribution through forward integration. The firm, in effect, builds on its distinctive competence to gain greater competitive advantage.

A firm can achieve vertical integration either internally or externally. Henry Ford, for example, used internal company resources to build his River Rouge Plant outside Detroit. The manufacturing process was integrated to the point that iron ore entered one end of the long plant and finished automobiles rolled out the other end into a huge parking lot. In contrast, DuPont, the huge chemical company, chose the external route to backward vertical integration by acquiring Conoco for oil needed in the production of DuPont's synthetic fabrics.

Although backward integration is usually more profitable than forward integration, it can reduce a corporation's strategic flexibility: by creating an encumbrance of expensive assets that might be hard to sell, it can thus create for the corporation an *exit barrier* to leaving that particular industry. With sales of its autos declining, General Motors, for example, has resorted to offering outside parts suppliers the use of its idle factories and workers.

In the 1990s, corporations seem to be moving away from vertical integration toward cooperative contractual relationships with suppliers and even with competitors. These relationships can range from **outsourcing**, where supplies are purchased from outsiders instead of made in-house (for example, Hewlett-Packard buys all its laser engines from Canon for HP's laser jet printers), to **strategic alliances**, in which partnerships, technology licensing agreements, and joint ventures are used to supplement a firm's capabilities (for example, Toshiba has used strategic alliances with GE, Siemens, Motorola, and Ericsson, among others, to become one of the world's leading electronic companies).

What Is Horizontal Integration? Growth can be achieved via **horizontal integration** by expanding the firm's products into other geographic locations and/or by increasing the range of products and services offered to current markets. A company can acquire market share, production facilities, distribution outlets, or specialized technology through internal development or externally through acquisitions or via joint ventures with another firm in the same industry. For example, after purchasing Zenith's computer operations, France's Groupe Bull acquired 19.9% of Packard Bell Electronics, the largest seller of personal computers in U.S. mass-merchandise stores. Bull thus gained access to 7000 retailers for its Zenith Data Systems subsidiary.[5] The *Company Spotlight on Maytag Corporation* feature discusses Maytag's use of horizontal integration to grow through acquisitions.

Why Use Diversification Strategies? If a company's current product lines do not have much growth potential, management may choose to diversify. There are two basic diversification strategies: concentric and conglomerate.

What Is Concentric (Related) Diversification? Growth through **concentric diversification** into a related industry may be an appropriate corporate strategy

COMPANY SPOTLIGHT

MAYTAG
Corporation

A Growth Strategy of Horizontal Integration Through External Means

Maytag management realized in 1978 that the company would be unable to continue competing effectively in the U.S. major home appliance industry if it remained only a high-quality niche manufacturer of automatic washers and dryers. The industry was rapidly consolidating around those appliance companies with a complete line of products at all price and quality levels in all three key lines of "white goods": laundry (washers and dryers), cooking (stoves and ovens), and cooling (refrigerators and freezers) appliances. Maytag's top management concluded that it would soon have to acquire other companies or risk being bought out itself. Given the long time-frame needed to acquire the technology as well as the manufacturing and marketing expertise necessary to produce and sell these other lines of appliances, Maytag chose to grow externally by acquiring Jenn-Air and Magic Chef in the mid-1980s. It was thus able to obtain Jenn-Air's popular down-draft ranges, Magic Chef's gas stoves and other appliances, and Admiral's refrigeration facilities—products Maytag needed to be a full-line home appliance manufacturer. Similarly, in 1989, Maytag's management concluded that the best way to ensure a global presence in major home appliances was to purchase Hoover, the well-known vacuum cleaner company with a solid position in white goods in Europe and Australia.

when a firm has a strong competitive position but industry attractiveness is low. By focusing on the characteristics that have given the company its distinctive competence, the company uses those very strengths as its means of diversification. The firm attempts to secure a strategic fit in a new industry where it can apply the product knowledge, manufacturing capabilities, and marketing skills that it used so effectively in the original industry. The corporation's products are related; they possess some common thread that allows synergy. The point of commonality may be similar technology, customer usage, distribution, managerial skills, or product similarity.

The firm may choose to diversify concentrically through either internal or external means. American Airlines, for example, has diversified both internally and externally out of the increasingly unprofitable airline business into a series of related businesses run by its parent company, AMR Corporation. Building on the expertise of its Sabre Travel Information Network, it built a computer reservations system for the French high-speed rail network and for the tunnel under the English Channel.

What Is Conglomerate (Unrelated) Diversification? When management realizes that the current industry is unattractive and that the firm lacks outstanding abilities or skills it could easily transfer to related products or services in other industries, the most likely strategy is **conglomerate diversification**—diversifying into an industry unrelated to its current one. Rather than maintaining a common thread throughout their organization, strategic managers who adopt this strategy are concerned primarily with financial considerations of cash flow or risk reduction.

The emphasis in conglomerate diversification is on financial considerations rather than on the product-market synergy common to concentric diversification. A cash-rich company with few opportunities for growth in its industry might, for example, move into another industry where opportunities are great but cash is hard to find. Another instance of conglomerate diversification might be when a company with a seasonal and therefore uneven cash flow purchases a firm in an unrelated industry with complementing seasonal sales that will level out the cash flow. The management of CSX Corporation (a railroad-dominated transportation company) considered the purchase of a natural gas transmission business (Texas Gas Resources) to be a good fit because most of the gas transmission revenue was realized in the winter months when railroads experience a seasonally lean period.

How Does a Firm Diversify? Some popular means of diversification are *mergers, acquisitions,* and *joint ventures*. A **merger** is a transaction involving two or more corporations in which stock is exchanged but from which only one corporation survives. Mergers usually occur between firms of somewhat similar size and are usually "friendly." The name of the resulting firm is likely to be derived from its composite firms. One example is the merging of Allied Corporation and Signal Companies to form Allied Signal.

An **acquisition** is the purchase of a company that is completely absorbed as an operating subsidiary or division of the acquiring corporation. Examples are Procter & Gamble's acquisition of Richardson-Vicks, known for its Oil of Olay and Vidal Sassoon brands, and Noxell Corporation, known for its Noxzema and

Cover Girl products. Acquisitions usually occur between firms of different sizes and can be either friendly or hostile. In hostile acquisitions, often called *takeovers*, the acquiring firm ignores the other firm's top management or board of directors and simply begins buying up the other firm's stock until it owns a controlling interest. The takeover target, in response, begins defensive maneuvers, such as buying up its own stock, calling in the Justice Department to initiate an antitrust suit in order to stop the acquisition, or looking for a friendly merger partner, often called a *white knight*.

A **joint venture** is a cooperative business activity, formed by two or more separate organizations for strategic purposes, that creates an independent business entity and allocates ownership, operational responsibilities, and financial risks and rewards to each member, while preserving their separate identity/autonomy. Joint ventures occur because the companies involved do not want to or cannot legally merge permanently. Joint ventures provide a way to temporarily combine the different strengths of partners to achieve an outcome of value to both. For example, the pharmaceutical firm Merck & Company agreed with the chemical giant DuPont Company to form, under joint ownership, a new company called DuPont Merck Pharmaceutical Company. Merck provided the new company its foreign marketing rights to some prescription medicines plus some cash. In return, Merck got access to all of DuPont's experimental drugs and its small but productive research operation.

What International Growth Strategies Are Available? Corporations use many of the same growth strategies mentioned earlier when they want to expand internationally. Joint ventures are, for example, very popular—especially when a country has restrictions on foreign ownership. The corporation can enter another country with fewer assets at stake and thus lower risk. Licensing is also a good method of establishing an international presence. Under a **licensing** agreement, the licensing firm grants rights to another firm in the host country to produce and/or sell a product. The licensee pays compensation to the licensing firm in return for technical expertise. This is an especially useful strategy if the trademark or brand name is well known, but the MNC does not have sufficient funds to finance its entry into the country directly. **Production sharing** can be used to combine the higher labor skills and technology available in developed countries with the lower cost labor available in developing countries. By locating a labor-intensive assembly plant in Ciudad Juarez, Mexico, and a packaging plant across the border in El Paso, Texas, companies like Hoover have been able to take advantage of Mexico's low labor costs. **Turnkey operations** are typically contracts for the construction of operating facilities in exchange for a fee. The facilities are transferred to the host country or firm when they are complete. The customer is usually a government agency of, for example, a Middle Eastern country that has decreed that a particular product be produced locally and under its control. **Management contracts** offer a means through which an MNC may use part of its personnel to assist a firm in a host country for a specified fee and period of time. Such arrangements are useful when a multinational corporation builds a manufacturing plant in a less developed country where people do not have the knowledge or skills needed to operate the facility.

When Are Stability Strategies Appropriate?

A corporation may choose stability over growth by continuing its current activities without any significant change in direction. The stability family of corporate strategies can be appropriate for a successful corporation operating in a reasonably predictable environment. Stability strategies can be very useful in the short run but can be dangerous if followed for too long. Some of the more popular of these strategies are the pause, proceed with caution, no change, and profit strategies.

What Is a Pause Strategy? A pause strategy is, in effect, a timeout—an opportunity to rest before continuing a growth or retrenchment strategy. It may be very appropriate as a *temporary strategy* to enable a company to consolidate its resources after prolonged rapid growth in an industry now facing an uncertain future. Dell Computer Corporation followed this strategy in 1993 after its growth strategy had resulted in more growth than it could handle. Explained CEO Michael Dell, "We grew 285% in two years, and we're having some growing pains." Selling personal computers by mail enabled it to underprice Compaq Computer and IBM, but it could not keep up with the needs of the $2 billion, 5600-employee company selling PCs in 95 countries. Dell was not giving up on its growth strategy, but merely putting it temporarily in limbo until the company could hire new managers, improve the structure, and build new facilities.

What Is a Proceed with Caution Strategy? A proceed with caution strategy is a very slow and deliberate attempt to make incremental improvements. It can be appropriate when the competitive environment is perceived as highly changeable and unpredictable. Management is therefore not likely to make sudden moves or take unjustified risks by either investing in or out of the industry. Ford Motor Company faced this situation when it recorded a record $2.3 billion loss in 1991. Instead of going into a radical retrenchment strategy calling for large layoffs and plant closings, Ford merely proceeded with caution. It had spent many years developing a lean workforce and quality products. Because management felt that the downturn in the industry was only temporary, the company was able to make some temporary adjustments until either the market improved or worsened.

What Is a No Change Strategy? A no change strategy is a decision to do nothing new—a choice to continue current operations and policies for the foreseeable future. Rarely articulated as a definite strategy, a no change strategy's success depends on a lack of significant change in a corporation's situation. The relative stability created by the firm's modest competitive position in an industry facing little or no growth encourages the company to continue on its current course, making only small adjustments for inflation in its sales and profit objectives. The company faces no obvious opportunities or threats and has no significant strengths or weaknesses. Few aggressive new competitors are likely to enter such an industry. The corporation has probably found a reasonably profitable and stable niche for its products. Unless the industry is undergoing consolidation, the relative comfort that a company in this situation experiences is likely to cause management to follow a no change strategy in which the future is expected to continue as an extension of the present. Most small-town businesses probably follow this strategy before a Wal-Mart moves into their areas.

What Is a Profit Strategy? A profit strategy is a decision to do nothing new in a worsening situation, but instead to act as though the company's problems are only temporary. The profit strategy is an attempt to artificially support profits when a company's sales are declining by reducing investment and short-term discretionary expenditures. Rather than announcing the company's poor position to stockholders and the investment community at large, top management may be tempted to follow this seductive strategy. Blaming the company's problems on a hostile environment (such as anti-business government policies, unethical competitors, finicky customers, and/or greedy lenders), management defers investments and/or cuts expenses, such as R&D, maintenance, and advertising, to keep profits at a stable level during this period. It may even sell one of its product lines for the cash flow benefits. Obviously the profit strategy is useful only to help a company get through a temporary difficulty. Unfortunately the strategy is seductive and if continued long enough will lead to a serious deterioration in a corporation's competitive position. The profit strategy is thus usually a top management's passive, short-term, and often self-serving response to the situation.

When Are Retrenchment Strategies Appropriate?

Management may pursue retrenchment strategies when the company has a weak competitive position in some or all of its product lines resulting in poor performance—sales are down and profits are becoming losses. These strategies generate a great deal of pressure to improve performance. Like the coach of a losing football team, the CEO here is typically under pressure to do something quickly or be fired. In an attempt to eliminate the weaknesses that are dragging the company down, management may follow one of several retrenchment strategies ranging from turnaround or becoming a captive company to selling out, bankruptcy, or liquidation.

What Is a Turnaround Strategy? The turnaround strategy emphasizes the improvement of operational efficiency and is probably most appropriate when a corporation's problems are pervasive but not yet critical. Analogous to a diet, the two basic phases of a turnaround strategy include contraction and consolidation.

Contraction is the initial effort to quickly "stop the bleeding" with a general, across-the-board cutback in size and costs. The second phase, consolidation, is the implementation of a program to stabilize the now leaner corporation. To streamline the company, management develops plans to reduce unnecessary overhead and to justify the costs of functional activities. This is a crucial time for the organization. If the consolidation phase is not conducted in a positive manner, many of the company's best people will leave. If, however, all employees are encouraged to get involved in productivity improvements, the firm is likely to emerge from this strategic retrenchment period a much stronger and better organized company. It has improved its competitive position and is able once again to expand the business.

What Is a Captive Company Strategy? A captive company strategy gives up independence in exchange for security. A company with a weak competitive position may not be able to engage in a full-blown turnaround strategy. The industry may not be sufficiently attractive to justify such an effort from either the current management or from investors. Nevertheless, a company in this situation faces poor sales and increasing losses unless it takes some action. Management desperately searches for an "angel" by offering to be a captive company to one of its larger customers in order to guarantee the company's continued existence with a long-term contract. In this way, the corporation may be able to reduce the scope of some of its functional activities, such as marketing, thus reducing costs significantly. The weaker company gains certainty of sales and production in return for becoming heavily dependent on one firm for at least 75% of its sales. For example, in order to become the sole supplier of an auto part to General Motors, Simpson Industries of Birmingham, Michigan, agreed to have its engine parts facilities and books inspected and its employees interviewed by a special team from GM. In return, nearly 80% of the company's production was sold to GM through long-term contracts.[6]

What Is a Selling Out/Divestment Strategy? If a corporation with a weak competitive position in the industry is unable either to pull itself up by its bootstraps or to find a customer to which it can become a captive company, it may have no choice but to sell out and leave the industry completely. If the corporation has multiple business lines and it chooses to sell off its weakest divisions, this is called **divestment**. The **selling out strategy** makes sense if management can still obtain a good price for its stockholders by selling out to another firm that may be expanding through horizontal integration. For example, Johnson Products, a pioneer in hair care products for African-American and other ethnic markets, found that over time it had lost its competitive position to larger cosmetics companies who had entered Johnson Products' niche. After numerous attempts to turn the company around, the Johnson family finally decided to sell out to Ivax Corporation while they could still get a decent price for the firm.

Why Choose a Bankruptcy or Liquidation Strategy? When a company finds itself in the worst possible situation with a poor competitive position in an industry with few prospects, management has only a limited number of alternatives—all of them distasteful. Because no one is interested in buying a weak company in an unattractive industry, the firm must pursue a bankruptcy or liquidation strategy. **Bankruptcy** involves giving up management of the firm to the courts in return for some settlement of the corporation's obligations. Top management hopes that after the court decides the claims on the company, the company will be stronger and better able to compete in a more attractive industry. Wang Laboratories, Inc., took this approach in 1992. Founded by An Wang, the company had been unable to make the transition from word processors to personal computers and finally collapsed after the death of its founder. The company emerged from bankruptcy in 1993 under a court-supervised reorganization plan requiring that the company focus on office software.

In contrast to bankruptcy, which seeks to perpetuate the corporation, **liquidation** is the termination of the firm. Because the industry is unattractive and the company too weak to be sold as a going concern, management may choose to convert as many salable assets as possible to cash, which is then distributed to the stockholders after all obligations are paid. The benefit of liquidation over bankruptcy is that the board of directors, as representatives of the stockholders, together with top management make the decisions instead of turning them over to the court, which may choose to ignore stockholders completely.

At times, top management must be willing to select one of these less desirable retrenchment strategies. Unfortunately many top managers are unwilling to admit that their company has serious weaknesses for fear that they may be blamed personally. Even worse, top management may not even perceive that crises are developing. When these top managers do eventually notice trouble, they are prone to attribute the problems to temporary environmental disturbances and tend to follow profit strategies. Even when things are going terribly wrong, top management is very tempted to avoid liquidation in hopes of a miracle. Thus a corporation needs a strong board of directors that, to safeguard stockholders' interests, can tell top management when to quit.

What Is Portfolio Analysis?

One of the most popular aids to developing corporate strategy in a corporation with many product lines in diverse industries is portfolio analysis. Over half of the Fortune 500 companies practice some form of portfolio analysis in strategy formulation.[7] The rate of use by companies located in other industrialized nations is probably similar. Portfolio analysis puts corporate headquarters into the role of an internal banker. In **portfolio analysis**, top management views its product lines and business units as a series of investments from which it expects to get a profitable return. The lines/units form a portfolio of investments that top management must constantly juggle to ensure the best return on the corporation's invested money.

Why Use the BCG Growth-Share Matrix?

The **BCG (Boston Consulting Group) Growth-Share Matrix** depicted in Figure 5.3 is the simplest way to portray a corporation's portfolio of investments. Each of the corporation's product lines or business units is plotted on the matrix according to both the *growth rate of the industry* in which it competes and its *relative market share*. A unit's relative competitive position is defined as its market share in the industry divided by that of the largest other competitor. By this calculation, a relative market share above 1.0 belongs to the market leader. The business growth rate is the percentage of market growth, that is, the percentage by which sales of a particular business unit classification of products have increased. The matrix assumes that, other things being equal, a growing market is an attractive one.

The line separating areas of high and low relative competitive position is set at 1.5 times. A product line or business unit must have relative strengths of this magnitude to ensure that it will have the dominant position needed to be a "star" or "cash cow." On the other hand, a product line or unit having a relative competitive position less than 1.0 has "dog" status.[8] Each product or unit is represented in Figure

FIGURE 5.3

BCG Growth Share Matrix

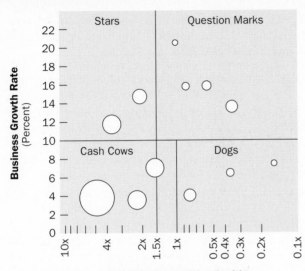

Source: Reprinted from *Long-Range Planning*, February 1977, B. Hedley, "Strategy and the Business Portfolio" p. 12. Copyright © 1977, with kind permission from Elsevier Science Ltd., The Boulevard, Langford Lane, Kidlington 0X5 1GB, UK.

5.3 by a circle, the area which represents the relative significance of each business unit or product line to the corporation in terms of assets used or sales generated.

The growth-share matrix has a lot in common with the product life cycle. As a product moves through its life cycle, it is categorized into one of four types for the purpose of funding decisions:

- **Question marks** (sometimes called "problem children" or "wildcats") are new products with the potential for success but that need a lot of cash for development. If one of these products is to gain enough market share to become a market leader and thus a star, money must be taken from more mature products and spent on a question mark.

- **Stars** are market leaders typically at the peak of their product life cycle and are usually able to generate enough cash to maintain their high share of the market. When their market growth rate slows, stars become cash cow products.

- **Cash cows** typically bring in far more money than is needed to maintain their market share. As these products move along the decline stage of their life cycle, they are "milked" for cash that will be invested in new question mark products. For example, IBM's mainframe computer business had been built on a 1964 design. Even though mainframes had become a mature business by the mid-1980s, they still accounted for over half of the company's total profits—profits IBM could invest in new products and developing technology. Question mark products that fail to obtain a dominant market share (and thus become a star) by the time the industry growth rate inevitably slows become dogs.

- **Dogs** are those products with low market share that do not have the potential (because they are in an unattractive industry) to bring in much cash. According to the BCG growth-share matrix, dogs should be either sold off or managed carefully for the small amount of cash they can generate.

Underlying the BCG growth-share matrix is the concept of the experience curve *(discussed in Chapter 4)*. The key to success is assumed to be market share. Firms with the highest market share tend to have a cost leadership position based on economies of scale, among other things. If a company uses the experience curve to its advantage, it should be able to manufacture and sell new products at a price low enough to garner early market share leadership. When a product becomes a star, it is destined to be very profitable, considering its inevitable future as a cash cow.

After the current positions of a company's product lines or business units have been plotted on a matrix, a projection can be made of their future positions, assuming no change in strategy. Management can then use the present and projected matrixes to identify major strategic issues facing the organization. The goal of any company is to maintain a balanced portfolio so that the firm can be self-sufficient in cash and always working to harvest mature products in declining industries to support new ones in growing industries.

Research into the growth-share matrix generally supports its assumptions and recommendations except for the advice that dogs should be promptly harvested or liquidated. A product with a low share in a declining industry can be very profitable if the product has a niche in which market demand remains stable and predictable. Some firms may also keep a dog because its presence creates an entry barrier for potential competitors. All in all, the BCG growth-share matrix is a popular technique because it is quantifiable and easy to use.

Nevertheless, the growth-share matrix has been criticized for several reasons:

- The use of highs and lows to make just four categories is too simplistic.
- The link between market share and profitability is not necessarily strong. Low-share businesses can be profitable, too (and vice versa).
- Growth rate is only one aspect of industry attractiveness. High-growth markets may not always be the best for every business unit or product line.
- It considers the product line or business unit only in relation to one competitor: the market leader. It misses small competitors with fast-growing market shares.
- Market share is only one aspect of overall competitive position.

Why Use the GE Business Screen?

General Electric developed a more complicated matrix with the assistance of the McKinsey and Company consulting firm. As depicted in Figure 5.4, the **GE Business Screen** includes nine cells based on long-term industry attractiveness and business strength/competitive position. The GE Business Screen, in contrast to the BCG growth-share matrix, includes much more data in its two key factors than just business growth rate and comparable market share. For example, at GE,

FIGURE
5.4

General Electric's Business Screen

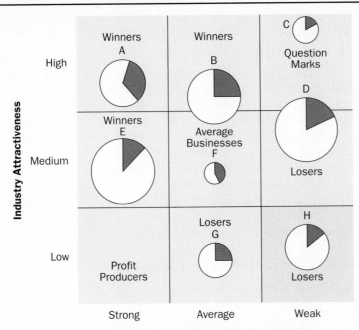

Source: Adapted from *Strategic Management in GE,* Corporate Planning and Development, General Electric Corporation. Reprinted with permission of General Electric Company.

industry attractiveness includes market growth rate, industry profitability, size, and pricing practices, among other possible opportunities and threats. Business strength or competitive position includes market share as well as technological position, profitability, and size, among other possible strengths and weaknesses.[9]

The individual product lines or business units are identified by a letter and are plotted as circles on the GE Business Screen. The area of each circle is in proportion to the size of the industry in terms of sales. The pie slices within the circles depict the market share of each product line or business unit.

To plot product lines or business units on the GE Business Screen, the following four steps are recommended:

Step 1. Select criteria to rate the industry for each product line or business unit. Assess overall industry attractiveness for each product line or business unit on a scale from 1 (very unattractive) to 5 (very attractive).

Step 2. Select the key factors needed for success in each product line or business unit. Assess business strength/competitive position for each product line or business unit on a scale of 1 (very weak) to 5 (very strong).

Step 3. Plot each product line's or business unit's current position on a matrix like that depicted in Figure 5.4.

Step 4. Plot the firm's future portfolio, assuming that present corporate and business strategies remain unchanged. Is there a performance gap between projected and desired portfolios? If so, this gap should serve as a stimulus for them to seriously review the corporation's current mission, objectives, strategies, and policies.

Overall, the nine-cell GE Business Screen is an improvement over the Boston Consulting Group Growth-Share Matrix. The GE Business Screen considers many more variables and does not lead to such simplistic conclusions. It recognizes, for example, that the attractiveness of an industry can be assessed in many different ways (other than simply using growth rate), and thus it allows users to select whatever criteria they feel are most appropriate to their situation. Nevertheless, it can get quite complicated and cumbersome. The numerical estimates of industry attractiveness and business strength/competitive position give the appearance of objectivity but are in reality subjective judgments that may vary from one person to another. Another shortcoming of this portfolio matrix is that it cannot effectively depict the positions of new products or business units in developing industries.

What Are the Advantages and Limitations of Portfolio Analysis?

Portfolio analysis is commonly used in strategy formulation because it offers certain **advantages:**

- It encourages top management to evaluate each of the corporation's businesses individually and to set objectives and allocate resources for each.
- It stimulates the use of externally oriented data to supplement management's judgment.
- It raises the issue of cash flow availability for use in expansion and growth.
- Its graphic depiction facilitates communication.

Portfolio analysis does, however, have some very real limitations that have caused some companies to reduce their use of the matrixes. These are some **limitations:**

- It is not easy to define product/market segments.
- It suggests the use of standard strategies that can miss opportunities or be impractical.
- It provides an illusion of scientific rigor when in reality positions are based on subjective judgments.
- Its value-laden terms like cash cow and dog can lead to self-fulfilling prophecies.
- It is not always clear what makes an industry attractive or what stage a product is at in its life cycle.
- Naively following the prescriptions of a portfolio model may actually reduce corporate profits if they are used inappropriately. For example, General Mills' Chief Executive H. Brewster Atwater cites his company's Bisquick brand of flour as a product that would have been written off years ago based on portfolio analysis. "This product is 57 years old. By all rights it should have been overtaken by newer products. But with the proper research to improve the product and promotion to keep customers excited, it's doing very well."[10]

How to Generate a TOWS (SWOT) Matrix?

Thus far, we have discussed how a firm assesses its situation and have reviewed various available corporate strategies. The next task is to identify alternative ways that an organization can use its specific strengths to capitalize on opportunities or to avoid threats and overcome its weaknesses. The **TOWS Matrix** (TOWS is just another way of using SWOT analysis) illustrates how the external opportunities and threats facing a particular corporation can be matched with that company's internal strengths and weaknesses to result in four sets of possible strategic alternatives. (See Figure 5.5.) This is a good way to use brainstorming to create alternative strategies that might not otherwise be considered. It forces strategic managers to create various kinds of growth as well as retrenchment strategies. It can be used at the corporate level as well as by business units.

To generate a TOWS Matrix for Maytag Corporation, for example, use the External Factor Analysis Summary (EFAS) listed in Table 3.2 from Chapter 3 and the Internal Factor Analysis Summary (IFAS) listed in Table 4.2 from Chapter 4. Take the following steps to build Figure 5.6:

1. In the block labeled **Opportunities**, list the external opportunities available in the corporation's current and future environment from EFAS Table 3.2.

FIGURE 5.5   **TOWS Matrix**

EXTERNAL FACTORS (EFAS) / INTERNAL FACTORS (IFAS)	Strengths (S) List 5 – 10 *internal* strengths here	Weaknesses (W) List 5 – 10 *internal* weaknesses here
Opportunities (O) List 5 – 10 *external* opportunities here	**SO Strategies** Generate strategies here that use **strengths** to take **advantage** of **opportunities**	**WO Strategies** Generate strategies here that take **advantage** of **opportunities** by **overcoming weaknesses**
Threats (T) List 5 – 10 *external* threats here	**ST Strategies** Generate strategies here that use **strengths** to **avoid threats**	**WT Strategies** Generate strategies here that **minimize weaknesses** and **avoid threats**

Source: Adapted from *Long-Range Planning*, April 1982, H. Weihrich, "The TOWS Matrix—A Tool for Situational Analysis" p. 60. Copyright 1982, with kind permission from Elsevier Science Ltd. The Boulevard, Langford Lane, Kidlington OX5 1GB, UK.

TABLE 4.2 Internal Strategic Factor Analysis Summary (IFAS): Maytag as Example

Internal Strategic Factors	Weight	Rating	Weighted Score	Comments
	1	2	3	4	5
Strengths				
• Quality Maytag culture	.15	5	.75	Quality key to success
• Experienced top management	.05	4	.20	Know appliances
• Vertical integration	.10	4	.40	Dedicated factories
• Employee relations	.05	3	.15	Good, but deteriorating
• Hoover's international orientation	.15	3	.45	Hoover name in cleaners
Weaknesses				
• Process-oriented R&D	.05	2	.10	Slow on new products
• Distribution channels	.05	2	.10	Superstores replacing small dealers
• Financial position	.15	2	.30	High debt load
• Global positioning	.20	2	.40	Hoover weak outside the United Kingdom and Australia
• Manufacturing facilities	.05	4	.20	Investing now
Total	1.00		3.05	

TABLE 3.2 External Strategic Factor Analysis Summary (EFAS): Maytag as Example

External Strategic Factors	Weight	Rating	Weighted Score	Comments
	1	2	3	4	5
Opportunities				
• Economic integration of European Community	.20	4	.80	Acquisition of Hoover
• Demographics favor quality appliances	.10	5	.50	Maytag quality
• Economic development of Asia	.05	1	.05	Low Maytag presence
• Opening of Eastern Europe	.05	2	.10	Will take time
• Trend to "Super Stores"	.10	2	.20	Maytag weak in this channel
Threats				
• Increasing government regulations	.10	4	.40	Well positioned
• Strong U.S. competition	.10	4	.40	Well positioned
• Whirlpool and Electrolux strong globally	.15	3	.45	Hoover weak globally
• New product advances	.05	1	.05	Questionable
• Japanese appliance companies	.10	2	.20	Only Asian presence is Australia
Total	1.00		3.15	

FIGURE 5.6   **Generating a TOWS Matrix for Maytag Corporation**

Strengths →

Weaknesses →

Opportunities →

Threats →

INTERNAL FACTORS (IFAS, Table 4.2) EXTERNAL FACTORS (EFAS, Table 3.2)	Strengths (S)	Weaknesses (W)
	■ Quality Maytag culture ■ Experienced top management ■ Vertical integration ■ Employee relations ■ Hoover's international orientation	■ Process-oriented R&D ■ Distribution channels ■ Financial position ■ Global positioning ■ Manufacturing facilities
Opportunities (O) ■ Economic integration of European Community ■ Demographics favor quality ■ Economic development of Asia ■ Opening of Eastern Europe ■ Trend toward super stores	**SO Strategies** ■ *Use worldwide Hoover distribution channels to sell both Hoover and Maytag major appliances.* ■ *Find joint venture partners in Eastern Europe and Asia.*	**WO Strategies** ■ *Expand Hoover's presence in continental Europe by improving Hoover quality and reducing manufacturing and distribution costs.* ■ *Emphasize superstore channel for all non-Maytag brands.*
Threats (T) ■ Increasing government regulation ■ Strong U.S. competition ■ Whirlpool and Electrolux positioned for global economy ■ New product advances ■ Japanese appliance companies	**ST Strategies** ■ *Acquire Raytheon's appliance business to increase U.S. market share.* ■ *Merge with a Japanese major home appliance company.* ■ *Sell off all non-Maytag brands and strongly defend Maytag's U.S. niche.*	**WT Strategies** ■ *Sell off Dixie-Narco Division to reduce debt.* ■ *Emphasize cost reduction to reduce break-even point.* ■ *Sell out to Raytheon or a Japanese firm.*

2. In the block labeled **Threats,** list the external threats facing the corporation now and in the future from EFAS Table 3.2.
3. In the block labeled **Strengths,** list the specific areas of current and future strength for the corporation from IFAS Table 4.2.
4. In the block labeled **Weaknesses,** list the specific areas of current and future weakness for the corporation from IFAS Table 4.2.
5. Generate a series of possible strategies for the corporation under consideration based on particular combinations of the four sets of strategic factors:
    - **SO strategies** are generated by thinking of ways a corporation could choose to use its strengths to take advantage of opportunities.
    - **ST strategies** consider a corporation's strengths as a way to avoid threats.
    - **WO strategies** attempt to take advantage of opportunities by overcoming weaknesses.
    - **WT strategies** are basically defensive and primarily act to minimize weaknesses and avoid threats.

In Conclusion . . .

KinderCare Learning Centers is a good example of a corporation that has experimented with many kinds of corporate strategy. The company had been founded to take advantage of the increasing numbers of dual-career couples who were turning to day-care centers to watch their children while they were at work. In comparison to some centers that were nothing more than baby-sitting services providing only minimal attention to the needs of the children, KinderCare offered pleasant surroundings staffed by well-trained personnel. Soon, KinderCare had over a thousand centers in almost 40 states in the United States. Not satisfied with its success, however, KinderCare's top management decided to take advantage of its relationship with working parents to diversify into the somewhat related businesses of banking, insurance, and retailing. Financed through junk bonds, the strategy failed to bring in enough cash to pay for its implementation. After years of losses, the company was driven to bankruptcy in the late 1980s. It emerged from bankruptcy in 1993—divested of its acquisitions and pledged to stay away from diversification. The new CEO initiated a concentration strategy with an emphasis on horizontal integration. KinderCare opened its first center catering expressly to commuters in a renovated supermarket near the Metro line to Chicago. It also offered to build child-care centers for big employers or to run existing facilities for a fee. Management planned to open its first overseas center in Britain with eventual expansion into New Zealand and Australia.

Discussion Questions

1. What industry forces might cause a propitious niche to disappear?
2. How does horizontal integration differ from vertical integration? From concentric diversification?
3. What are the tradeoffs between an internal and an external growth strategy?

4. Is stability really a strategy or is it just a term for no strategy?
5. Compare and contrast SWOT analysis with portfolio analysis.

Key Terms

SWOT
distinctive or core competencies
SFAS Matrix
propitious niche
corporate strategy
growth strategies
stability strategies
retrenchment strategies
concentration
diversification
vertical integration
outsourcing
strategic alliances
horizontal integration
concentric diversification
conglomerate diversification
mergers
acquisitions
joint ventures

licensing
production sharing
turnkey operations
management contracts
pause strategy
proceed with caution strategy
no change strategy
profit strategy
turnaround strategy
captive company strategy
divestment
selling out strategy
bankruptcy
liquidation
portfolio analysis
BCG Growth Share Matrix
GE Business Screen
TOWS (SWOT) Matrix

6

Strategy Formulation: Business and Functional Strategy

When Donald Lamberti incorporated Casey's General Stores in 1967 in Des Moines, Iowa, he formulated a strategy unknown at that time in the convenience store industry. Instead of targeting the large, growing metropolitan areas of the eastern, western, and southern United States where potential sales were high, he chose to focus on the small towns in the agricultural heartland of the Midwest. Contrary to all the conventional wisdom arguing against beginning a business in a declining market, Lamberti avoided direct competition with 7-Eleven and moved into these increasingly ignored small markets.

By 1993, Casey's operated 819 convenience stores in the upper midwestern United States. Lamberti decided to expand offerings from just gasoline and basic groceries to include fast food and bakeries. In many small towns of the Midwest, Casey's was now the only retail business left. These were towns too small for even Wal-Mart to covet. Like any convenience store, prices were somewhat higher than in larger, more specialized stores in the cities. But small-town people did not want to have to drive 10 to 20 miles for a loaf of bread or a pizza. At a time when other convenience stores were struggling to show a profit and avoid bankruptcy, Casey's recorded continuing growth and profitability.

Casey's General Stores is successful because its strategic managers formulated a new strategy designed to give it an advantage in a very competitive industry. Casey's uses a differentiation focus competitive strategy in which a company focuses on a particular market area to provide a differentiated product or service. This strategy is one of several business-level strategies to be discussed in this chapter as a continuation of the strategy formulation process begun in Chapter 5.

6.1 ▶ Business/Competitive Strategy

Business strategy (often called **competitive strategy**) focuses on improving the competitive position of a company's products or services within the specific industry or market segment that the company or business unit serves. Just as corporate strategy asks **what** industry(ies) the company should be in, business/competitive strategy asks **how** the company or its units should compete in each industry. In addition, business/competitive strategy raises the following questions:

- Should we compete on the basis of low cost, or should we differentiate our products or services on some basis other than cost, such as quality or service?
- Should we compete head to head with our major competitors for the biggest but most sought-after share of the market, or should we focus on a niche in which we can satisfy a less sought-after but also profitable segment of the market?

What Are Porter's Generic Competitive Strategies?

Michael Porter proposes two "generic" competitive strategies for outperforming other corporations in a particular industry: lower cost and differentiation.[1] These strategies are called generic because any type or size of business firm, even not-for-profit organizations, can pursue them.

- **Lower cost** is the ability of a company or a business unit to design, produce, and market a comparable product more efficiently than its competitors.
- **Differentiation** is the ability to provide unique and superior value to the buyer in terms of product quality, special features, or after-sale service.

Porter further proposes that a firm's competitive advantage in an industry is determined by its **competitive scope**, that is, the breadth of the company's or business unit's target market. Before using one of the two generic competitive strategies of lower cost or differentiation, the firm or unit must choose the range of product varieties it will produce, the distribution channels it will employ, the types of buyers it will serve, the geographic areas in which it will sell, and the array of related industries in which it also will compete. This should reflect an understanding of the firm's unique resources. Simply put, a company or business unit can choose a *broad target* (that is, aim at the middle of the mass market) or a *narrow target* (that is, aim at a market niche). Combining these two types of target markets with the two competitive strategies results in the four variations of generic strategies depicted in Figure 6.1. When the lower cost and differentiation strategies have a broad mass-market target, they are simply called *cost leadership* and *differentiation*. When they are focused on a market niche (narrow target), however, they are called *cost focus* and *focused differentiation*.

Cost Leadership is a low-cost competitive strategy that aims at the broad mass market and requires "aggressive construction of efficient-scale facilities, vigorous pursuit of cost reductions from experience, tight cost and overhead control,

FIGURE
6.1
Porter's Generic Competitive Strategies

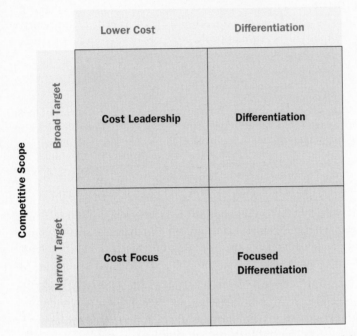

Source: Reprinted with the permission of The Free Press, a division of Simon & Schuster, from *The Competitive Advantage of Nations* by Michael E. Porter. Copyright © 1990 by Michael E. Porter.

avoidance of marginal customer accounts, and cost minimization in areas like R&D, service, sales force, advertising, and so on."[2] Because of its lower costs, the cost leader is able to charge a lower price for its products than its competitors and still make a satisfactory profit. Some companies successfully following this strategy are Wal-Mart (retailing), Timex (watches), and Gateway 2000 (personal computers). Having a low-cost position also gives a company or business unit a defense against rivals. Lower costs allow the company to continue to earn profits during times of heavy competition. Its high market share gives it more bargaining power relative to its suppliers (because it buys in large quantities). Its low price also serves as a barrier to entry because few new entrants will be able to match the leader's cost advantage. As a result, cost leaders are likely to earn above-average returns on investment.

Differentiation is aimed at the broad mass market and involves the creation of a product or service that its industry perceives as unique. The company or business unit may then charge a premium for its product. This specialty can be associated with design or brand image, technology, features, dealer network, or customer service. Differentiation is a viable strategy for earning above-average returns in a specific business because the resulting brand loyalty lowers customers' sensitivity to price. Increased costs can usually be passed on to the buyers. Buyer loyalty also serves as an entry barrier—new firms must develop their own distinctive competence to differentiate their products in some way in order to compete successfully. Examples of the successful use of a differentiation strategy are Walt Disney Productions, Maytag appliances, and Mercedes-Benz automobiles. Research does suggest that a differentiation strategy is more likely to generate higher profits than is a low-cost strategy because differentiation creates a better entry barrier. A low-cost strategy is more likely, however, to generate increases in market share.[3]

Cost Focus is a low-cost competitive strategy that focuses on a particular buyer group or geographic market and attempts to serve only this niche, to the exclusion of others. In using cost focus, the company or business unit seeks a cost advantage in its target segment. A good example of this strategy is Fadal Engineering. Fadal focuses its efforts on building and selling no-frills machine tools to small manufacturers. Fadal achieved cost focus by minimizing overhead and R&D and by focusing marketing efforts strictly on its market niche. The cost focus strategy is valued because of a belief that a company or business unit that focuses its efforts is better able to serve its narrow strategic target more *efficiently* than can its competition. It does, however, require a tradeoff between profitability and overall market share.

Like cost focus, **Differentiation Focus** concentrates on a particular buyer group, product line segment, or geographic market. This is the competitive strategy successfully followed by Casey's General Stores, Morgan Motor Car Company (manufacturer of classic British sports cars), and local health food stores. In using differentiation focus, the company or business unit seeks differentiation in a targeted market segment. This strategy is valued because of a belief that a company or a business unit that focuses its efforts is better able to serve the special needs of a narrow strategic target more *effectively* than can its competition.

What Risks Are Associated with Competitive Strategies?

No one competitive strategy is guaranteed to achieve success, and some companies that have successfully implemented one of Porter's competitive strategies have found that they could not sustain the strategy. As shown in Table 6.1, each of the generic strategies has its risks. For example, a company following a differentiation strategy must ensure that the higher price it charges for its higher quality is not priced too far above the competition or else customers will not see the extra quality as worth the extra cost. This is what the term *cost proximity* in Table 6.1 means.

What Are the Issues in Competitive Strategies?

Porter argues that to be successful, a company or business unit must achieve one of the generic competitive strategies. Otherwise, the company or business unit is **stuck in the middle** of the competitive marketplace with no competitive advantage

TABLE 6.1   **Risks of Generic Competitive Strategies**

Risks of Cost Leadership	Risks of Differentiation	Risks of Focus
Cost leadership is not sustained: • Competitors imitate. • Technology changes. • Other bases for cost leadership erode. Proximity in differentiation is lost.	Differentiation is not sustained: • Competitors imitate. • Bases for differentiation become less important to buyers. Cost proximity is lost.	The focus strategy is imitated: The target segment becomes structurally unattractive: • Structure erodes. • Demand disappears. Broadly targeted competitors overwhelm the segment: • The segment's differences from other segments narrow. • The advantages of a broad line increase.
Cost focusers achieve even lower cost in segments.	Differentiation focusers achieve even greater differentiation in segments.	New focusers subsegment the industry.

Source: Reprinted with the permission of The Free Press, a division of Simon & Schuster, from *Competitive Advantage: Creating and Sustaining Superior Performance* by Michael E. Porter. Copyright © 1985 by Michael E. Porter.

and is doomed to below average performance. An example of a company stuck in the middle was Tandy Corporation. Tandy's strategy of selling personal computers to the average person had failed to generate the large amount of sales and profits that top management had desired. Its computers had neither the exciting new features found on Compaq's products nor the low price of the PC clones like those sold through the mail by Dell or Gateway. Sales were stagnating. Attempting to increase its sales to business through its GRiD Systems subsidiary while keeping up its Radio Shack sales, Tandy was confronted with the dilemma of trying to be all things to all people—and failing. Deciding at last that computers were distracting it from its primary business of consumer electronics retailing, management sold the company's computer operations to AST Research in 1993.

Research generally supports Porter's contention that a firm that fails to achieve a generic strategy is going to be stuck in the middle with no competitive advantage. But what about companies that attempt to achieve both a low cost *and* a high differentiation position? The Japanese auto companies of Toyota, Nissan, and Honda are often presented as examples of successful firms able to achieve both of these generic strategies. Although Porter agrees that a company or a business unit may achieve low cost and differentiation simultaneously, he argues that this state is often temporary. Porter does admit, however, that many different kinds of potentially profitable competitive strategies are possible. Although only one company can successfully pursue the mass market cost leadership strategy (because it is so dependent on achieving dominant market share), others can pursue an almost unlimited number of differentiation and focus strategies (depending on the range of possible desirable features and the number of identifiable market niches).

Most entrepreneurial ventures follow focus strategies. The successful ones differentiate their product from other competitors in the areas of quality and service and focus the product on customer needs in a segment of the market so that they achieve a dominant share of that part of the market. Adopting guerrilla-warfare tactics, these companies go after opportunities in market niches too small to justify retaliation from the market leaders. Table 6.2 lists some suggestions for entrepreneurial competitive strategies.

What Is the Relationship Between Industry Structure and Competitive Strategy?

Although each of Porter's generic competitive strategies may be used in any industry, in some instances certain strategies are more likely to succeed than others. In a **fragmented industry**, for example, where many small and medium-sized local companies compete for relatively small shares of the total market, focus strategies will likely predominate. Fragmented industries are typical for products in the early stages of their life cycle. If few economies are to be gained through size, no large firms will emerge and entry barriers will be low, allowing a stream of new entrants into the industry. If a company can overcome the limitations of a fragmented market, however, it can reap the benefits of a cost leadership or differentiation

TABLE 6.2

Some Guidelines for Entrepreneurial Competitive Strategies

- Focus on industries facing substantial technological or regulatory changes, especially those with recent exits by established competitors.
- Seek industries whose smaller firms have relatively weak competitive positions.
- Seek industries that are in early, high-growth stages of evolution.
- Seek industries in which it is possible to create high barriers to subsequent entry.
- Seek industries with heterogeneous products that are relatively unimportant to the customer's overall success.
- Seek to differentiate your products from those of your competitors in ways that are meaningful to your customers.
- Focus such differentiation efforts on product quality, marketing approaches, and customer service—and charge enough to cover the costs of doing so.
- Seek to dominate the market segments in which you compete. If necessary, either segment the market differently or change the nature and focus of your differentiation efforts to increase your domination of the segments you serve.
- Stress innovation, especially new product innovation, that is built on existing organizational capabilities.
- Seek natural, organic growth through flexibility and opportunism that builds on existing organizational strengths.

Source: C. W. Hofer and W. R. Sandberg, "Improving New Venture Performance: Some Guidelines for Success," *American Journal of Small Business* (Summer 1987), pp. 17, 19. Copyright © 1987 by C. W. Hofer and W. R. Sandberg. Reprinted by permission.

strategy. Until Pizza Hut used advertising to differentiate itself from local competitors, the pizza fast-food business was a fragmented industry composed primarily of locally owned pizza parlors, each with its own distinctive product and service offering. Subsequently Domino's used the cost leader strategy to achieve U.S. national market share.

As an industry matures, fragmentation is overcome and the industry tends to become a **consolidated industry** dominated by a small number of large companies. Although many industries begin by being fragmented, battles for market share and creative attempts to overcome local or niche market boundaries often result in a few companies' obtaining increasingly larger market shares. When product standards become established for minimum quality and features, competition shifts to a greater emphasis on cost and service. Slower growth combined with overcapacity and knowledgeable buyers put a premium on a firm's ability to achieve cost leadership or differentiation along the dimensions most desired by the market. Research and development shifts from product to process improvements. Overall product quality improves and costs are reduced significantly. This is the type of industry in which cost leadership and differentiation tend to be combined to various degrees. A firm can no longer gain high market share simply through low price. The buyers are more sophisticated and demand a certain minimum level of quality for the price paid. The same is true for firms emphasizing high quality. Either the quality must be high enough and valued by the customer enough to justify the higher price or the price must be dropped (through lowering costs) to compete effectively with the lower priced products. This consolidation is taking place worldwide in the automobile, airline, and home appliance industries.

What Are Competitive Tactics?

A **tactic** is a specific operating plan detailing *how* a strategy is to be implemented in terms of *when* and *where* it is to be put into action. By their nature, tactics are narrower in their scope and shorter in their time horizon than are strategies. Tactics may therefore be viewed (like policies) as a link between the formulation and implementation of strategy. Some of the tactics available to implement competitive strategies are those dealing with timing (when) and market location (where).

What Are Timing Tactics?

The first company to manufacture and sell a new product or service is called the **first mover**. Some of the advantages of being a first mover are that the company is able to establish a reputation as a leader in the industry, move down the learning curve to assume the cost leader position, and earn temporarily high profits from buyers who value the product or service very highly. Being a first mover does, however, have its disadvantages. These disadvantages are, conversely, advantages enjoyed by late mover firms. **Late movers** may be able to imitate others' technological advances (and thus keep R&D costs low), minimize risks by waiting until a new market is established, and take advantage of the natural inclination of the first mover to ignore market segments.

What Are Market Location Tactics?

A company or business unit can implement a competitive strategy either offensively or defensively. An **offensive tactic** usually takes place in an established competitor's market location. A defensive tactic usually takes place within a company's current market position as a defense against possible attack by a rival.[4]

What Are Offensive Tactics? Some of the methods used to attack a competitor's position are:

- **Frontal Assault:** The attacking firm goes head to head with its competitor. It matches the competitor in every category from price to promotion to distribution channel. To be successful, the attacker must not only have superior resources, but it must also be willing to persevere. This tactic is generally very expensive and may serve to awaken a sleeping giant (as MCI and Sprint did to AT&T in long-distance telephone service), depressing profits for all in the industry.

- **Flanking Maneuver:** Rather than going straight for a competitor's position of strength with a frontal assault, a firm may attack a part of the market where the competitor is weak. Cyrix Corporation followed this tactic with its entry into the microprocessor market—a market then almost totally dominated by Intel. Rather than going directly after Intel's microprocessor business, Cyrix developed a math coprocessor for Intel's 386 chip that would run 20 times faster than Intel's microprocessor. To be successful, the flanker must be patient and willing to carefully expand out of the relatively undefended market niche or else face retaliation by an established competitor.

- **Encirclement:** Usually evolving from a frontal assault or flanking maneuver, encirclement occurs as an attacking company or business unit encircles the competitor's position in terms of products or markets or both. The encircler has greater product variety (a complete product line ranging from low to high price) and/or serves more markets (it dominates every secondary market). Honda successfully took this approach in motorcycles by taking every market segment except for the heavyweight segment in the United States controlled by Harley-Davidson. To be successful, the encircler must have the wide variety of abilities and resources necessary to attack multiple market segments.

- **Bypass Attack:** Rather than directly attacking the established competitor frontally or on its flanks, a company or business unit may choose to change the rules of the game. This tactic attempts to cut the market out from under the established defender by offering a new type of product that makes the competitor's product unnecessary. For example, instead of competing directly against Microsoft's Windows 95 operating system, Netscape chose to use Java "applets" in its Internet browser so that an operating system and specialized programs were no longer necessary to run applications on a personal computer.

- **Guerrilla Warfare:** Instead of a continual and extensive resource-expensive attack on a competitor, a firm or business unit may choose to "hit and run."

Guerrilla warfare involves small, intermittent assaults on a competitor's different market segments. In this way, a new entrant or small firm can make some gains without seriously threatening a large, established competitor and evoking some form of retaliation. To be successful, the firm or unit conducting guerrilla warfare must be patient enough to accept small gains and to avoid pushing the established competitor to the point that it must make a response or else lose face. Microbreweries, which make beer for sale to local customers, use this tactic against national brewers like Anheuser-Busch.

What Are Defensive Tactics? According to Porter, **defensive tactics** aim to lower the probability of attack, divert attacks to less-threatening avenues, or lessen the intensity of an attack. Instead of increasing competitive advantage per se, they make a company's or business unit's competitive advantage more sustainable by causing a challenger to conclude that an attack is unattractive. These tactics deliberately reduce short-term profitability to ensure long-term profitability.[5]

- **Raise Structural Barriers:** Entry barriers act to block a challenger's logical avenues of attack. According to Porter, some of the most important are to (1) offer a full line of products in every profitable market segment to close off any entry points, (2) block channel access by signing exclusive agreements with distributors, (3) raise buyer switching costs by offering low-cost training to users, (4) raise the cost of gaining trial users by keeping prices low on items new users most likely will purchase, (5) increase scale economies to reduce unit costs, (6) foreclose alternative technologies through patenting or licensing, (7) limit outside access to facilities and personnel, (8) tie up suppliers by obtaining exclusive contracts or purchasing key locations, (9) avoid suppliers that also serve competitors, and (10) encourage the government to raise barriers such as safety and pollution standards or favorable trade policies.

- **Increase Expected Retaliation:** This tactic is an action that increases the perceived threat of retaliation for an attack. For example, management may strongly defend any erosion of market share by drastically cutting prices or matching a challenger's promotion through a policy of accepting any price-reduction coupons for a competitor's product. This counterattack is especially important in markets that are important to the defending company or business unit. For example, when Clorox Company challenged Procter & Gamble Company in the detergent market with Clorox Super Detergent, P&G retaliated by test marketing its liquid bleach Lemon Fresh Comet in an attempt to scare Clorox into retreating from the detergent market.

- **Lower the Inducement for Attack:** This third tactic reduces a challenger's expectations of future profits in the industry. Like Southwest Airlines, a company can deliberately keep prices low and constantly invest in cost-reducing measures. Keeping prices very low gives a new entrant little profit incentive.

How Is a Business/Competitive Strategy Chosen?

Before selecting one of these generic competitive strategies (and the appropriate competitive tactic) for a company or business unit, management should assess its feasibility in terms of company or business unit resources and capabilities. Table 6.3 lists some of the commonly required skills and resources as well as organizational requirements. Because these resources usually exist within a firm's functional areas, we now examine functional strategy as a way to achieve business/ competitive strategy.

6.2 Functional Strategy

Functional strategy maximizes resource productivity so that a distinctive competence will develop to give a company or business unit a competitive advantage. Within the constraints of corporate and business/competitive strategies, functional strategies pull together the various activities and competencies of each function (typically housed within a department) to improve performance. For example, a manufacturing department is concerned with developing a strategy to reduce costs and improve the quality of its output. Marketing, in comparison, is typically concerned with developing strategies to increase sales. These functional strategic

TABLE 6.3   Requirements for Generic Competitive Strategies

Generic Strategy	Commonly Required Skills and Resources	Common Organizational Requirements
Overall Cost Leadership	Sustained capital investment and access to capital Process engineering skills Intense supervision of labor Products designed for ease of manufacture Low-cost distribution system	Tight cost control Frequent, detailed control reports Structured organization and responsibilities Incentives based on meeting strict quantitative targets
Differentiation	Strong marketing abilities Product engineering Creative flair Strong capability in basic research Corporate reputation for quality or technological leadership Long tradition in the industry or unique combination of skills drawn from other businesses Strong cooperation from channels	Strong coordination among functions in R&D, product development, and marketing Subjective measurement and incentives instead of quantitative measures Amenities to attract highly skilled labor, scientists, or creative people
Focus	Combination of the above policies directed at the particular strategic target	Combination of the above policies directed at the particular strategic target

Source: Reprinted with the permission of The Free Press, a division of Simon & Schuster from *Competitive Strategy: Techniques for Analyzing Industries and Competitors* by Michael E. Porter. Copyright © 1980 by The Free Press.

decisions need to be made if functional managers are to implement corporate and business/competitive strategies properly.

What Is the Role of Outsourcing?

Where should a function be housed? Should it be integrated within the organization or purchased from an outside contractor? **Outsourcing** is purchasing from someone else a product or service that had been previously provided internally. Increasingly, outsourcing is considered to be an important part of strategic decision making. For example, DuPont contracts out project engineering and design to Morrison Knudsen, AT&T contracts its credit card processing to Total System Services, Northern Telecom its electronic-component manufacturing to Comptronix, and Eastman Kodak its computer support services to Businessland. Sophisticated strategists, according to Quinn, are no longer thinking just of market share or vertical integration as the keys to strategic planning:

> Instead they concentrate on identifying those few core service activities where the company has—or can develop: (1) a continuing strategic edge and (2) long-term streams of new products to satisfy future customer demands. They develop these competencies in greater depth than anyone else in the world. Then they seek to eliminate, minimize, or outsource activities where the company cannot be preeminent, unless those activities are essential to support or protect the chosen areas of strategic focus.[6]

The key to outsourcing is to purchase from outside only those activities that are not key to the company's distinctive competence. Otherwise, the company may give up the very core technologies or capabilities that made it successful in the first place—thus putting itself on the road to eventual decline as a "hollow corporation." Therefore, in deciding on functional strategy, the strategic manager must (1) identify the company's or business unit's core competencies, (2) ensure that the competencies are continually being strengthened, and (3) manage the competencies in such a way that best preserves the competitive advantage they create. An outsourcing decision depends on the fraction of total value added by the activity under consideration and by the amount of competitive advantage in that activity for the company or business unit. Only when the fraction of total value is small and the competitive advantage in the activity is low, should a company or unit outsource.

What Marketing Strategies Can Be Employed?

Marketing strategy deals with pricing, selling, and distributing a product. Using a **market development strategy**, a company or business unit can (1) capture a larger share of an existing market for current products through market saturation and market penetration or (2) develop new markets for current products. Consumer product giants such as Procter & Gamble, Colgate-Palmolive, and Unilever are experts at using advertising and promotion to implement a market saturation or penetration strategy in order to gain the dominant market share in a product category. As seeming masters of the product life cycle, these companies extend product life almost indefinitely through "new and improved" variations of product and packaging that appeal to most market niches. These companies also follow the second market development strategy by taking a successful product they market in one part of the world and marketing it elsewhere. Noting the success of their presoak detergents in Europe, both P&G and Colgate successfully introduced this type of laundry product to North America under the trade names of Biz and Axion.

Using the **product development** strategy, a company or unit can (1) develop new products for *existing markets* or (2) develop new products for *new markets*. Church and Dwight has had great success following the first product development strategy by developing new products to sell to its current customers. Acknowledging the widespread appeal of its Arm & Hammer brand baking soda, the company generated new uses for its sodium bicarbonate by reformulating it as toothpaste, deodorant, and detergent. The company has also successfully followed the second product development strategy by developing pollution reduction products (using sodium compounds) for sale to coal-fired electrical plants.

Numerous other marketing strategies exist. For advertising and promotion, for example, a company or business unit can choose between a "push" or a "pull" marketing strategy. Many large food and consumer products companies in the United States and Canada have followed a **push strategy** by spending a large amount of money on trade promotion in order to gain or hold shelf space in retail outlets. Trade promotion includes discounts, in-store special offers, and advertising allowances designed to "push" products through the distribution system. The Kellogg Company recently decided to change its emphasis from a push to a **pull strategy**, in which advertising "pulls" the products through the distribution channels. The company now spends more money on consumer advertising designed to build brand awareness so that shoppers will ask for the products.

Other marketing strategies deal with distribution and pricing. As shown in the *Company Spotlight on Maytag Corporation* feature, the corporation chose not to sell its Maytag brand home appliances through Sears' "Brand Central" because management did not want to alienate existing Maytag dealers.

When pricing a new product, a company or business unit can follow one of two strategies. For new-product pioneers, **skim pricing** offers the opportunity to "skim the cream" from the top of the demand curve with a high price while the product is novel and competitors are few. **Penetration pricing**, in contrast, attempts to hasten market development and offers the pioneer the opportunity to use the experience curve to gain market share with a low price and dominate the industry. Depending on corporate and business unit objectives and strategies, either of these choices may be desirable to a particular company or unit. Penetration pricing is, however, more likely than skim pricing to raise a unit's operating profit in the long term.[7]

What Financial Strategies Can Be Employed?

Financial strategy examines the financial implications of corporate and business-level strategic options and identifies the best financial course of action. It can also provide competitive advantage through a lower cost of funds and a flexible ability

In the late 1980s, Sears instituted its new *Brand Central* format to sell white goods. In addition to offering its own private brands, the retail giant offered nationally known brands such as General Electric, Whirlpool, Amana, Jenn-Air, and Speedqueen. Except for its Jenn-Air products, Maytag Corporation chose not to join Sears' Brand Central effort. Some industry experts thought this to be a strange decision given that Sears alone sold one out of every four U.S. major home appliances. Why would Maytag ignore this key sales outlet?

Leonard Hadley, Chief Operating Officer of Maytag Corporation at the time, explained that the company did not want to antagonize its carefully nurtured appliance dealers who had always considered Sears their major retail competition. The corporation's emphasis on quality and higher price rather than market share as the Maytag unit's business competitive strategy made the Maytag brand more dependent on appliance dealers than either General Electric or Whirlpool. In addition, some Maytag people feared that Sears might use the Maytag brand image to attract customers into the stores, but then persuade them to buy a less expensive Sears brand carrying a higher markup.

to raise capital to support a business strategy. Financial strategy usually attempts to maximize the financial value of the firm.

The desired level of debt versus equity versus internal long-term financing via cash flow is a key issue in financial strategy. Many small and medium-sized companies, such as Urschel Laboratories, try to avoid all external sources of funds in order to avoid outside entanglements and to keep control of the company within the family.

A popular financial strategy is the leveraged buyout (LBO). In a **leveraged buyout,** a company is acquired in a transaction financed largely by debt—usually obtained from a third party such as an insurance company. Ultimately the debt is paid with money generated from the acquired company's operations or by sales of its assets. The acquired company, in effect, pays for its own acquisition! Management of the LBO is then under tremendous pressure to keep the highly leveraged company profitable. Unfortunately the huge amount of debt on the acquired company's books may actually cause its eventual decline unless it goes public once again.

The management of dividends to stockholders is an important part of a corporation's financial strategy. Corporations in fast-growing industries, such as computers and computer software, often do not declare dividends. They use the money they might have spent on dividends to finance rapid growth. If the company is successful, its growth in sales and profits is reflected in a higher stock price—eventually resulting in a hefty capital gain when stockholders sell their common stock.

Other corporations, such as electric utilities, that do not face rapid growth must support the value of their stock by offering generous and consistent dividends.

What Research and Development (R&D) Strategies Are Available?

R&D strategy deals with product and process innovation and improvement. One of the R&D choices is to be either a **technological leader** (pioneers an innovation) or a **technological follower** (imitates the products of competitors). Porter suggests that making the decision to become a technological leader or follower can be a way of achieving either overall low cost or differentiation. (See Table 6.4.)

One example of an effective use of the leader R&D functional strategy to achieve a differentiation competitive advantage is Nike, Inc. Nike spends more than most companies in the industry on R&D in order to differentiate its athletic shoes from its competitors in terms of performance. As a result, its products have become the favorite of the serious athlete.

What Operations Strategies May Be Used?

Operations strategy determines how and where a product or service is to be manufactured, the level of vertical integration, the deployment of physical resources, and relationships with suppliers. To begin with, a firm's manufacturing strategy is affected by the product or process life cycle. This concept describes the increase in production volume ranging from lot sizes as low as one in a *job shop* (one-of-a-kind production using skilled labor) through *connected line batch flow* (components are standardized; each machine functions like a job shop but is positioned in the same order as the parts are processed) to lot sizes as high as 100,000 or more per year for *flexible manufacturing systems* (parts are grouped into manufacturing

TABLE 6.4

Research and Development Strategy and Competitive Advantage

	Technological Leadership	**Technological Followership**
Cost Advantage	Pioneer the lowest cost product design Be the first firm down the learning curve Create low-cost ways of performing value activities	Lower the cost of the product or value activities by learning from the leader's experience Avoid R&D costs through imitation
Differentiation	Pioneer a unique product that increases buyer value Innovate in other activities to increase buyer value	Adapt the product or delivery system more closely to buyer needs by learning from the leader's experience

Source: Reprinted with the permission of The Free Press, a division of Simon & Schuster, from *Competitive Advantage: Creating and Sustaining Superior Performance* by Michael E. Porter. Copyright © 1985 by Michael E. Porter.

families to produce a wide variety of mass-produced items) and *dedicated transfer lines* (highly automated assembly lines making one mass-produced product using little human labor). According to this concept, the product becomes standardized into a commodity over time in conjunction with increasing demand, as flexibility gives way to efficiency. Nevertheless, a company's competitive business strategy can be the key determinant of the manufacturing process.[8]

Operations strategy also should deal with the optimum level of technology the firm should use in its operations processes. Advanced Manufacturing Technology (AMT) is revolutionizing operations worldwide and should continue to have a major impact as corporations strive to integrate diverse business activities using computer integrated design and manufacturing (CAD/CAM) principles. The use of CAD/CAM, flexible manufacturing systems, computer numerically controlled systems, automatic-guided vehicles, robotics, manufacturing resource planning (MRP II), optimized production technology, and just-in-time delivery contribute to increased flexibility, quick response time, and higher productivity. Such investments also act to increase operating leverage and could cause significant problems if the company is unable to achieve economies of scale or scope.

What Human Resource Strategies Can Be Used?

HRM strategy addresses the issue of whether a company or business unit should hire a large number of low-skilled employees who receive low pay, perform repetitive jobs, and most likely quit after a short time (the McDonald's restaurant strategy) or hire skilled employees who receive relatively high pay and are cross-trained to participate in self-managed work teams. Many companies are not only using increasing numbers of part-time and temporary employees, they are also experimenting with leasing employees from employee leasing companies. To reduce costs and obtain increased flexibility, companies in the United States leased around two million workers in 1994.[9]

As work increases in complexity, the more suited it is for teams. A recent survey of 476 Fortune 1000 U.S. companies revealed that, although only 7% of their workforce was organized into self-managed teams, half the companies reported that they would be relying significantly more on them in the years ahead.[10] Other HRM strategies deal with the question of promotion from within or recruitment of managers from outside the company.

6.3 ▶ Strategies to Avoid

Several strategies, which could be considered corporate, business, or functional, are very dangerous. Managers who have made a poor analysis or lack creativity may be trapped into considering them.

- **Follow the Leader:** Imitating the strategy of a leading competitor might seem a good idea, but it ignores a firm's particular strengths and weaknesses as well as the possibility that the leader may be wrong. Fujitsu Ltd., the world's second-largest computer maker, was driven since the 1960s by the sole ambition of catching up to IBM. Like IBM, Fujitsu competed primarily as a mainframe computer maker. So devoted was it to catching IBM, however, it failed to notice that the mainframe business was reaching maturity and by 1993 was rapidly going into decline.

- **Hit Another Home Run:** If a company is successful because it pioneered an extremely successful product, it has a tendency to search for another superproduct that will ensure growth and prosperity. Like betting on long shots at the horse races, the probability of finding a second winner is slight. Polaroid spent a lot of money developing an "instant" movie camera, but the public ignored it.

- **Arms Race:** Entering into a spirited battle with another firm for an increase in market share might increase sales revenue, but that increase will probably be more than offset by increases in advertising, promotion, R&D, and manufacturing costs. Since the deregulation of airlines, price wars and rate "specials" have contributed to the low profit margins or bankruptcy of many major airlines, such as Eastern and Continental.

- **Do Everything:** When faced with several interesting opportunities, management might tend to leap at all of them. At first, a corporation might have enough resources to develop each idea into a project, but money, time, and energy are soon exhausted as each of the many projects demand large infusions of resources.

- **Losing Hand:** A corporation might have invested so much in a particular strategy that top management is unwilling to accept the fact that the strategy is not successful. Believing that it has too much invested to quit, the corporation continues to throw "good money after bad." Pan American Airlines, for example, chose to sell its Pan Am Building and Intercontinental Hotels, the most profitable parts of the corporation, to keep its money-losing airline flying. Continuing to suffer losses, the company followed this strategy of shedding assets for cash until it had sold off everything and went bankrupt.

6.4 ▶ Selection of the Best Strategy

After potential strategic alternatives have been identified and evaluated in terms of their pros and cons, one must be selected for implementation. By this point, many feasible alternatives probably will have emerged. How does management determine the best strategy?

Perhaps the most important criterion is the ability of the proposed strategy to deal with the specific strategic factors developed earlier in the SWOT analysis. If the alternative doesn't take advantage of environmental opportunities and corporate strengths and lead away from environmental threats and corporate weaknesses, it will probably fail.

Another important consideration in the selection of a strategy is the ability of each alternative to satisfy agreed-on objectives with the least use of resources and with the fewest negative side effects. It is therefore important to develop a tentative implementation plan so that the difficulties that management is likely to face are addressed. This should be done in light of societal trends, the industry, and the company's situation based on the construction of scenarios.

How to Construct Corporate Scenarios

Corporate scenarios are *pro forma* balance sheets and income statements that forecast the effect that each alternative strategy and its various programs will likely have on division and corporate return on investment. In a survey of Fortune 500 firms, 78% reported using scenarios and 84% reported using computer simulation models in strategic planning. Most of these were simply spreadsheet-based simulation models.[11]

Corporate scenarios are simply extensions of the industry scenarios discussed in Chapter 3. If, for example, industry scenarios suggest that a strong market demand is likely to emerge for certain products, a series of alternative strategy scenarios can be developed for a specific firm. The alternative of acquiring another company having these products can be compared with the alternative of developing the products internally. Using three sets of estimated sales figures (optimistic, pessimistic, and most likely) for the new products over the next five years, the two alternatives can be evaluated in terms of their effect on future company performance as reflected in its probable future financial statements. Pro forma (estimated future) balance sheets and income statements can be generated with spreadsheet software, such as Lotus 1-2-3 or Excel, on a personal computer.

To construct a corporate scenario, follow these steps:

- **First,** use the *industry scenarios* discussed earlier in Chapter 3 and develop a set of assumptions about the task environment. At 3M, for example, the general manager of each business unit is required annually to describe what his or her industry will look like in 15 years. *Optimistic, pessimistic,* and *most likely* assumptions should be listed for key economic factors such as the GDP (gross domestic product), CPI (consumer price index), prime interest rate, and for other key external strategic factors such as governmental regulation and industry trends. These same underlying assumptions should be listed for each of the alternative scenarios to be developed.

- **Second,** develop *common-size financial statements* (**discussed in Chapter 10**) for the company's or business unit's previous years. These common-size financial statements are the basis for the projections of pro forma financial statements. Use the historical common-size percentages to estimate the level of revenues, expenses, and other categories in estimated pro forma statements for future years. For each strategic alternative, develop a set of optimistic, pessimistic, and most likely assumptions about the impact of key variables on the company's future financial statements. Forecast three sets of sales and cost of goods sold figures for at least five years into the future. Look at historical data and make adjustments based on the environmental assumptions made. Do the same for other figures that can vary significantly. For the rest, assume that they will continue in their historical relationship to sales or some other key determining factor. Plug in expected inventory levels, accounts receivable, accounts payable, R&D expenses, advertising and promotion expenses, capital expenditures, and debt payments (assuming that debt is used to finance the strategy), among others. Consider not only historical trends, but also programs that might be needed to implement each alternative strategy (such as building a new manufacturing facility or expanding the sales force). Table 6.5 presents a form to use in developing pro forma financial statements using historical averages from common-size financial statements.

- **Third,** construct detailed *pro forma financial statements* for each strategic alternative. Using a spreadsheet program, list the actual figures from this year's financial statements in the left column. To the right of this column, list the optimistic figures for year one, year two, year three, year four, and year five. Repeat this same process with the same strategic alternative but now list the pessimistic figures for the next five years. Do the same with the most likely figures. Then develop a similar set of optimistic (O), pessimistic (P), and most likely (ML) pro forma statements for the second strategic alternative. This process generates six different pro forma scenarios reflecting three different situations (O, P, and ML) for two strategic alternatives. Next, calculate financial ratios and common-size income statements, and balance sheets to

TABLE 6.5   Scenario Box for Use in Generating Financial Pro Forma Statements

Factor	Last Year	Historical Average	Trend Analysis	Projections[1] 19— O	P	ML	19— O	P	ML	19— O	P	ML	Comments
GDP													
CPI													
Other													
Sales—units													
Sales—dollars													
COGS													
Advertising and marketing													
Interest expense													
Plant expansion													
Dividends													
Net profits													
EPS													
ROI													
ROE													
Other													

Note 1: **O** = Optimistic; **P** = Pessimistic; **ML** = Most Likely.

Source: T. L. Wheelen and J. D. Hunger, "Scenario Box for Use in Generating Financial Pro Forma Statements." Copyright © 1993 by Wheelen and Hunger Associates. Reprinted by permission.

accompany the pro forma statements. To determine the feasibility of the scenarios, compare the assumptions underlying the scenarios with these financial statements and ratios. For example, if cost of goods sold drops from 70% to 50% of total sales revenue in the pro forma income statements, this drop should result from a change in the production process or a shift to cheaper raw materials or labor costs, rather than from a failure to keep the cost of goods sold in its usual percentage relationship to sales revenue when the predicted statement was developed.

The result of this detailed scenario construction should be anticipated net profits, cash flow, and net working capital for each of three versions of the two alternatives for five years into the future. A strategist might want to go further into the future if the strategy is expected to have a major impact on the company's financial statements beyond five years. The result of this work should provide sufficient information on which to base forecasts of the likely feasibility and probable profitability of each of the strategic alternatives.

Obviously these corporate scenarios can quickly become very complicated, especially if three sets of acquisition prices and development costs are calculated. Nevertheless, this sort of detailed "what if" analysis is needed in order to realistically compare the projected outcome of each reasonable alternative strategy and its attendant programs, budgets, and procedures. Regardless of the quantifiable pros and cons of each alternative, the actual decision probably will be influenced by one or more of the following subjective factors.

Why Consider Management's Attitude Toward Risk?

The attractiveness of a particular strategic alternative is partially a function of the amount of risk it entails. **Risk** is composed not only of the *probability* that the strategy will be effective, but also of the *amount of assets* the corporation must allocate to that strategy, and the *length of time* the assets will be unavailable for other uses. The greater the assets involved and the longer they are committed, the more likely top management is to demand a high probability of success. This demand might be one reason that innovations seem to occur more often in small firms than in large, established corporations. An entrepreneur managing a small firm is willing to accept greater risk than would professional managers running a large firm of diversified ownership. It is one thing to take a chance if you are the primary stockholder and are not concerned with periodic changes in the value of the company's common stock. It is something else if the corporation's stock is widely held and acquisition-hungry competitors or takeover artists surround the company like sharks every time the company's stock price falls below some external assessment of the firm's value!

What Pressures from the External Environment Affect Decisions?

The attractiveness of a strategic alternative is affected by its perceived compatibility with the key stakeholders in a corporation's task environment. Creditors want to be paid on time. Unions exert pressure for comparable wage and employment security. Governments and interest groups demand social responsibility. Stock-holders want dividends. Management must consider all of these pressures in select-ing the best alternative.

To assess the importance of stakeholder concerns in a particular decision, strategic managers should ask four questions: (1) Which stakeholders are most crucial for corporate success? (2) How much of what they want are they likely to get under this alternative? (3) What are they likely to do if they don't get what they want? (4) What is the probability that they will do it?

Strategy-makers should be better able to choose strategic alternatives that minimize external pressures and maximize stakeholder support. In addition, top management can propose a *political strategy* to influence its key stakeholders. Some of the most commonly used political strategies are constituency building, po-litical action committee (PAC) contributions, advocacy advertising, lobbying, and coalition building.

What Pressures from the Corporate Culture Affect Decisions?

If a strategy is incompatible with the corporate culture, it probably will not suc-ceed. Foot-dragging and even sabotage could result, as employees fight to resist a radical change in corporate philosophy. Precedents tend to restrict the kinds of ob-jectives and strategies that management can seriously consider. The "aura" of the founders of a corporation can linger long past their lifetimes because they have im-printed their values on a corporation's members.

In considering a strategic alternative, strategy-makers must assess its com-patibility with the corporate culture. If there is little fit, management must decide if it should (1) *take a chance on ignoring the culture*, (2) *manage around the culture and change the implementation plan*, (3) *try to change the culture to fit the strategy*, or (4) *change the strategy to fit the culture*. Further, a decision to proceed with a particular strategy without a commitment to change the culture or manage around the culture (both very tricky and time consuming) is danger-ous. Nevertheless, restricting a corporation to only those strategies that are com-pletely compatible with its culture might eliminate the most profitable alternatives from consideration. (**See Chapter 8 for more information on managing corporate culture.**)

How Do the Needs and Desires of Key Managers Affect Decisions?

Even the most attractive alternative might not be selected if it is contrary to the needs and desires of important top managers. People's egos may be tied to a partic-ular proposal to the extent that they strongly lobby against all other alternatives. Key executives in operating divisions, for example, might be able to influence other people in top management to favor a particular alternative and to ignore ob-jections to it.

People tend to maintain the status quo, which means that decision makers continue with existing goals and plans beyond the point when an objective ob-server would recommend a change in course. People may ignore negative informa-tion about a particular course of action to which they are committed because they want to appear competent and they strongly value consistency. It may take a crisis or an unlikely event to cause strategic decision makers to seriously consider an alternative they had previously ignored or discounted. For example, it wasn't until the CEO of ConAgra, a multinational food products company, had a heart attack that ConAgra started producing the Healthy Choice line of low-fat, low-cholesterol, low-sodium frozen-food entrees.

What Is the Process of Strategic Choice?

> There is an old story at General Motors about Alfred Sloan. At a meeting with his key executives, Sloan proposed a controversial strategic decision. When asked for comments, each executive responded with supportive comments and praise. After announcing that they were all in apparent agreement, Sloan stated that they were not going to proceed with the decision. Either his executives didn't know enough to point out potential downsides of the decision, or they were agreeing to avoid upsetting the boss and disrupting the cohesion of the group. The decision was delayed until a debate could occur over the pros and cons.[12]

Strategic choice is the evaluation of alternative strategies and the selection of the best alternative. There is mounting evidence that when an organization faces a dynamic environment, the best strategic decisions are not arrived at through consensus—they actually involve a certain amount of heated disagreement and even conflict. Because unmanaged conflict often carries a high emotional cost, authorities in decision making propose that strategic managers use *programmed conflict* to raise different opinions, regardless of the personal feelings of the people involved. To help strategic managers avoid the consensus trap that Alfred Sloan found in the example mentioned earlier, two techniques are suggested: devil's advocate and dialectical inquiry.

What Is Devil's Advocate?

The devil's advocate originated in the medieval Roman Catholic Church as a way of ensuring that impostors were not canonized as saints. One trusted person was selected to find and present all reasons why the person could not be canonized. When applied to strategic decision making, the **devil's advocate** (who may be an individual or a group) is assigned to identify potential pitfalls and problems with a proposed alternative strategy in a formal presentation.

What Is Dialectical Inquiry?

The dialectic philosophy, which can be traced back to Plato and Aristotle and more recently to Hegel, involves combining two conflicting views—the *thesis* and the *antithesis*—into a *synthesis*. When applied to strategic decision making, **dialectical inquiry** requires that two proposals using different assumptions be generated for each alternative strategy under consideration. After advocates of each position present and debate the merits of their arguments before key decision makers, either one of the alternatives or a new compromise alternative is selected as the strategy to be implemented.

6.5 Development of Policies

The selection of the best strategic alternative is not the end of strategy formulation. Management now must establish policies that define the ground rules for implementation. Flowing from the selected strategy, these policies provide guidance for decision making and actions throughout the organization. At General Electric, for example, Chairman Welch insists that GE be Number One or Number Two wherever it competes. This policy gives clear guidance to managers throughout the organization. Another example of such a policy is Casey's General Stores' policy that a new service or product line may be added to its stores only when the product or service can be justified in terms of increasing store traffic.

Policies tend to be rather long lived and can even outlast the particular strategy that created them. Interestingly, these general policies, such as "The customer is always right" or "Research and development should get first priority on all budget requests," can become, in time, part of a corporation's culture. Such policies can make the implementation of specific strategies easier, but they can also restrict top management's strategic options in the future. For this reason, a change in policies should quickly follow any change in strategy. Managing policy is one way to manage the corporate culture.

In Conclusion . . .

When Sheri Poe founded Rykä, Inc., she knew that to succeed she had to follow a business strategy of focus differentiation. How else was her company to compete with Nike and Reebok? Poe explained:

> At that time (1987), women's athletic shoes were sized-down versions of men's; but a woman's body is obviously different, and when she's not wearing shoes designed for her physiology, the constant pounding of a workout will make her more likely to develop nagging injuries. . . . What Rykä developed was a fitness shoe built specifically for a woman, a patented design for better shock absorption and durability. . . .

> In any industry, the key is to have a strong niche; that way, if anyone copies the product, yours will still be viewed as the original. Staying a step ahead as the megabucks companies' attempt to invade your niche is essential to long-term success in a crowded market.[13]

Discussion Questions

1. Is it possible for a company or business unit to follow a cost leadership strategy and a differentiation strategy simultaneously? Why or why not?

2. What are the advantages and disadvantages of being a first mover in an industry? Give some examples of first mover and late mover firms. Were they successful?

3. Why is penetration pricing more likely than skim pricing to raise a company's or a business unit's operating profit in the long run?

4. What are the pros and cons of R&D leadership versus follower-ship as a functional strategy?

5. What is the relationship of policies to strategies?

Key Terms

business or competitive strategy
competitive scope
cost leadership
differentiation
cost focus
differentiation focus
stuck in the middle
fragmented industry
consolidated industry
tactic
first mover
late mover
offensive tactics
defensive tactics
functional strategy
outsourcing
marketing strategies
market development strategy

product development
push strategy
pull strategy
skim pricing
penetration pricing
financial strategy
leveraged buyout
R&D strategy
technological leader
technological follower
operations strategy
HRM strategy
corporate scenarios
risk
strategic choice
devil's advocate
dialectical inquiry

7

Strategy Implementation: Organizing for Action

Based on the huge success of its Hollywood, California, Universal Studios tour, MCA, Inc., had planned since 1969 to establish a bigger version of the studio tour in Orlando, Florida. MCA bought land in central Florida, but management's reservations about the project delayed construction until the late 1980s—too late to beat Walt Disney World and its Disney-MGM Studios operation. Finally deciding to go ahead in 1989, the year the Disney-MGM studio tour opened, top management rushed to open the project well before it was ready. The importance of proper implementation was ignored as everyone hurried to meet management's deadline. Three months after opening its 444-acre combination studio tour and theme park, customers were still demanding refunds on poorly operating rides and attractions. The rides, which were based on Universal's movies *Jaws*, *Earthquake*, and *King Kong*, rarely operated as planned. One group of customers, having paid the full-price $29 admission, charged up to assembled television cameras, thrust down their thumbs, and shouted: "We're going to Disney World!" After expecting the Florida operation to add as much as $25 million a year to MCA's earnings, management revised its estimates and was hoping merely to break even. It took two more years before the studio tour began to live up to management's expectations.

7.1 What Is Strategy Implementation?

Strategy implementation is the sum total of the activities and choices required for the execution of a strategic plan. It is *the process by which strategies and policies are put into action through the development of programs, budgets, and procedures.* Although implementation is usually considered after strategy has been formulated, implementation is a key part of strategic management. The Orlando

Universal Tours is one example of how a good strategy can result in a disaster through poor strategy implementation. Strategy formulation and strategy implementation should thus be considered as two sides of the same coin.

To begin the implementation process, strategy-makers must consider three questions:

- *Who* are the people who will carry out the strategic plan?
- *What* must be done?
- *How* are they going to do what is needed?

Management should have addressed these questions and similar ones initially when they analyzed the pros and cons of strategic alternatives, but the questions must be addressed again before management can make appropriate implementation plans. Unless top management can answer these basic questions satisfactorily, even the best-planned strategy is unlikely to provide the desired outcome.

A survey of 93 Fortune 500 firms revealed that over half of the corporations experienced the following ten problems (listed in order of frequency) when they attempted to implement a strategic change:

1. Slower implementation than originally planned
2. Unanticipated major problems
3. Ineffective coordination of activities
4. Competing activities and crises that distracted attention away from implementation
5. Insufficient capabilities of the involved employees
6. Inadequate training and instruction of lower level employees
7. Uncontrollable external environmental factors
8. Inadequate leadership and direction by departmental managers
9. Poor definition of key implementation tasks and activities
10. Inadequate monitoring of activities by the information system[1]

7.2 Who Implements Strategy?

Depending on how the corporation is organized, those who implement strategy will probably be a much more diverse group of people than those who formulate it. In most large, multi-industry corporations, the implementers will be everyone in the organization. Vice-presidents of functional areas and directors of divisions or SBUs will work with their subordinates to put together large-scale implementation plans. Plant managers, project managers, and unit heads will put together plans for their specific plants, departments, and units. Therefore, every operational manager down to the first-line supervisor and every employee will be involved in some way in the implementing of corporate, business, and functional strategies.

Most of the people in the organization who are crucial to successful strategy implementation probably had little, if anything, to do with the development of the corporate and even business strategy. Therefore, they might be entirely ignorant of the vast amount of data and work that went into the formulation process. Unless changes in mission, objectives, strategies, and policies and their importance to the company are communicated clearly to all operational managers, resistance and foot-dragging can result. Managers might hope to convince top management to abandon its new plans and return to its old ways. This is one reason why involving middle managers in the formulation as well as in the implementation of strategy tends to result in better organizational performance.

7.3 What Must Be Done?

The managers of divisions and functional areas work with their fellow managers to develop **programs**, **budgets**, and **procedures** for the implementation of strategy. They also work to achieve synergy among the divisions and functional areas in order to establish and maintain a company's distinctive competence.

How to Develop Programs, Budgets, and Procedures?

Programs

The purpose of a program is to make the strategy action oriented. For example, assume Ajax Continental chose forward vertical integration as its best strategy for growth. It purchased existing retail outlets from another firm (Jones Surplus) instead of building its own. To integrate the new stores, the company would now have to develop various programs, for example:

1. A restructuring program to move the Jones Surplus stores into Ajax Continental's marketing chain of command so that store managers report to regional managers, who report to the merchandising manager, who reports to the vice-president in charge of marketing
2. An advertising program ("Jones Surplus is now a part of Ajax Continental. Prices are lower. Selection is better.")
3. A training program for newly hired store managers as well as for those Jones Surplus managers the corporation has chosen to keep
4. A program to develop reporting procedures that will integrate the Jones Surplus stores into Ajax Continental's accounting system
5. A program to modernize the Jones Surplus stores and to prepare them for a "grand opening"

Budgets

After programs are developed, the budget process begins. Planning a budget is the last real check a corporation has on the feasibility of its selected strategy. An ideal strategy might be found to be completely impractical only after specific implementation programs are costed in detail.

Procedures

After program, divisional, and corporate budgets are approved, standard operating procedures (SOPs) must be developed. They typically detail the various activities that must be carried out to complete a corporation's programs. In the case of

Ajax Corporation's acquisition of Jones Surplus' retail outlets, new operating procedures must be established for, among others, in-store promotions, inventory ordering, stock selection, customer relations, credits and collections, warehouse distribution, pricing, paycheck timing, grievance handling, and raises and promotions. These procedures ensure that the day-to-day store operations will be consistent over time (that is, next week's work activities will be the same as this week's) and consistent among stores (that is, each store will operate in the same manner as the others). For example, to ensure that its policies are carried out to the letter in every one of its fast-food retail outlets, McDonald's has done an excellent job of developing very detailed procedures (and policing them!).

How Does a Company Achieve Synergy?

One of the goals to be achieved in strategy implementation is synergy between and among functions and business units, which is why corporations commonly reorganize after an acquisition. **Synergy** is said to exist for a divisional corporation if the return on investment (ROI) of each division is greater than what the return would be if each division were an independent business. The acquisition or development of additional product lines is often justified on the basis of achieving some advantages of scale in one or more of a company's functional areas. For example, when Ralston Purina acquired Union Carbide's Eveready and Energizer lines of batteries, Ralston's CEO argued that his company would earn better profit margins on batteries than Union Carbide would because of Ralston's expertise in developing and marketing branded consumer products. Ralston Purina felt it could lower the battery costs by taking advantage of synergies in advertising, promotion, and distribution.

7.4 ▶ How Is Strategy to Be Implemented? Organizing for Action

Before plans can lead to actual performance, top management must ensure that the corporation is appropriately organized, programs are adequately staffed, and activities are being directed toward the achievement of desired objectives. Organizing activities are reviewed briefly in this chapter. *(Staffing, directing, and control activities are discussed in Chapters 8 and 9.)*

A change in corporate strategy will likely require some sort of change in organizational structure and in the skills needed in particular positions. Strategic managers must therefore closely examine how their company is structured to decide what, if any, changes should be made in the way work is accomplished. Should activities be grouped differently? Should the authority to make key decisions be centralized at headquarters or decentralized to managers in distant locations? Should the company be managed tightly with many rules and controls or loosely with few rules and controls? Should the corporation be organized into a tall structure with many layers of managers, each having a narrow span of control (that is, few employees to supervise) for better control of subordinates; or should it be organized into a flat structure with fewer layers of managers, each having a wide span of control (that is, more employees to supervise) to give more freedom to subordinates? For example, Ford had a fairly tall structure with 15 layers of managers, whereas Toyota had a relatively flat structure (for an automaker) of seven layers. Was Toyota's or Ford's structure "better"?

Does Structure Follow Strategy?

In a classic study of large U.S. corporations such as DuPont, General Motors, Sears, and Standard Oil, Alfred Chandler concluded that changes in corporate strategy lead to changes in organizational structure.[2] He also concluded that organizations follow a pattern of development from one kind of structural arrangement to another as they expand. According to him, these structural changes occur because inefficiencies caused by the old structure have, by being pushed too far, become too obviously detrimental to live with. Chandler therefore proposed the following sequence of what occurs:

1. New strategy is created.
2. New administrative problems emerge.
3. Economic performance declines.
4. New appropriate structure is invented.
5. Profit returns to its previous level.

Chandler found that in their early years, corporations such as DuPont tend to have a centralized functional organizational structure that is well suited to producing and selling a limited range of products. As they add new product lines, purchase their own sources of supply, and create their own distribution networks, they become too complex for highly centralized structures. To remain successful, this type of organization needs to shift to a decentralized structure with several semiautonomous divisions (referred to in Chapter 4 as the *divisional structure*).

Alfred P. Sloan, past CEO of General Motors, detailed how GM conducted such structural changes in the 1920s.[3] He saw decentralization of structure as "centralized policy determination coupled with decentralized operating management." After top management developed a strategy for the total corporation, the individual divisions, such as Chevrolet, Buick, and so on, were free to choose how to implement that strategy. Patterned after DuPont, GM found the decentralized multidivisional structure to be extremely effective in allowing the maximum amount of freedom for product development. Return on investment (ROI) was used as a financial control. (*ROI is discussed in more detail in Chapter 9.*)

Research generally supports Chandler's proposition that structure follows strategy (as well as the reverse proposition that structure influences strategy). As mentioned earlier, changes in the environment tend to be reflected in changes in a corporation's strategy, thus leading to changes in a corporation's structure. Strategy, structure, and the environment need to be closely aligned; otherwise, organizational performance will likely suffer. For example, a business unit following a differentiation strategy needs more freedom from headquarters to be successful than does another unit following a low-cost strategy.[4]

Although it is agreed that organizational structure must vary with different environmental conditions, which, in turn, affect an organization's strategy, there is no agreement about an optimal organizational design. What was appropriate for DuPont and General Motors in the 1920s might not be appropriate today. Firms in the same industry do, however, tend to organize themselves in a similar manner. For example, automobile manufacturers tend to emulate General Motors' divisional concept, whereas consumer goods producers tend to emulate the brand management concept (a type of matrix structure) pioneered by Procter & Gamble Company. The general conclusion seems to be that firms following similar strategies in similar industries tend to adopt similar structures.

What Are the Stages of Corporate Development?

Successful corporations tend to follow a pattern of structural development as they grow and expand. Beginning with the *simple structure* of the entrepreneurial firm (in which everybody does everything), they usually (if they are successful) get larger and organize along *functional* lines with marketing, production, and finance departments. With continuing success, the company adds new product lines in different industries and organizes itself into interconnected *divisions*. The differences among these three **stages of corporate development** in terms of typical problems, objectives, strategies, reward systems, and other characteristics are specified in detail in Table 7.1.

What Is Stage I? Simple Structure

Stage I is typified by the entrepreneur, who founds the company to promote an idea (product or service). The entrepreneur tends to make all the important decisions personally and is involved in every detail and phase of the organization. The Stage I company has little formal structure, which allows the entrepreneur to directly supervise the activities of every employee (see **Figure 4.2 for an illustration of the simple, functional, and divisional structures**). Planning is usually short range or reactive. The typical managerial functions of planning, organizing, directing, staffing, and controlling are usually performed to a very limited degree, if at all. The greatest strengths of a Stage I corporation are its flexibility and dynamism. The drive of the entrepreneur energizes the organization in its struggle for growth. Its greatest weakness is its extreme reliance on the entrepreneur to decide general strategies as well as detailed procedures. If the entrepreneur falters, the company usually flounders. This is often referred to as a *crisis of leadership.*[5]

Stage I describes Oracle Corporation, the computer software firm, under the management of its co-founder and CEO Lawrence Ellison. The company adopted a pioneering approach to retrieving data called structured query language (SQL). When IBM made SQL its standard, Oracle's success was assured. Unfortunately Ellison's technical wizardry was not sufficient to manage the company. Often working at home, he lost sight of details outside his technical interests. Although the company's sales were rapidly increasing, its financial controls were so weak that management had to restate an entire year's results to rectify irregularities. After the company recorded its first loss, Ellison hired a set of functional managers to run the company while he retreated to focus on new product development.

TABLE 7.1   **Factors Differentiating Stage I, II, and III Companies**

Function	Stage I	Stage II	Stage III
1. Sizing up: Major problems	Survival and growth dealing with short-term operating problems.	Growth, rationalization, and expansion of resources, providing for adequate attention to product problems.	Trusteeship in management and investment and control of large, increasing, and diversified resource. Also, important to diagnose and take action on problems at division level.
2. Objectives	Personal and subjective.	Profits and meeting functionally oriented budgets and performance targets.	ROI, profits, earnings per share.
3. Strategy	Implicit and personal; exploitation of immediate opportunities seen by owner-manager.	Functionally oriented moves restricted to "one product" scope; exploitation of one basic product or service field.	Growth and product diversification; exploitation of general business opportunities.
4. Organization: Major characteristic of structure	One unit, "one-man show."	One unit, functionally specialized group.	Multiunit general staff office and decentralized operating divisions.
5. (a) Measurement and control	Personal, subjective control based on simple accounting system and daily communication and observation.	Control grows beyond one person; assessment of functional operations necessary; structured control systems evolve.	Complex formal system geared to comparative assessment of performance measures, indicating problems and opportunities and assessing management ability of division managers.
5. (b) Key performance indicators	Personal criteria, relationships with owner, operating efficiency, ability to solve operating problems.	Functional and internal criteria such as sales, performance compared to budget, size of empire, status in group, personal relationships, etc.	More impersonal application of comparisons such as profits, ROI, P/E ratio, sales, market share, productivity, product leadership, personnel development, employee attitudes, public responsibility.
6. Reward–punishment system	Informal, personal, subjective; used to maintain control and divide small pool of resources to provide personal incentives for key performers.	More structured; usually based to a greater extent on agreed policies as opposed to personal opinion and relationships.	Allotment by "due process" of a wide variety of different rewards and punishments on a formal and systematic basis Companywide policies usually apply to many different classes of managers and workers with few major exceptions for individual cases.

Source: D. H. Thain, "Stages of Corporate Development," *Business Quarterly* (Winter 1969). Reprinted with permission of *Business Quarterly*, published by the Western Business School, The University of Western Ontario, London, Canada.

What Is Stage II? Functional Structure

At **Stage II**, a team of managers who have functional specializations replaces the entrepreneur. The transition to this stage requires a substantial managerial style change for the chief officer of the company, especially if he or she was the Stage I entrepreneur. Otherwise, having additional staff members yields no benefits to the organization. Lawrence Ellison's retreat from top management at Oracle Corporation to new product development manager is one way that technically brilliant founders are able to get out of the way of the newly empowered functional managers. Once into Stage II, the corporate strategy favors protectionism through dominance of the industry, often through vertical or horizontal integration. The great strength of a Stage II corporation lies in its concentration and specialization in one industry. Its great weakness is that all of its eggs are in one basket.

By concentrating on one industry while that industry remains attractive, a Stage II company, like Oracle Corporation in computer software, can be very successful. Once a functionally structured firm diversifies into other products in different industries, however, the advantages of the functional structure break down. A *crisis of autonomy* can now develop, in which people managing diversified product lines need more decision-making freedom than top management is willing to delegate to them. The company needs to move to a different structure.

What Is Stage III? Divisional Structure

The **Stage III** corporation focuses on managing diverse product lines in numerous industries; it decentralizes the decision-making authority. These organizations grow by diversifying their product lines and expanding to cover wider geographic areas. They move to a divisional structure with a central headquarters and decentralized operating divisions—each division or business unit is a functionally organized Stage II company. They may also use a conglomerate structure if top management chooses to keep its collection of Stage II subsidiaries operating autonomously. Headquarters attempts to coordinate the activities of its operating divisions through performance- and results-oriented control and reporting systems, and by stressing corporate planning techniques. The divisions are not tightly controlled but are held responsible for their own performance results. Therefore, to be effective, the company has to have a decentralized decision process. The greatest strength of a Stage III corporation is its almost unlimited resources. Its most significant weakness is that it is usually so large and complex that it tends to become relatively inflexible. General Electric, DuPont, and General Motors are Stage III corporations.

What Are the Blocks to Changing Stages?

Corporations often find themselves in difficulty because they are blocked from moving into the next logical stage of development. Blocks to development may be internal, such as lack of resources, lack of ability, or a refusal of top management to delegate decision making to others, or they may be external, such as economic conditions, labor shortages, and lack of market growth. For example, Chandler noted in his study that the successful founder/CEO in one stage was rarely the person who created the new structure to fit the new strategy, and that, as a result, the transition from one stage to another was often painful. This was true of General Motors Corporation under the management of William Durant, Ford Motor Company under Henry Ford I, Polaroid Corporation under Edwin Land, and Apple Computer under Steven Jobs. This difficulty in moving to a new stage is compounded by the founder's tendency to maneuver around the need to delegate by carefully hiring, training, and grooming his or her own team of managers. The team tends to maintain the founder's influence throughout the organization long after the founder is gone. This is what happened at Walt Disney Productions when the family continued to emphasize Walt's policies and plans long after he was dead. Although this may often be an organization's strength, it may also be a weakness—to the extent that the culture supports the status quo and blocks needed change.

Is There An Organizational Life Cycle?

Instead of considering stages of development in terms of structure, the organizational life cycle approach places the primary emphasis on the dominant issue facing the corporation. Organizational structure is only a secondary concern. The **organizational life cycle** describes how organizations grow, develop, and eventually decline. It is the organizational equivalent of the product life cycle in marketing. The stages of the organizational life cycle are *Birth* (Stage I), *Growth* (Stage II), *Maturity* (Stage III), *Decline* (Stage IV), and *Death* (Stage V). The impact of these stages on corporate strategy and structure is summarized in Table 7.2. Note that the first three stages are similar to the three commonly accepted stages of corporate development. The only significant difference is the addition of decline and death stages to complete the cycle. Even though a company's strategy may still be sound, its aging structure, culture, and processes may be such that they prevent the strategy from being executed properly—thus the company moves into decline.

Movement from growth to maturity to decline and finally to death is not, however, inevitable. A *Revival* phase may occur sometime during the maturity or

TABLE 7.2	**Organizational Life Cycle**				
	Stage I	**Stage II**	**Stage III**	**Stage IV**	**Stage V**
Dominant Issue	Birth	Growth	Maturity	Decline	Death
Popular Strategies	Concentration in a niche	Horizontal and vertical integration	Concentric and conglomerate diversification	Profit strategy followed by retrenchment	Liquidation or bankruptcy
Likely Structure	Entrepreneur-dominated	Functional management emphasized	Decentralization into profit or investment centers	Structural surgery	Dismemberment of structure

decline stages. Managerial and product innovations can extend the corporation's life cycle. This often occurs during the implementation of a turnaround strategy. At Maytag Corporation, for example, the revival phase was initiated in the 1970s under the leadership of Daniel Krumm while Maytag was still in its mature stage of development. As pointed out in the *Company Spotlight on Maytag Corporation* feature, the transition from aggressive growth to a rather passive and compla-

COMPANY SPOTLIGHT

MAYTAG
Corporation

**Initiating a
Revival Phase**

Maytag Company expanded during the 1920s into a national company. In terms of the organizational life cycle, this was Maytag Company's *growth stage*. Throughout the 1920s and 1930s, Maytag Company had an average U.S. market share of over 40% in washing machines. During the Great Depression of the 1930s, Maytag never suffered a loss. By World War II, Maytag had become the most successful washing machine company in the U.S. and had reached its *maturity stage*. Unfortunately the innovative genius and entrepreneurial drive of the company's early years were no longer present. After World War II, Bendix, a newcomer to the industry, introduced an automatic washing machine that used an automatic spin cycle instead of a hand-cranked wringer to squeeze excess rinse water out of clothes. Maytag, however, was reluctant to convert to automatic washers. This reluctance cost the company its leadership of the industry. By 1954, Maytag's share of the U.S. washer market had dropped to only 8%. It continued through the 1960s as a relatively small (compared to its competition) but profitable company.

Taking over as company President in 1972, Daniel Krumm was not satisfied with Maytag's situation. Although the company had added products to its original line of washers, Krumm saw Maytag as merely a successful niche manufacturer in a maturing U.S. market and vulnerable to aggressive actions by larger competitors. Consequently Maytag's management adopted a strategy to become a full-line manufacturer and develop a stronger position in the U.S. appliance industry. The decision was made to grow by acquisition within the appliance industry. The *revival phase* of Maytag's organizational life had begun.

In 1981, Maytag purchased Hardwick Stove Company, followed by Jenn-Air a year later and Magic Chef in 1986. In 1988, the top management of the new Maytag Corporation decided to extend the corporation's growth strategy by buying the Hoover Company. In this one step, Maytag Corporation moved into the international home appliance marketplace with nine manufacturing operations in the U.K., France, Australia, Mexico, Colombia, and Portugal. Maytag Corporation was now positioned as one of the "Big Five" U.S. appliance manufacturers able to have a strong presence in the developing global home appliance industry.

cent maturity in the 1950s and 1960s left the company vulnerable to competitive advances and the possibility of being acquired.

Unless a company is able to resolve the critical issues facing it in the decline stage, it is likely to move into Stage V, corporate death—also known as bankruptcy. This is what happened to TWA, Macy's Department Stores, Baldwin-United, Eastern Airlines, Colt's Manufacturing, Orion Pictures, and Wheeling-Pittsburgh Steel, as well as to many other firms. As in the cases of Johns Manville and International Harvester, both of which went bankrupt in the 1980s, a corporation might nevertheless rise like a phoenix from its own ashes and live again (as Manville Corporation and Navistar International Corporation, respectively). The company may be reorganized or liquidated, depending on individual circumstances.

Few corporations move through these five stages in sequence. Some corporations, for example, might never move past Stage II. Others, like General Motors, might go directly from Stage I to Stage III. Many entrepreneurial ventures jump from Stage I into Stages IV and V. The key is for management to be able to identify when the firm is changing stages and to make the appropriate strategic and structural adjustments to maintain or even improve corporate performance.

What Are Advanced Types of Organizational Structures?

The basic structures (simple, functional, divisional, and conglomerate) *were discussed earlier in Chapter 4*. The previous sections described how a business corporation tends to grow and develop from a Stage I simple structure to a functional structure and finally to a Stage III divisional structure. The divisional structure is not, however, the last word in organization design. Advanced structures may help a company better implement new strategies so that it can avoid decline. A new strategy may require more flexible characteristics than a divisional structure can offer. Under conditions of (1) increasing environmental uncertainty, (2) greater use of sophisticated technological production methods, (3) the increasing size and scope of worldwide business corporations, (4) a greater emphasis on multi-industry competitive strategy, and (5) a more educated cadre of managers and employees, new advanced forms of organizational structure emerged and are continuing to emerge during the latter half of the twentieth century. Although many variations and hybrid structures exist, three forms stand out as real advances in organizational structure: *strategic business units*, *matrix structure*, and the *network* (or cluster) structure. One or a combination of these forms may eventually become an additional stage in corporate development.

What Is a Strategic Business Unit (SBU)?

In 1971, General Electric (GE) successfully developed a method for structuring a large and complex business corporation as a variant of the divisional structure. Referred to as **strategic business units**, or SBUs, organizational groups composed of discrete, independent product-market segments served by the firm were identified and given primary responsibility and authority for managing their own functional areas. An SBU may be of any size or level, but it must have (1) *a unique* *mission*, (2) *identifiable competitors*, (3) an *external market focus*, and (4) *control of its business functions*.[6]

The idea is to decentralize on the basis of strategic elements rather than on the basis of size, product characteristics, or span of control and to create horizontal linkages among units previously kept separate. Following GE's lead, other firms, such as Honeywell, Mead Corporation, Eastman Kodak, Campbell Soup, Union Carbide, and Armco Steel, have implemented the concept of the strategic business unit. General Foods introduced the concept by organizing certain products on the basis of menu segments: breakfast food, beverage, main meal, dessert, and pet foods.

What Is a Matrix Structure?

Most organizations find that organizing around either functions (in the functional structure) or around products and geography (in the divisional structure) provides an appropriate organizational structure. The strategic business unit form is simply a more advanced version of the divisional structure pioneered by General Motors and DuPont. SBUs provide horizontal links for related product divisions so that the organization as a whole can better address changing product-market issues. The matrix structure, in contrast, may be very appropriate when organizations conclude that neither functional nor divisional forms, even when combined with horizontal linking mechanisms, are right for their situations. In **matrix structures**, functional and product forms are combined simultaneously at the same level of the organization. (See Figure 7.1.) Employees have two superiors, a product or project manager and a functional manager. The "home" department—engineering, manufacturing, or sales—is usually functional and is reasonably permanent. People from these functional units are often assigned on a temporary basis to one or more product units or projects. The product units or projects are usually temporary and act like divisions in that they are differentiated on a product-market basis.

Pioneered in the aerospace industry, the matrix structure was developed to combine the stability of the functional structure with the flexibility of the product form. The matrix structure is very useful when the external environment (especially its technological and market aspects) is very complex and changeable. It does, however, produce conflicts revolving around duties, authority, and resource allocation. To the extent that the goals to be achieved are vague and the technology used is poorly understood, a continuous battle for power is likely to exist between product and functional managers. The matrix structure is likely to be used in an organization or within an SBU when the following three conditions exist:

- Cross-fertilization of ideas across projects or products is needed.
- Resources are scarce.
- The abilities to process information and to make decisions need improvement.[7]

Although a corporation may not organize itself as a full-blown matrix organization, it is becoming common to use some of the horizontal connections common to a matrix structure. It may use *cross-functional work teams* (like Chrysler Corporation in product development) or *brand management* (like Procter & Gamble and other consumer products companies).

FIGURE
7.1

Matrix and Network Structures

135

Matrix Structure

Network Structure

What Is a Network Structure?

Perhaps the newest and most radical organizational design, the **network structure** (see Figure 7.1), is an example of what could be termed a nonstructure because it virtually eliminates in-house business functions. The network structure becomes most useful when the firm's environment is unstable and is expected to remain so. Under such conditions, the need for innovation and quick response usually is strong. The company draws up long-term contracts with suppliers and distributors to replace services that it could provide for itself through vertical integration. Electronic markets and sophisticated information systems reduce the transaction costs of the marketplace, thus justifying a *buy* over a *make* decision. Rather than being located in a single building or area, an organization's business functions are scattered worldwide. The organization is, in effect, only a shell, with a small headquarters acting as a "broker," electronically connected to some completely owned divisions, partially owned subsidiaries, and other independent companies. In its ultimate form, the network organization is a series of independent firms or business units linked by computers in an information system that designs, produces, and markets a product or service.

An example of a complete network organization is Just Toys. The New York City company licenses characters like Disney's Little Mermaid, Hanna-Barbera's Flintstones, and Marvel Entertainment's Spiderman to make bendable polyvinyl chloride figures called *Bend-Ems*. The company contracts out the manufacturing and administrative work for Bend-Ems and employs only 30 people. If a toy isn't selling well, production can be reduced and shipments stopped almost immediately. It would take Mattel and Hasbro months to react in a similar situation. Other companies like Nike, Reebok, and Benetton use the network structure in their operations function by subcontracting manufacturing to other companies in low-cost locations around the world. For control purposes, Benetton maintains what it calls an "umbilical cord" by providing all its subcontractors with production planning, planning materials requirements, bills of labor, standard prices and costs, and technical assistance to make sure their quality is up to Benetton's standards.

The network organization structure gives a company the increased flexibility and adaptability it needs to cope with rapidly changing technology and shifting patterns of international trade and competition. It allows a company to concentrate on its distinctive competencies, while gathering efficiencies from other firms who are concentrating their efforts in their areas of expertise. The network does, however, have disadvantages. The availability of numerous potential partners can be a potential source of trouble. If a particular firm overspecializes, it runs the risk of becoming a "hollow" corporation—a firm without a clearly defined essential contribution to its product or service.

Why Is Reengineering Important to Strategy Implementation?

Reengineering is the radical redesign of business processes to achieve major gains in cost, service, or time. It is not in itself a type of structure, but it is an effective way to implement a turnaround strategy. Reengineering strives to break away from the old rules and procedures that develop and become ingrained in every organization over the years. These may be a combination of policies, rules, and procedures that have never been seriously questioned since they were established years earlier. These may range from "Credit decisions are made by the credit department" to "Local inventory is needed for good customer service." These rules of organization and work design were based on assumptions about technology, people, and organizational goals that may no longer be relevant. Rather than attempting to fix existing problems through minor adjustments and fine-tuning existing processes, the key to reengineering is to ask "If this were a new company, how would we run this place?"

Michael Hammer, who popularized the concept, suggests the following principles for reengineering:

- **Organize around outcomes, not tasks:** Design a person's or a department's job around an objective or outcome instead of a single task or series of tasks.
- **Have those who use the output of the process perform the process:** With computer-based information systems, processes can now be reengineered so that the people who need the result of the process can do it themselves.
- **Subsume information-processing work into the real work that produces the information:** People or departments that produce information can also process it for use instead of just sending raw data to others in the organization to interpret.
- **Treat geographically dispersed resources as though they were centralized:** With modern information systems, companies can provide flexible service locally while keeping the actual resources in a centralized location for coordination purposes.
- **Link parallel activities instead of integrating their results:** Instead of having separate units perform different activities that must eventually come together, have them communicate while they work so that they can do the integrating.
- **Put the decision point where the work is performed and build control into the process:** The people who do the work should make the decisions and be self-controlling.
- **Capture information once and at the source:** Instead of each unit developing its own database and information processing activities, the information can be put on a network so all can have access to the data.[8]

Several companies have had success with reengineering. Union Carbide, for example, used the concept to reduce fixed costs by $400 million over three years. GTE expected reengineering to double its revenues and to cut its costs in half. Nevertheless, because reengineering is almost always accompanied by a significant amount of pain, between 50% and 70% of reengineering efforts fail to achieve their goals.[9]

How to Design Jobs to Implement Strategy?

Organizing a company's activities and people to implement strategy involves more than simply redesigning a corporation's overall structure; it also involves redesigning the way jobs are done. With the increasing emphasis on reengineering, many companies are beginning to rethink their work processes with an eye toward phasing unnecessary people and activities out of the process. Process steps that had traditionally been performed sequentially can be improved by performing them concurrently using cross-functional work teams. Harley-Davidson, for example, has managed to reduce total plant employment by 25% while reducing by 50% the time needed to build a motorcycle. Restructuring through fewer people requires broadening the scope of jobs and encouraging teamwork. The design of jobs and subsequent job performance are therefore increasingly being considered as sources of competitive advantage.

Job design refers to the study of individual tasks in an attempt to make them more relevant to the company and to the employee(s). In an effort to minimize some of the adverse consequences of task specialization, corporations have turned to new job design techniques: **job enlargement** (combining tasks to give a worker more of the same type of duties to perform), **job rotation** (moving workers through several jobs to increase variety), and **job enrichment** (altering jobs by giving the worker more autonomy and control over activities). Although each of these methods has its adherents, none of them seems to work in all situations.

The **job characteristics model** is an advanced approach to job enrichment based on the belief that tasks can be described in terms of certain objective characteristics and that these characteristics affect employee motivation. For the job to be motivating, (1) the worker needs to feel a sense of responsibility, feel the task to be meaningful, and receive useful feedback on performance, and (2) the job has to satisfy needs that are important to the worker. The model proposes that managers follow five principles for redesigning work:

- Combine tasks to increase task variety and enable workers to identify with what they are doing.
- Form natural work units to make a worker more responsible and accountable for the performance of the job.
- Establish client relationships so the worker will know what performance is required and why.
- Vertically load the job by giving workers increased authority and responsibility over their activities.
- Open feedback channels by providing workers information on how they are performing.[10]

Although several other approaches to job design exist besides the job characteristics model, practicing managers seem increasingly to follow the prescriptions of the model as a way of improving productivity and product quality. For example, Corning, Inc., the glass manufacturer, introduced team-based production in its Blacksburg, Virginia, plant in 1989. With union approval, Corning reduced job classifications from 47 to four to enable production workers to rotate jobs after learning new skills. The workers were divided into 14-member teams that, in effect, managed themselves. The plant had only two levels of management: Plant Manager Robert Hoover and two line leaders who only advised the teams. Employees worked demanding 12½ hour shifts, alternating three-day and four-day weeks. The teams made managerial decisions, imposed discipline on fellow workers, and were given the task of learning three "skill modules" within two years or else lose their jobs. As a result of this new job design, a Blacksburg team, made up of workers with interchangeable skills, can retool a line to produce a different type of filter in only ten minutes—six times faster than workers in a traditionally designed filter plant. The Blacksburg plant earned a $2 million profit in its first eight months of production, instead of losing the $2.3 million projected for the start-up period. The plant performed so well that Corning's top management acted to convert the company's 27 other factories to team-based production.[11]

7.5 International Issues in Strategy Implementation

Strategic alliances, such as joint ventures and licensing agreements, between a multinational company (MNC) and a local partner in a host country are becoming an increasingly popular means for an MNC to gain entry into other countries, especially less developed countries. The key to the successful implementation of these strategies is the selection of the local partner. Each party needs to assess not only the strategic fit of each company's project strategy, but also the fit of each company's respective resources. A successful joint venture may require as many as two years of prior contacts between both parties.

How Do International Considerations Affect Organizational Design?

A company's stage of development in international activities and the types of industries in which the company is involved strongly influence the design of an organization's structure. The issue of centralization versus decentralization becomes especially important for a multinational corporation operating in both multidomestic and global industries.

Are There Stages of International Development?

Multinational corporations tend to evolve through five common **stages of international development,** both in their relationships with widely dispersed geographic markets and in the manner in which they structure their operations and programs.

- **Stage 1:** The primarily domestic company exports some of its products through local dealers and distributors in the foreign countries. The impact on the organization's structure is minimal because everything is handled through an export department at corporate headquarters.
- **Stage 2:** Success in Stage 1 leads the company to establish its own sales company with offices in other countries to eliminate the middlemen and to take more control over its marketing. Because exports have now become more important, the company establishes an export division to oversee foreign sales offices.
- **Stage 3:** Success in earlier stages leads the company to establish manufacturing facilities in addition to sales and service offices in key countries. By now, the

company adds an international division with responsibilities for most of the business functions conducted in other countries.

- **Stage 4:** Now a full-fledged multinational corporation, the company increases its investments in other countries. It establishes a local operating division or company in the host country, such as Ford of Britain, to better serve the market and the product line is expanded. Local manufacturing capacity is established. Managerial functions (product development, finance, marketing, and so on) are organized locally. As time goes by, the parent company acquires other related businesses, broadening the base of the local operating division. As the subsidiary in the host country successfully develops a strong regional presence, it achieves greater autonomy and self-sufficiency.

- **Stage 5:** A few of the most successful multinational corporations move into a fifth stage in which they have worldwide personnel, R&D, and financing strategies. Typically operating in a global industry, the MNC denationalizes its operations and plans product design, manufacturing, and marketing around worldwide considerations. Global considerations now dominate organizational design. The global MNC structures itself in a matrix form around some combination of geographic areas, product lines, and functions. All managers are now responsible for dealing with international as well as domestic issues.

Research provides some support for the stages of international development concept but does not necessarily support the particular sequence of stages just listed. Firms may leapfrog across stages. As an example, a company may initiate local production in a foreign country without having gone through the steps of exporting or having local sales subsidiaries. In addition, any one corporation can be at different stages simultaneously, with different products in different markets at different levels. Nevertheless, the concept is useful for illustrating some of the structural changes corporations undergo when they increase their involvement in international activities.

Is Centralization or Decentralization Better Internationally?

A basic dilemma facing the multinational corporation is how to organize authority centrally so that it operates as a vast interlocking system that achieves synergy and at the same time decentralize authority so that local managers can make the decisions necessary to meet the demands of the local market or host government. To deal with this problem, MNCs tend to structure themselves either along product groups or geographic areas. They may even combine both in a matrix structure—the design chosen by 3M Corporation. One side of 3M's matrix represents the company's product divisions; the other side includes the company's international country and regional subsidiaries.

Two examples of the usual international structures are Nestlé and American Cyanamid. Nestlé's structure is one in which significant power and authority have been decentralized to geographic entities. This structure is similar to that depicted in Figure 7.2, in which each geographic set of operating companies has a different group of products. In contrast, American Cyanamid has a series of product groups with worldwide responsibilities. To depict Cyanamid's structure, the geographical entities in Figure 7.2 would have to be replaced by product groups or strategic business units.

The **product-group structure** enables the company to introduce and manage a similar line of products around the world. This enables the corporation to *centralize* decision making along product lines. The **geographic-area structure**, in contrast, allows a company to tailor products to regional differences and to achieve regional coordination. This *decentralizes* decision making to the local subsidiaries.

Simultaneous pressures for decentralization to be locally responsive and centralization to be maximally efficient are causing interesting structural adjustments in most large corporations. This is what is meant by the phrase "Think globally, act locally." Companies are attempting to decentralize those operations closest to

FIGURE 7.2   **Geographic Area Structure for a Multinational Corporation**

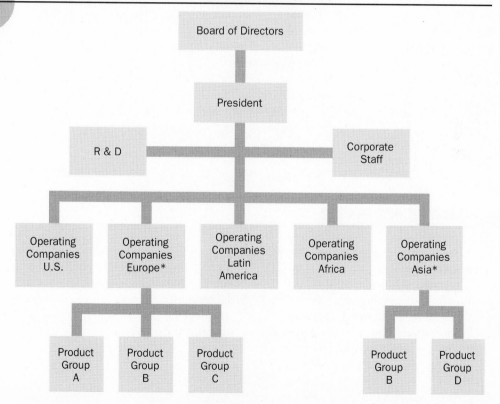

*Note: Because of space limitations, product groups for only Europe and Asia are shown here.

the customers—manufacturing and marketing. At the same time, the companies are consolidating less visible internal functions, such as research and development, finance, and information systems, to achieve significant economies of scale.

In Conclusion . . .

When the Nabisco Biscuit Company decided to introduce a new line of fat-free cookies, no one in management had any idea that it would cause the company so many problems. SnackWell's Devil's Food Cookie Cakes were introduced in 1992 as a very special type of cookie. The cookie center was covered completely with marshmallow, then drenched with chocolate icing, followed by a chocolate glaze. Because each cookie was completely covered, it would stick to a conveyor belt—and thus could not be baked using conventional methods. These devil's food cookies could only be made on equipment available only in one of Nabisco's bakeries. The process took four hours compared to 30 minutes for chocolate chip cookies.

The devil's food cookies were an immediate hit with consumers. SnackWell's had the authentic-tasting chocolate that most fat-free cookies lacked, and the marshmallow center kept the cookies moist. Unfortunately the company couldn't produce the cookies fast enough. More than a year after the introduction of the cookie, Nabisco was still unable to meet demand. Management had three production lines running overtime at the bakery and was adding a fourth in 1993. Meanwhile, the company was introducing a new SnackWell's Double Fudge Cookie Cake containing two layers of cake with fat-free fudge in the middle. This was a much easier cookie to make, but management wasn't taking any chances this time. Until Nabisco could accurately judge market demand for the new product, it was being sold only in the northeastern United States. Admitted a company spokesperson: "We've learned our lesson."[12]

Discussion Questions

1. How should a corporation attempt to achieve synergy among functions and business units?

2. What are the advantages and disadvantages of the network structure?

3. How should an owner-manager prepare a company for its movement from Stage I to Stage II?

4. How can a corporation keep from sliding into the decline part of the organizational life cycle?

5. Is reengineering just another management fad or does it offer something of lasting value?

Key Terms

strategy implementation
programs
budgets
procedures
synergy
stages of corporate development
organizational life cycle
strategic business units
matrix structure
network structure

reengineering
job design
job enlargement
job rotation
job enrichment
job characteristics model
stages of international development
product-group structure
geographic-area structure

8

Strategy Implementation: Staffing and Directing

Not long ago, Clark Equipment Company was on the brink of bankruptcy. The diversified manufacturing company realized that, in addition to other problems, its corporate office was significantly overstaffed. When top management identified the different specialty departments within the corporate office, they found that there were enough people to operate a law firm, an accounting firm, a data processing/telecommunications company, a trucking line, and a printing and graphics business. Instead of simply firing half or more of the people, Clark took a more positive approach. It informed the specialty departments that they had two years to (1) develop 50% of their business outside of Clark and to (2) earn their own cost of capital. If they achieved both these objectives, they could choose to become a Clark operating company, undertake an employee buyout of the unit, or find themselves a new owner. If they failed to attain these objectives, the choice of becoming a Clark company was no longer an option. Management also told them that after one year the operating divisions would no longer be required to use corporate staff department services but could get the same services elsewhere. Top management also announced that the corporate personnel and purchasing departments would be phased out in one year and the responsibilities given to the operating divisions. Clark helped people transfer to an operating division or leave the company under a voluntary corporate separation plan. These programs reduced the corporate office staff from 500 to under 100 people. Jim Rinehart, former CEO of Clark, explained why the downsizing was a success at Clark. First, the company's survival was at stake. The employees were well aware of the company's problems and the need for significant change. Second, management used a participative process by asking people to suggest ways to save the company. Third, management presented the members of the different specialty units with choices and then gave them time to consider their options.[1]

This example from Clark Equipment Company illustrates how to implement a successful retrenchment strategy with carefully considered programs. This chapter discusses strategy implementation in terms of staffing and directing. Staffing focuses on the selection and use of employees. Directing emphasizes the use of programs to better align employee interests and attitudes with a new strategy.

8.1 ▶ Staffing

The implementation of new strategies and policies often calls for new human resource management priorities and a different utilization of personnel. This may mean hiring new people with new skills, firing people with inappropriate or substandard skills, and/or training existing employees to learn new skills.

If a corporation plans to implement growth strategies, new people may need to be hired and trained. Experienced people with the necessary skills need to be promoted to newly created managerial positions. If the corporation adopts a retrenchment strategy, however, a large number of people may need to be laid off or fired, and top management and divisional managers need to specify the criteria to be used in making these personnel decisions. Should employees be fired on the basis of low seniority or on the basis of poor performance? Sometimes corporations find it easier to close an entire division than to choose which individuals to fire.

Does Staffing Follow Strategy?

As in the case of structure, staffing requirements are also likely to follow a change in strategy.

How Do Hiring and Training Requirements Change?

Once a new strategy is formulated, either different kinds of people may be needed or the current employees may need to be retrained to implement the new strategy. Consider the introduction of team-based production at Corning's filter plant mentioned earlier in Chapter 7. Employee selection and training were crucial to the success of the new manufacturing strategy. Plant Manager Robert Hoover sorted through 8000 job applications before hiring 150 people with the best problem-solving ability and a willingness to work in a team setting. Those selected received extensive training in technical and interpersonal skills. During the first year of production, 25% of all hours worked were devoted to training at a cost of $750,000.[2]

Training and development is one way to implement a company's corporate or business strategy. It is very important for a differentiation strategy that emphasizes quality or customer service. For example, Motorola, with annual sales of $13.3 billion, spends $120 million on employee education. The company is especially concerned with attaining the highest quality possible in all its operations. The company estimates that every $1 it spends on training delivers $30 in productivity gains within three years.

Training is also important when implementing a retrenchment strategy. As suggested earlier, successful downsizing means that the company has to invest in its remaining employees. General Electric's Aircraft Engine Group used training to maintain its share of the market even though it had cut its workforce from 42,000 to 33,000 between 1991 and 1993.[3]

How Does a Company Match the Manager to the Strategy?

The most appropriate type of general manager needed to effectively implement a new corporate or business strategy depends on the strategic direction that firm or business unit desires. Executives with a particular mix of skills and experiences may be classified as an **executive type** and paired with a specific corporate strategy. For example, a corporation following a concentration strategy that emphasizes vertical or horizontal integration would probably want an aggressive new chief executive with a great deal of experience in that particular industry—a *dynamic industry expert*. A diversification strategy, in contrast, might call for someone with an analytical mind who is highly knowledgeable in other industries and can manage diverse product lines—an *analytical portfolio manager*. A corporation choosing to follow a stability strategy would probably want as its CEO a person with a conservative style, a production or engineering background, and experience with controlling budgets, capital expenditures, inventories, and standardization procedures—a *cautious profit planner*. Weak companies in a relatively attractive industry tend to turn to a challenge-oriented executive to save the company—a *turnaround specialist*. If a company cannot be saved, a *professional liquidator* might be called on by a bankruptcy court to close the firm and liquidate its assets.

This approach is in agreement with Chandler who proposed (**in Chapter 7**) that the most appropriate CEO of a company changes as a firm moves from one stage of development to another. Because priorities certainly change over an organization's life, successful corporations need to select managers who have skills and characteristics appropriate to the organization's particular stage of development and position in its life cycle.

Nevertheless, one study of 173 firms over a 25-year period revealed that CEOs in these companies tended to have the same functional specialization as the former CEO, especially when the past CEO's strategy continued to be successful. This may be a pattern for successful corporations.[4] In particular, it explains why so many prosperous companies tend to recruit their top executives from one particular background. At Procter & Gamble, for example, the route to the CEO's position has always been through brand management. In other firms, the route may be through manufacturing, marketing, accounting, or finance, depending on what the corporation has always considered its principal functional areas.

How Important Are Selection and Management Development?

Selection and development are important not only to ensure that people with the right mix of skills and experiences are hired initially, but also to help them grow on the job and be prepared for future promotions.

Executive Succession: Should a CEO Come from Inside the Company?

Executive succession is the process of replacing a key top manager. Given that the typical large U.S. corporation changes its chief executive every eight years, firms need to plan for this eventuality.[5] Particularly companies that usually promote from within must prepare their current managers for promotion. Prosperous firms tend to look outside for CEO candidates only if they have no obvious internal candidates. Firms in trouble, however, tend to choose outsiders to lead them. Boards realize that the best way to move to a new strategy and to ensure its implementation is to hire a new CEO with no connections to the current strategy.

How Can Abilities Be Identified and Potential Developed?

A company can identify and prepare its people for important positions in several ways. One approach is to establish a sound **performance appraisal system** to identify good performers with promotion potential. A survey of 34 corporate planners and human resource executives from 24 large U.S. corporations revealed that approximately 80% made some attempt to identify managers' talents and behavioral tendencies, so that they could match a manager as closely as possible with a given competitive strategy.[6]

Many large organizations are using **assessment centers** to evaluate a person's suitability for an advanced position. Corporations such as AT&T, Standard Oil, IBM, Sears, and GE have successfully used assessment centers. Because each is specifically tailored to its corporation, these assessment centers are unique. They use special interviews, management games, in-basket exercises, leaderless group discussions, case analyses, decision-making exercises, and oral presentations to assess the potential of employees for specific positions. Promotions into these positions are based on performance levels in the assessment center. Many assessment centers have proved to be highly predictive of subsequent job performance.

Many large corporations use **job rotation**, the moving of people from one job to another, to ensure that employees are gaining the appropriate mix of experiences to prepare them for future responsibilities. For example, companies that pursue related diversification strategies through internal development make greater use of interdivisional transfers of people than do companies that grow through unrelated acquisitions. Apparently the companies that grow internally attempt to transfer important knowledge and skills throughout the corporation in order to achieve some sort of synergy.[7]

Does Retrenchment Create Problems?

Downsizing (sometimes called "rightsizing") refers to the planned elimination of positions or jobs. Companies commonly use this program to implement retrenchment strategies. Because the financial community is likely to react favorably to announcements of downsizing from a company in difficulty, such a program may provide some short-term benefits such as raising the company's stock price. If not done properly, however, downsizing may result in less rather than in more productivity. One study of downsizing revealed that at 20 out of 30 automobile-related U.S. industrial companies, either the wrong jobs were eliminated or blanket offers of early retirement prompted managers, even those considered invaluable, to leave. After the layoffs, the employees who were left had to do not only their work, but also the work of the people who had gone. Because the survivors often didn't know how to do the work of those who had left, morale and productivity plummeted.[8] In addition, cost-conscious executives tend to defer maintenance, skimp on training, delay new product introductions, and avoid risky new businesses—all of which decrease sales and eventually profits. A situation can thus develop in which retrenchment feeds on itself and acts to further weaken the company instead of strengthening it.

Proposed guidelines for successful downsizing are as follows:

- **Eliminate Unnecessary Work Instead of Making Across-the-Board Cuts:** Spend the time to research where money is going and eliminate the task, not the workers, if it doesn't add value to what the firm is producing.
- **Contract Out Work That Others Can Do Cheaper:** For example, Bankers Trust of New York contracts out to a division of Xerox its mail room and printing services and some of its payroll and accounts payable activities.
- **Plan for Long-Run Efficiencies:** Don't simply eliminate all postponable expenses, such as maintenance, R&D, and advertising, in the unjustifiable hope that the environment will become more supportive.
- **Communicate the Reasons for Actions:** Tell employees not only why the company is downsizing, but also what the company is trying to achieve.
- **Invest in the Remaining Employees:** Because most "survivors" in a corporate downsizing probably will be doing different tasks after the change, firms need to draft new job specifications, performance standards, appraisal techniques, and compensation packages. Additional training will be needed to ensure that everyone has the proper skills to deal with expanded jobs and responsibilities.
- **Develop Value-Added Jobs to Balance Out Job Elimination:** When no other jobs are currently available within the organization to transfer employees, management must consider some other staffing alternatives. Harley-Davidson, for example, worked with the company's unions to find other work for surplus employees by moving work previously done by suppliers into Harley plants.

What Are International Issues in Staffing?

Because of cultural differences, managerial style and human resource practices must be tailored to fit the particular situations in other countries. Most multinational corporations (MNCs) attempt to fill managerial positions in their subsidiaries with well-qualified citizens of the host countries. Unilever and IBM take this approach. This policy serves to placate nationalistic governments and to better attune management practices to the host country's culture. The danger in using primarily foreign nationals to staff managerial positions in subsidiaries is the increased likelihood of suboptimization (the local subsidiary ignores the needs of the larger parent corporation). This makes it difficult for a multinational corporation to meet its long-term, worldwide objectives. To a local national in an MNC subsidiary, the corporation as a whole is an abstraction. Communication and coordination across subsidiaries become more difficult. As it becomes harder to coordinate the activities of several international subsidiaries, an MNC will have serious problems operating in a global industry.

Another approach to staffing the managerial positions of multinational corporations is to use people with an international orientation, regardless of their country of origin or host country assignment. This is a widespread practice among European firms. For example, A.B. Electrolux, a Swedish firm, had a French director in its Singapore factory. This approach to using third-country nationals allows for more opportunities for promotion than does Unilever's policy of hiring local people, but it can result in a greater number of misunderstandings and conflicts with the local employees and with the host country's government.

To improve their chances of success using expatriates, multinational corporations are now emphasizing intercultural training for managers being assigned to a foreign country. This training is one of the commonly cited reasons for the lower expatriate failure rates—6% or less—for European and Japanese MNCs, which have emphasized cross-cultural experiences, compared with 35% for U.S.-based MNCs.[9]

8.2 Directing

Implementation also involves directing people to use their abilities and skills most effectively and efficiently to achieve organizational objectives. Without direction, people tend to do their work according to their personal view of what tasks should be done, how, and in what order. They may approach their work as they have in the past or emphasize those tasks that they most enjoy—regardless of the corporation's priorities. Direction may take the form of management leadership, communicated norms of behavior from the corporate culture, or agreements among workers in autonomous work groups. It may also be accomplished more formally through action planning or through programs such as Management By Objectives (MBO) and Total Quality Management (TQM).

How Can a Company Manage Corporate Culture?

Because an organization's culture can exert a powerful influence on the behavior of all employees, it can strongly affect a company's ability to shift its strategic direction. A problem for a strong culture is that a change in mission, objectives, strategies, or policies is not likely to be successful if it is in opposition to the accepted culture of the company. Corporate culture has a strong tendency to resist change because its very reason for existence often rests on preserving stable relationships and patterns of behavior.

There is no one best corporate culture. An optimal culture is one that best supports the mission and strategy of the company of which it is a part. This means that, like structure and staffing, *corporate culture should follow strategy*. Unless the strategy is in complete agreement with the culture, a significant change in strategy should thus be followed by a modification of the organization's culture. Although corporate culture can be changed, it may often take a long time and require much effort. A key job of management is therefore to evaluate (1) what a particular strategy change will mean to the corporate culture, (2) whether or not a change in culture will be needed, and (3) whether or not an attempt to change the culture will be worth the likely costs.

How Can One Assess Strategy–Culture Compatibility?

When implementing a new strategy, management should consider the following questions regarding the corporation's culture:

1. **Is the planned strategy compatible with the company's current culture?**
   If *yes*, full steam ahead. Tie organizational changes into the company's culture by identifying how the new strategy will achieve the mission better than the current strategy does.
2. **If the strategy is not compatible with the current culture, can the culture be easily modified to make it more compatible with the new strategy?**
   If *yes*, move forward carefully by introducing a set of culture-changing activities, such as minor structural modifications, training and development activities, and/or hiring new managers who are more compatible with the new strategy. When Procter & Gamble's top management decided to implement a strategy aimed at reducing costs, for example, it changed how some things were done but did not eliminate its brand management system. The culture was able to adapt to these modifications over a couple of years and productivity increased.
3. **If the culture cannot be easily changed to make it more compatible with the new strategy, is management willing and able to make major organizational changes and accept probable delays and a likely increase in costs?**
   If *yes*, manage around the culture by establishing a new structural unit to implement the new strategy. At General Motors, for example, top management realized that in order to be more competitive, the company had to make some radical changes. Because the current structure, culture, and procedures were very inflexible, management decided to establish a completely new division (GM's first new division since 1918) called Saturn to build its new auto. In cooperation with the United Auto Workers, an entirely new labor agreement was developed based on decisions reached by consensus. Carefully selected employees received from 100 to 750 hours of training, and a whole new culture was built piece by piece.
4. **If management is not willing to make the major organizational changes required to manage around the culture, are they still committed to implementing the strategy?**

If *yes*, find a joint-venture partner or contract with another company to carry out the strategy. If *no*, formulate a different strategy.

How Can Communication Be Used to Manage Culture?

Communication is crucial to effectively managing change. The rationale for strategic changes should be communicated to workers not only in newsletters and speeches but also in training and development programs. Companies in which major cultural changes have successfully taken place had the following characteristics in common:

● The CEO and other top managers had a strategic vision of what the company could become and communicated this vision to employees at all levels. The current performance of the company was compared to that of its competition and constantly updated.

● The vision was translated into the key elements necessary to accomplish that vision. For example, if the vision called for the company to become a leader in quality or service, aspects of quality and service were pinpointed for improvement and appropriate measurement systems were developed to monitor them. These measures were communicated widely through contests, formal and informal recognition, and monetary rewards, among other devices.[10]

How Can Diverse Cultures Be Managed When Following an Acquisition Growth Strategy?

When merging with or acquiring another company, top management must consider a potential clash of cultures. To assume that the firms can simply be integrated into the same reporting structure is dangerous. The greater the gap between the cultures of acquired and acquiring firms, the faster executives in the acquired firms quit their jobs and valuable talent is lost.

The four general methods of managing two different cultures are integration, assimilation, separation, and deculturation. (See Figure 8.1.) The choice of which method to use should be based on (1) *how much members of the acquired firm value the preservation of their own culture* and (2) *their perception of the attractiveness of the acquirer*.[11]

Integration   Integration involves a relatively balanced give-and-take of cultural and managerial practices between the merger partners and no strong imposition of cultural change on either company. It allows the two cultures to merge while preserving the separate cultures of both firms in the resulting culture. This is what occurred when the Seaboard and Chesapeake & Ohio railroads merged to form CSX Corporation. The top executives were so concerned that both cultures be equally respected that they kept referring to the company as a "partnership of equals."

Assimilation   In assimilation, one organization dominates the other. The domination is not forced but is welcomed by members of the acquired firm, who may feel

FIGURE
8.1

Methods of Managing the Culture of an Acquired Firm

**How Much Members of the Acquired Firm Value
Preservation of Their Own Culture**

	Very Much	Not at All
Very Attractive	Integration	Assimilation
Not at All Attractive	Separation	Deculturation

(vertical axis label: **Perception of the Attractiveness of the Acquirer**)

Source: A. Nahavandi and A. R. Malekzadeh, "Acculturation in Mergers and Acquisitions," *Academy of Management Review* (January 1988), p. 83. Copyright © 1988 by the Academy of Management. Reprinted by permission.

for many reasons that their culture and managerial practices have not produced success. The acquired firm surrenders its culture and adopts the culture of the acquiring company. The *Company Spotlight on Maytag Corporation* describes this method of acculturation when Admiral, a subsidiary of Magic Chef, joined Maytag Corporation.

Separation   In separation, two companies' cultures are structurally separated without cultural exchange. In the case of the Shearson–American Express merger, both parties agreed to keep the fast-paced Shearson completely separate from the planning-oriented American Express.

Deculturation   Deculturation, the most common and most destructive method of dealing with two different cultures, involves the disintegration of one company's culture as a result of unwanted and extreme pressure from the other to impose its culture and practices. A great deal of confusion, conflict, resentment, and stress of-

Maytag's corporate culture had been dominated almost from the beginning of the company by the concept of quality. Maytag employees took great pride in being known as the "dependability people." Over the years, Maytag Company consistently advertised that their repairmen were "lonely" because Maytag brand products rarely, if ever, needed repair.

Admiral's history had, however, been quite different. Prior to Maytag's purchase of Magic Chef (and thus Admiral) in 1986, Admiral had been owned by three different corporations. Its manufacturing plant in Galesburg, Illinois, had deteriorated to a dismal level by the time Maytag acquired it. Refrigerators sometimes rolled off the assembly line with screws driven in crooked and temperature balances askew!

Maytag's management had always wanted to have its own Maytag brand refrigerator—that was one reason why it purchased Magic Chef—but it was worried that Admiral might not be able to produce a quality product to Maytag's specifications. To improve Admiral's quality, Maytag's top management decided to integrate Admiral directly into Maytag Company operations. As a result, all Admiral functional departments, except marketing, reported directly to the Maytag Company president.

Under the direction of Leonard Hadley, while he was serving as Maytag Company President, a project was initiated to design and manufacture a Maytag brand refrigerator at the Admiral plant. When Hadley first visited Admiral's facilities to discuss the design of a Maytag line of refrigerators, Admiral personnel asked Hadley when the name on their plant's water tower would be changed from Admiral to Maytag. Hadley (acknowledging Maytag's cultural concerns regarding quality) responded: "When you earn it."

The refrigerator resulting from the Maytag–Admiral collaboration was a huge success. The project crystallized corporate management's philosophy for forging synergies among the Maytag companies while simultaneously allowing the individual expertise of those units to flourish. Admiral's employees were willing to accept the dominance of Maytag's strong quality-oriented culture because they respected it. In turn, they expected to be treated with some respect for their tradition of skill in refrigeration technology.

COMPANY SPOTLIGHT

MAYTAG Corporation

Assimilating Admiral's Culture

ten accompanies this method. Such a merger typically results in poor performance by the acquired company and its eventual divestment.

What Is Action Planning?

Activities can be directed toward accomplishing strategic goals through action planning. At a minimum, an **action plan** states what actions are going to be taken, by whom, during what timeframe, and with what expected results. Having selected a program to implement a particular strategy, the company should develop an action plan to put the program in place.

Take the example of a company that chose forward vertical integration through the acquisition of a retailing chain as its growth strategy. Now that it owns its own retail outlets, it must integrate them into the company. One of the many programs it would have to develop is a new advertising program for the stores. The resulting action plan to develop a new advertising program should include the following elements:

1. **Specific actions to be taken to make the program operational:** One action might be to contact three reputable advertising agencies and ask them to prepare a proposal for a new radio and newspaper ad campaign based on the theme "Jones Surplus is now a part of Ajax Continental. Prices are lower. Selection is better."

2. **Dates to begin and end each action:** Time would have to be allotted not only to select and contact three agencies, but to allow them sufficient time to prepare a detailed proposal. For example, allow one week to select and contact the agencies and three months for them to prepare detailed proposals to present to the company's marketing director. Also allow some time to make a decision on which proposal to accept.

3. **Person (identified by name and title) responsible for carrying out each action:** List someone—such as Jan Lewis, advertising manager—who can be put in charge of the program.

4. **Person responsible for monitoring the timeliness and effectiveness of each action:** Indicate that Jan Lewis is responsible for ensuring that the proposals are of good quality and are priced within the planned program budget. She is the primary company contact for the ad agencies and is expected to report on the progress of the program once a week to the company's marketing director.

5. **Expected financial and physical consequences of each action:** Estimate when a completed ad campaign will be ready to show top management and how long it will take after approval to begin to air the ads. Estimate also the expected increase in store sales over the six-month period after the ads are first aired. Indicate if "recall" measures will be used to help assess the ad campaign's effectiveness and how, when, and by whom the recall data will be collected and analyzed.

6. **Contingency plans:** Indicate how long it will take to get another acceptable ad campaign ready to show top management if none of the initial proposals is acceptable.

Action plans are important for several reasons. First, they serve as a link between strategy formulation and evaluation and control. Second, the action plan specifies what needs to be done differently from the way operations are currently carried out. Third, during the evaluation and control process that comes later, an action plan helps appraise performance and identify any remedial actions, as needed. In addition, the explicit assignment of responsibilities for implementing and monitoring the programs may improve motivation. Figure 8.2 illustrates a written action plan.

FIGURE
8.2

Example of an Action Plan

Action Plan for Jan Lewis, Advertising Manager, Ajax Continental

Program Objective: To Run a New Advertising and Promotion Campaign for the Combined Jones Surplus/Ajax Continental Retail Stores for the Coming Christmas Season Within a Budget of $XX.

Program Activities:

1. Identify Three Best Ad Agencies for New Campaign.
2. Ask Three Ad Agencies to Submit a Proposal for a New Advertising and Promotion Campaign for Combined Stores.
3. Agencies Present Proposals to Marketing Manager.
4. Select Best Proposal and Inform Agencies of Decision.
5. Agency Presents Winning Proposal to Top Management.
6. Ads Air on TV and Promotions Appear in Stores.
7. Measure Results of Campaign in Terms of Viewer Recall and Increase in Store Sales.

Action Steps	Responsibility	Start-End
1. A. Review previous programs	Lewis & Carter	1/1–2/1
B. Discuss with boss	Lewis	2/1–2/3
C. Decide on 3 agencies	Lewis	2/4
2. A. Write specifications for ad	Lewis	1/15–1/20
B. Assistant writes ad request	Carter	1/20–1/30
C. Contact ad agencies	Lewis	2/5–2/8
D. Send request to 3 agencies	Carter	2/10
E. Meet with agency acct execs	Lewis & Carter	2/16–2/20
3. A. Agencies work on proposals	Account Executives	2/23–5/1
B. Agencies present proposals	Carter	5/1–5/15
4. A. Select best proposal	Lewis	5/15–5/20
B. Meet with winning agency	Lewis	5/22–5/30
C. Inform losers	Carter	6/1
5. A. Fine-tune proposal	Account Executives	6/1–7/1
B. Present to management	Lewis	7/1–7/3
6. A. Ads air on TV	Lewis	9/1–12/24
B. Floor displays in stores	Carter	8/20–8/30
7. A. Gather recall measures of ads	Carter	9/1–12/24
B. Evaluate sales data	Carter	1/1–1/10
C. Prepare analysis of campaign	Carter	1/10–2/15

What Is Management By Objectives (MBO)?

Management By Objectives (MBO) is an organizationwide approach to help assure purposeful action toward desired objectives. MBO links organizational objectives and the behavior of individuals. Because it is a system that links plans with performance, MBO is a powerful implementation technique.

The process of MBO involves (1) establishing and communicating organizational objectives, (2) setting individual objectives (through superior-subordinate interaction) that help implement organizational ones, (3) developing an action plan of activities needed to achieve the objectives, and (4) periodically (at least quarterly) reviewing performance as it relates to the objectives and including the results in the annual performance appraisal. MBO provides an opportunity for the corporation to connect the objectives of people at each level to those at the next higher level. Therefore, MBO ties together corporate, business, and functional objectives and the strategies developed to achieve them.

One of the real benefits of MBO is that it can reduce the amount of internal politics operating within a large corporation. Political actions can cause conflict and divide the very people and groups who should be working together to implement strategy. People are less likely to jockey for position if the company's mission and objectives are clear and they know that the reward system is based not on game playing, but on achieving clearly communicated, measurable objectives.

What Is Total Quality Management (TQM)?

Total Quality Management (TQM) is an operational philosophy that stresses commitment to *customer satisfaction* and *continuous improvement*. TQM is committed to quality and excellence and to being the best in all functions. There are four *objectives* of TQM:

1. Better, less variable quality of the product and service
2. Quicker, less variable response in processes to customer needs
3. Greater flexibility in adjusting to customers' shifting requirements
4. Lower cost through quality improvement and elimination of nonvalue-adding work[12]

Because TQM aims to reduce costs as well as improve quality, it can be used as a program to implement both an overall low cost or a differentiation business strategy.

According to TQM, faulty processes, not poorly motivated employees, cause defects in quality. To succeed in a company, the program usually involves a significant change in corporate culture, requiring strong leadership from top management, employee training, empowerment of lower level employees (giving people more control over their work), and teamwork. The emphasis in TQM is on prevention, not correction. Inspection for quality still takes place, but the emphasis is on improving the process to prevent errors and deficiencies. Thus **quality circles** or quality improvement teams are formed to identify problems and suggest how to improve the processes that may be causing the problems.

The essential *ingredients* of TQM are:

- **An intense focus on customer satisfaction:** Everyone (not just people in the sales and marketing departments) understands that their jobs exist only because of customer needs. Thus *all employees* must approach their jobs in terms of how their work will affect customer satisfaction.
- **Customers are internal as well as external:** An employee in the shipping department may be the internal customer of another employee who completes the assembly of a product, just as a person who buys the product is a customer of the entire company. An employee must be just as concerned with pleasing the internal customer as with pleasing the external customer.
- **Accurate measurement of every critical variable in a company's operations:** Employees have to be trained in what to measure, how to measure, and how to interpret the data. A rule of TQM is "you only improve what you measure."
- **Continuous improvement of products and services:** Everyone realizes that operations need to be continuously monitored to find ways to improve products and services.
- **New work relationships based on trust and teamwork:** A key is the idea of *empowerment*—giving employees wide latitude in how they go about in achieving the company's goals.

What Are the International Considerations in Directing?

In a study of 53 different national cultures, Hofstede found that he could explain the success or failure of certain management practices on the basis of the following five cultural dimensions.[13]

1. **Power Distance (PD)** is the extent to which a society accepts an unequal distribution of power in organizations. People in nations with high PD scores tend to prefer autocratic to more participative managers.
2. **Uncertainty Avoidance (UA)** is the extent to which a society feels threatened by uncertain and ambiguous situations. People in nations with high UA scores tend to want career stability, formal rules, and clear-cut measures of performance.
3. **Individualism–Collectivism (IC)** is the extent to which a society values individual freedom and independence of action compared with a tight social framework and loyalty to the group. People in nations scoring high on individualism tend to value individual success through competition, whereas people scoring low on individualism tend to value group success through collective cooperation.
4. **Masculinity–Femininity (M-F)** is the extent to which society is oriented toward money and things (which Hofstede labels masculine) or toward people (which Hofstede labels feminine). People in nations scoring high on masculinity tend to value clearly defined sex roles where men dominate, and to emphasize

performance and independence, whereas people scoring low on masculinity (and thus high on femininity) tend to value equality of the sexes where power is shared and to emphasize the quality of life and interdependence.

5. **Confucian Dynamism (CD)** is the extent to which society follows the principles commonly ascribed to Confucius. These principles are (a) the arrangement of relationships by status and a sensitivity to social contracts; (b) the importance placed on hard work, education, and persistence; (c) the importance of thrift; and (d) the treatment of others as one would like to be treated.

These **dimensions of national culture** may help to explain why some management practices work well in some countries but not in others. Management By Objectives (MBO), which originated in the United States, has succeeded in Germany, according to Hofstede, because the idea of replacing the arbitrary authority of the boss with the impersonal authority of mutually agreed-upon objectives fits the small power distance and strong uncertainty avoidance that are dimensions of the German culture. It has failed in France, however, because the French are used to large power distances—to accepting orders from a highly personalized authority. Some of the difficulties experienced by U.S. companies in using Japanese-style quality circles may stem from the extremely high value U.S. culture places on individualism.

Multinational corporations must pay attention to the many differences in cultural dimensions around the world and appropriately adjust their management practices. Cultural differences can easily go unrecognized by a headquarters staff that may interpret these differences as personality defects, whether the people in the subsidiaries are locals or expatriates. Hofstede and Bond conclude: "Whether they like it or not, the headquarters of multinationals are in the business of multicultural management."[14]

In Conclusion . . .

Mary Baechler, founder and president of Racing Strollers, Inc., became concerned that her company was not properly implementing its entrepreneurial strategy. To improve service to her customers, Baechler implemented a new delivery program:

> Anyone in our company can stop production if he thinks there's a flaw. Any employee can send a stroller that's on order via Federal Express (at $87 a pop!) if he feels we have not met our delivery commitments. Beyond our lifetime guarantee for frames and one-year guarantee on wheels, our customer service people can do whatever it takes, up to $300 per customer, to make things right for the customer (we track costs religiously so that we can keep this up). We stay in contact after each repair, and the customer gets a postcard to send that comes directly to me and lets me know if we took care of matters to the customer's satisfaction. And we keep trying, until that customer is doing great. Those postcards are an immediate report card and the best part of my day.[15]

Discussion Questions

1. What skills should a person have for managing a business unit following a differentiation strategy? Why? What should a company do if no one is available internally and the company has a policy of promotion from within?

2. When should someone from outside the company be hired to manage the company of one of its business units?

3. What are some ways to implement a retrenchment strategy without creating a lot of resentment and conflict with labor unions?

4. How can corporate culture be changed?

5. What value does Total Quality Management have in implementing strategy?

Key Terms

executive types
executive succession
performance appraisal system
assessment centers
job rotation
downsizing
strategy–culture compatibility

action plan
Management By Objectives (MBO)
Total Quality Management (TQM)
quality circles
dimensions of national culture

9

Evaluation and Control

During the spring of 1992, Jim Canna-vino, the manager in charge of IBM's personal computer business, insisted that his was the most profitable PC business in the world. Unfortunately his comment was based on the very strange way in which IBM allocated its costs to products. For example, IBM's system of accounting allocated all of a particular technology's R&D spending to the first group that used the technology; other IBM units then were able to use that technology free. As IBM found itself facing declining profits, it changed its cost allocation system to a more realistic one. In the fall of 1992, IBM disclosed that its PC business was actually unprofitable. IBM's competitors commented that the business had probably been losing money on and off for years—IBM just didn't know it![1]

The **evaluation and control process** ensures that the company is achieving what it set out to accomplish. It compares performance with desired results and provides the feedback necessary for management to evaluate the results and take corrective action, as needed. This process can be viewed as a five-step feedback model, as depicted in Figure 9.1.

1. **Determine what to measure:** Top managers and operational managers must specify implementation processes and results to be monitored and evaluated. The processes and results must be measurable in a reasonably objective and consistent manner. The focus should be on the most significant elements in a process—the ones that account for the highest proportion of expense or the greatest number of problems. Measurements must be found for all important areas regardless of difficulty.
2. **Establish standards of performance:** Standards used to measure performance are detailed expressions of strategic objectives. They are *measures* of accept-

able performance results. Each standard usually includes a *tolerance range*, which defines any acceptable deviations. Standards can be set not only for final output, but also for intermediate stages of production output.

3. **Measure actual performance:** Measurements must be made at predetermined times.

4. **Compare actual performance with the standard:** If the actual performance results are within the desired tolerance range, the measurement process stops here.

5. **Take corrective action:** If the actual results fall outside the desired tolerance range, action must be taken to correct the deviation. The action must not only correct the deviation, but also prevent its recurrence. The following issues must be resolved:

   a. Is the deviation only a chance fluctuation?

   b. Are the processes being carried out incorrectly?

   c. Are the processes appropriate for achieving the desired standard?

Top management is often better at the first two steps of the control model than they are in the last three follow-through steps. The tendency to establish a control system and then delegate the implementation to others can have unfortunate results.

9.1 Evaluation and Control in Strategic Management

Evaluation and control information consists of performance data and activity reports (gathered in Step 3 of Figure 9.1). Operational managers must know about any inappropriate use of strategic management processes that causes undesired performance so that they can correct the employee activity. Top management need not be involved. If, however, the processes themselves cause the undesired

FIGURE 9.1   **Evaluation and Control Process**

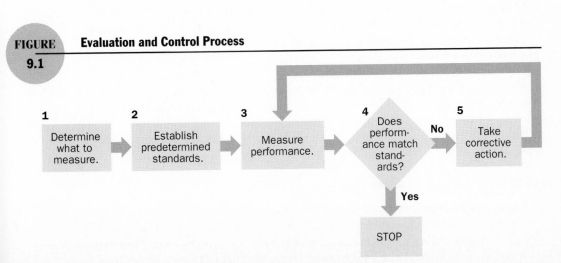

performance, both top managers and operational managers must know about it so that they can develop new implementation programs or procedures.

Evaluation and control information must be relevant to what is being monitored. The IBM example demonstrates how the use of inappropriate data clouded the perceptions of the head of IBM's PC unit and may have led to poor strategic decision making. Evaluation and control is not an easy process. One of the obstacles to effective control is the difficulty in developing appropriate measures of important activities and outputs.

The application of the control process to strategic management depicted in Figure 9.2 provides strategic managers with a series of questions to use in evaluating strategies formulated and implemented. Such a strategy review is usually initiated when a gap appears between a company's financial objectives and the expected results of current activities. After answering the proposed set of questions, a manager should have a good idea of where the problem originated and what must be done to solve it.

9.2 Measuring Performance

Performance is the end result of activity. Which measures to select to assess performance depends on the organizational unit to be appraised and the objectives to be achieved. The objectives that were established earlier in the strategy formulation part of the strategic management process (dealing with profitability, market share, and cost reduction, among others) should certainly be used to measure corporate performance once the strategies have been implemented.

When Should Measures Be Used?

Some measures, such as *return on investment (ROI)*, are appropriate for evaluating the corporation's or division's ability to achieve a profitability objective. This type of measure, however, is inadequate for evaluating additional corporate objectives such as social responsibility or employee development. Even though profitability is a corporation's major objective, ROI can be computed only *after* profits are totaled for a period. It tells what happened after the fact—not what *is* happening or what *will* happen. A firm, therefore, needs to develop measures that predict likely profitability. These are referred to as **steering controls** because they measure variables that influence future profitability. One example of this type of control is the use of control charts in Statistical Process Control (SPC). In SPC, workers and managers maintain charts and graphs detailing quality and productivity on a daily basis. They are thus able to adjust the system before it gets out of control.

How Do Behavior and Output Controls Differ?

Controls can be established to focus either on actual performance results (output) or on the activities that generate the performance (behavior). **Behavior controls** specify *how* something is to be done through policies, rules, standard operating procedures, and orders from a superior. **Output controls** specify *what* is to be

FIGURE
9.2

Evaluating an Implemented Strategy

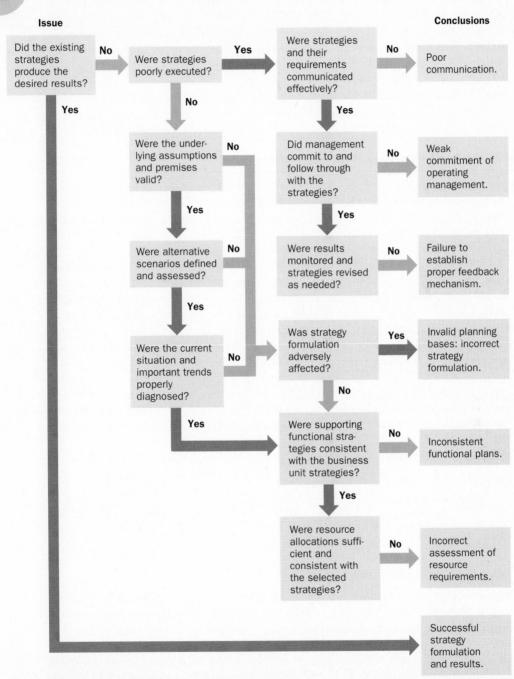

Issue   Conclusions

Did the existing strategies produce the desired results? → **No** → Were strategies poorly executed? → **Yes** → Were strategies and their requirements communicated effectively? → **No** → Poor communication.

Yes

Were strategies poorly executed? → **No** → Were the underlying assumptions and premises valid?

Were strategies and their requirements communicated effectively? → **Yes** → Did management commit to and follow through with the strategies? → **No** → Weak commitment of operating management.

Were the underlying assumptions and premises valid? → **No** → Did management commit to and follow through with the strategies?

Yes

Were alternative scenarios defined and assessed? → **No** → Were results monitored and strategies revised as needed?

Did management commit to and follow through with the strategies? → **Yes** → Were results monitored and strategies revised as needed? → **No** → Failure to establish proper feedback mechanism.

Yes

Were the current situation and important trends properly diagnosed? → **No** → Was strategy formulation adversely affected?

Was strategy formulation adversely affected? → **Yes** → Invalid planning bases: incorrect strategy formulation.

No

Were the current situation and important trends properly diagnosed? → **Yes** → Were supporting functional strategies consistent with the business unit strategies?

Was strategy formulation adversely affected? → **No** → Were supporting functional strategies consistent with the business unit strategies? → **No** → Inconsistent functional plans.

Yes

Were supporting functional strategies consistent with the business unit strategies? → **Yes** → Were resource allocations sufficient and consistent with the selected strategies? → **No** → Incorrect assessment of resource requirements.

Did the existing strategies produce the desired results? → **Yes** → Successful strategy formulation and results.

Source: Jeffrey A. Schmidt, "The Strategic Review," *Planning Review* (July/August 1988), p. 15. Copyright © 1988 by The Planning Forum, Oxford, Ohio.

accomplished by focusing on the end result of the behaviors through the use of objectives and performance targets or milestones. Behavior and output controls are not interchangeable. Behavior controls (such as following company procedures, making sales calls to potential customers, and getting to work on time) are most appropriate when performance results are hard to measure and a clear cause–effect connection exists between activities and results. Output controls (such as sales quotas, specific cost reduction or profit objectives, and surveys of customer satisfaction) are most appropriate when specific output measures are agreed upon and no clear cause–effect connection exists between activities and results.

What Are the Primary Measures of Corporate Performance?

The most commonly used measure of corporate performance (in terms of profits) is **return on investment** (ROI). It is simply the result of dividing net income before taxes by total assets. Although ROI has several advantages, it also has several distinct limitations. (See Table 9.1.) Although ROI gives the impression of objectivity and precision, it can be easily manipulated.

Earnings per share (EPS), dividing net earnings by the amount of common stock, also has several deficiencies as an evaluation of past and future performance. First, because alternative accounting principles are available, EPS can have several different but equally acceptable values, depending on the principle selected for its computation. Second, because EPS is based on accrual income, the conversion of income to cash can be near term or delayed. Therefore, EPS does not consider the present value of money. **Return on equity** (ROE), dividing net income by total equity, also has its share of limitations because it is also derived from accounting-based data. In addition, EPS and ROE are often unrelated to a company's stock price. Because of these and other limitations, ROI, EPS, and ROE by themselves are not adequate measures of corporate performance.

What Are Stakeholder Measures?

Each stakeholder has its own set of criteria to determine how well the corporation is performing. These criteria typically deal with the direct and indirect impact of corporate activities on stakeholder interests. Top management should establish one or more simple measures for each stakeholder category so that it can keep track of stakeholder concerns. (See Table 9.2.)

What Is Shareholder Value?

Because of the belief that accounting-based numbers such as return on investment, return on equity, and earnings per share are not reliable indicators of a corporation's economic value, many corporations are using shareholder value as a better measure of corporate performance and strategic management effectiveness. Real **shareholder value** is defined as the present value of the anticipated future stream of cash flows from the business plus the value of the company if liquidated. Assuming that the purpose of a company is to increase shareholder wealth, shareholder value analysis concentrates on cash flow as the key measure of performance. The

TABLE 9.1	**Advantages and Limitations of Using ROI as a Measure of Corporate Performance**

Advantages

1. ROI is a single comprehensive figure influenced by everything that happens.

2. It measures how well the division manager uses the property of the company to generate profits. It is also a good way to check on the accuracy of capital investment proposals.

3. It is a common denominator that can be compared with many entities.

4. It provides an incentive to use existing assets efficiently.

5. It provides an incentive to acquire new assets only when doing so would increase the return.

Limitations

1. ROI is very sensitive to depreciation policy. Depreciation write-off variances between divisions affect ROI performance. Accelerated depreciation techniques increase ROI, conflicting with capital budgeting discounted cash-flow analysis.

2. ROI is sensitive to book value. Older plants with more depreciated assets have relatively lower investment bases than newer plants (note also the effect of inflation), thus increasing ROI. Note that asset investment may be held down or assets disposed of in order to increase ROI performance.

3. In many firms that use ROI, one division sells to another. As a result, transfer pricing must occur. Expenses incurred affect profit. Because, in theory, the transfer price should be based on the total impact on firm profit, some investment center managers are bound to suffer. Equitable transfer prices are difficult to determine.

4. If one division operates in an industry that has favorable conditions and another division operates in an industry that has unfavorable conditions, the former division automatically "looks" better than the other.

5. The time span of concern here is short range. The performance of division managers should be measured in the long run. This is top management's time span capacity.

6. The business cycle strongly affects ROI performance, often despite managerial performance.

Source: "Advantages and Limitations of ROI as a Measure of Corporate Performance" from *Organizational Policy and Strategic Management: Text and Cases*, 2nd ed. by James M. Higgins, copyright © 1984 by The Dryden Press. Reproduced by permission of the publisher.

value of a corporation is thus the value of its cash flows discounted back to their present value, using the business's cost of capital as the discount rate. As long as the returns from a business exceed its cost of capital, the business will create value and be worth more than the capital invested in it.

Economic value added (EVA) has become an extremely popular shareholder value method of measuring corporate and divisional performance and may be on its way to replacing ROI as the standard performance measure. Simply put, EVA is after-tax operating profit minus the total annual cost of capital. It measures the difference between the prestrategy and poststrategy value of the business. If the difference, discounted by the cost of capital, is positive, the strategy is generating value for the shareholders. Among the many companies using the new measure are Coca-Cola, AT&T, Quaker Oats, Briggs & Stratton, and CSX. Explained by Roberto Goizueta, CEO of Coca-Cola, "We raise capital to make concentrate, and sell it at an operating profit. Then we pay the cost of that capital. Shareholders pocket the difference."[2] Unlike ROI, one of EVA's most powerful properties is its

TABLE 9.2

A Sample Scorecard for "Keeping Score" with Stakeholders

Stakeholder Category	Possible Near-Term Measures	Possible Long-Term Measures
Customers	Sales ($ and volume)	Growth in sales
	New customers	Turnover of customer base
	Number of new customer needs met ("tries")	Ability to control price
Suppliers	Cost of raw material	Growth rates of:
	Delivery time	Raw material costs
	Inventory	Delivery time
		Inventory
	Availability of raw material	New ideas from suppliers
Financial community	EPS	Ability to convince Wall Street of strategy
	Stock price	
	Number of "buy" lists	Growth in ROE
	ROE	
Employees	Number of suggestions	Number of internal promotions
	Productivity	Turnover
	Number of grievances	
Congress	Number of new pieces of legislation that affect the firm	Number of new regulations that affect industry
	Access to key members and staff	Ratio of "cooperative" vs. "competitive" encounters
Consumer advocate	Number of meetings	Number of changes in policy due to C.A.
	Number of "hostile" encounters	
	Number of times coalitions formed	Number of C.A.-initiated "calls for help"
	Number of legal actions	
Environmentalists	Number of meetings	Number of changes in policy due to environmentalists
	Number of hostile encounters	
	Number of times coalitions formed	Number of environmentalist "calls for help"
	Number of EPA complaints	
	Number of legal actions	

Source: R. E. Freeman, *Strategic Management: A Stakeholder Approach* (Boston: Ballinger Publishing Company, 1984), p. 179. Copyright © 1984 by R. E. Freeman. Reprinted by permission.

strong relationship to stock price. Managers can improve their company's or business unit's EVA by (1) earning more profit without using more capital, (2) using less capital, and (3) investing capital in high-return projects.

How Is Top Management Evaluated?

Through its strategy, audit, and compensation committees, a board of directors closely evaluates the job performance of the CEO and the top management team. Of course, the board is concerned primarily with overall profitability as measured quantitatively by return on investment, return on equity, earnings per share, and shareholder value. The absence of short-run profitability is certainly a factor contributing to the firing of any CEO, but the board is also concerned with other factors.

Members of the compensation committees of today's boards of directors generally agree that measuring a CEO's ability to establish strategic direction, build a management team, and provide leadership is more critical in the long run than are a few quantitative measures. The board should evaluate top management not only on the typical output-oriented quantitative measures, but also on behavioral measures—factors relating to its strategic management practices. Unfortunately less than 30% of companies systematically evaluate their CEO's performance.[3]

The specific measures that a board uses to evaluate its top management should be based on the objectives agreed on earlier by both the board and top management. If better relations with the local community and improved safety practices in work areas were selected as objectives for the year (or for five years), these items should be included in the evaluation. In addition, other factors that tend to lead to profitability might be included, such as market share, product quality, or investment intensity.

What Is the Value of a Management Audit?

Used by various consulting firms as a way to measure performance, audits of corporate activities are frequently suggested for use by boards of directors as well as by others in managerial positions. **Management audits** have been developed to evaluate activities such as corporate social responsibility, functional areas such as the marketing department, and divisions such as the international division—and the corporation itself in a strategic audit. (**See Appendix 10.C for an example of a strategic audit.**)

What Are the Primary Measures of Divisional and Functional Performance?

Companies use a variety of techniques to evaluate and control performance in divisions, SBUs, and functional areas. If a corporation is composed of SBUs or divisions, it will use many of the same performance measures (ROI or EVA, for instance) that it uses to assess overall corporation performance. To the extent that it can isolate specific functional units, such as R&D, the corporation may develop responsibility centers. It will also use typical functional measures such as market share and sales per employee (marketing), unit costs and percentage of defects (operations), percentage of sales from new products and number of patents (R&D), and turnover and job satisfaction (HRM).

During strategy formulation and implementation, top management approves a series of programs and supporting *operating budgets* from its business units. These operating budgets list the costs and expenses for each proposed program in dollar terms. During evaluation and control, management contrasts actual expenses with planned expenditures and assesses the degree of variance, typically on a monthly basis. In addition, top management probably will require *periodic statistical reports* summarizing data on key factors, such as the number of new customer contracts, volume of received orders, and productivity figures.

What Are Responsibility Centers?

Control systems can be established to monitor specific functions, projects, or divisions. For example, budgets typically are used to control the financial indicators of performance. **Responsibility centers** are used to isolate a unit so that it can be evaluated separately from the rest of the corporation. Each responsibility center has its own budget, is evaluated on its use of budgeted resources, and is headed by a manager who is responsible for its performance. The center uses resources (measured in terms of costs or expenses) to produce a service or a product (measured in terms of volume or revenues). The way in which the corporation's control system measures these resources and services or products determines which of the five major types of responsibility centers is used.

1. **Standard cost centers:** Primarily used in manufacturing facilities, standard (or expected) costs are computed for each operation on the basis of historical data. In evaluating the center's performance, its total standard costs are multiplied by the units produced; the result is the expected cost of production, which is then compared to the actual cost of production.

2. **Revenue centers:** Production, usually in terms of unit or dollar sales, is measured without considering resource costs (e.g., salaries). The center is thus judged in terms of *effectiveness* rather than *efficiency*. The effectiveness of a sales region, for example, is determined by comparing its actual sales to its projected or previous year's sales. Profits are not considered because sales departments have limited influence over the cost of the products they sell.

3. **Expense centers:** Resources are measured in dollars without considering service or product costs. Thus budgets are prepared for *engineered* expenses (costs that can be calculated) and for *discretionary* expenses (costs that can be only estimated). Typical expense centers are administrative, service, and research departments. They cost an organization money, but they contribute only indirectly to revenues.

4. **Profit centers:** Performance is measured in terms of the difference between revenues (which measure production) and expenditures (which measure resources). A profit center is typically established whenever an organizational unit controls both its resources and its products or services. By having such centers, a company can be organized into divisions of separate product lines. The manager of each division is given autonomy to the extent that she or he is able to keep profits at a satisfactory (or better) level.

   Some organizational units that are not usually considered potentially autonomous can, for the purpose of profit-center evaluations, be made so. A manufacturing department, for example, can be converted from a standard cost center (or expense center) into a profit center: it is allowed to charge a **transfer price** for each product it "sells" to the sales department. The difference between the manufacturing cost per unit and the agreed-upon transfer price is the unit's "profit." Transfer pricing is commonly used in vertically integrated corporations and can work well when a price can be easily determined for a designated amount of product.

5. Investment centers: Because many divisions in large manufacturing corporations use significant assets to make their products, their asset base should be factored into their performance evaluation. Thus to focus only on profits, as in the case of profit centers, is insufficient. An investment center's performance is measured in terms of the difference between its resources and its services or products. For example, two divisions in a corporation made identical profits, but one division owns a $3 million plant, whereas the other owns a $1 million plant. Both make the same profits, but one is obviously more efficient: the smaller plant provides the shareholders with a better return on their investment. The most widely used measure of investment center performance is return on investment (ROI).

Most single-business corporations, such as Apple Computer, tend to use a combination of cost, expense, and revenue centers. In these corporations, most managers are functional specialists and manage against a budget. Total profitability is integrated at the corporate level. Multidivisional corporations with one dominating product line, such as Anheuser-Busch, which have diversified into a few small businesses but which still depend on a single product line (such as beer) for most of their revenue and income, generally use a combination of cost, expense, revenue, and profit centers. Multidivisional corporations, such as General Electric, tend to emphasize investment centers—although in various units throughout the corporation other types of responsibility centers will also be used. One problem with using responsibility centers, however, is that the separation needed to measure and evaluate a division's performance can make it difficult to achieve the level of cooperation among divisions needed to attain synergy for the corporation as a whole. (This problem is discussed later in this chapter under suboptimization.)

How Is Benchmarking Used to Evaluate Performance?

According to Xerox Corporation, the company that pioneered this concept in the United States, **benchmarking** is "the continual process of measuring products, services, and practices against the toughest competitors or those companies recognized as industry leaders."[4] Benchmarking, an increasingly popular program, is based on the concept that to reinvent something that someone else is already using makes no sense. It involves openly learning how other companies do something better and not only imitating but perhaps even improving on their techniques. The benchmarking process usually involves the following steps:

- **Identify the area or process to be examined:** It should be an activity which has the potential to determine a business unit's competitive advantage.
- **Find behavioral and output measures of the area or process and obtain measurements.**
- **Select an accessible set of competitors and best-in-class companies against which to benchmark:** These may very often be companies that are in completely different industries but perform similar activities. For example, when Xerox wanted to improve its order fulfillment, it went to L. L. Bean, the successful mail order firm, to learn how they achieved excellence in this area.

- Calculate the differences among the company's performance measurements and those of the best-in-class: Determine why the differences exist.
- Develop tactical programs for closing performance gaps.
- Implement the programs and then compare the resulting new measurements with those of the best-in-class companies.

Manco, Inc., a small Cleveland-area producer of duct tape, regularly benchmarks itself against Wal-Mart, Rubbermaid, and PepsiCo to enable it to better compete with giant 3M. The American Productivity & Quality Center, a Houston research group, recently established a "best practices database" of 600 leading techniques from 250 companies.[5]

9.3   Strategic Information Systems

Before performance measures can have any impact on strategic management, they must first be communicated to the people responsible for formulating and implementing strategic plans. Strategic information systems—computer-based or manual, formal or informal—can perform this function. One of the main reasons given for the bankruptcy of International Harvester was the inability of the corporation's top management to precisely determine its income by major class of similar products. Because of this inability, management kept trying to fix ailing businesses and was unable to respond flexibly to major changes and unexpected events. In contrast, one of the main reasons for the success of Toys 'R' Us has been management's use of the company's sophisticated information system to control purchasing decisions. Cash registers in the more than 300 U.S. Toys 'R' Us stores transmit information daily to computers at the company's headquarters. Consequently managers know every morning exactly how many of each item were sold the day before, how many have been sold so far in the year, and how this year's sales compare to last year's. The information system allows automatic reordering by computer without managerial input. It also allows the company to experiment with new toys without committing to big orders in advance. In effect, the system allows the customers to decide through their purchases what gets reordered.

At the divisional or SBU level of a corporation, the information system should be used to support, reinforce, or enlarge its business-level strategy through its decision support system. An SBU pursuing a strategy of *overall cost leadership* could use its information system to reduce costs by either improving labor productivity or using other resources such as inventory or machinery. For example, Merrill Lynch developed PRISM software to provide its 500 U.S. retail offices quick access to financial information in order to boost the efficiency of its brokers. Another SBU, in contrast, might wish to pursue a *differentiation* strategy. It could use its information system to add uniqueness to the product or service and contribute to quality, service, or image through the functional areas. Federal Express wanted to use superior service to gain a competitive advantage. It invested heavily in several types of information systems to measure and track the performance of its delivery service. Together, these information systems gave Federal Express the fastest error-response time in the overnight delivery business.

9.4 ▶ Problems in Measuring Performance

Measuring performance is a crucial part of evaluation and control. The lack of quantifiable objectives or performance standards and the inability of the information system to provide timely, valid information are two obvious control problems. Without objective and timely measurements, making operational, let alone strategic, decisions would be extremely difficult. Nevertheless, the use of timely, quantifiable standards does not guarantee good performance. The very act of monitoring and measuring performance can cause side effects that interfere with overall corporate performance. Among the most frequent negative side effects are a short-term orientation and goal displacement.

Why Is Short-Term Orientation a Problem?

In many situations, top executives report that they analyze *neither* the long-term implications of present operations on the strategy they have adopted *nor* the operational impact of a strategy on the corporate mission. Long-run evaluations are often not conducted because executives (1) don't realize their importance, (2) believe that short-run considerations are more important than long-run considerations, (3) aren't personally evaluated on a long-term basis, or (4) don't have the time to make a long-run analysis.[6] There is no real justification for the first and last "reasons." If executives realize the importance of long-run evaluations, they make the time needed to conduct them. Even though many chief executives point to immediate pressures from the investment community and to short-term incentive and promotion plans to support the second and third reasons, evidence does not always support their claims.

Nevertheless, at times the stock market does not value a particular strategic investment. See the *Company Spotlight on Maytag Corporation* feature for the response of the investment community to Maytag's acquisition of Hoover (in terms of Maytag's stock market price).

Many accounting-based measures do, however, encourage a short-term emphasis. Table 9.1 indicates that one of the limitations of ROI as a performance measure is its short-term nature. In theory, ROI is not limited to the short run, but in practice using this measure to realize long-term benefits for the company is often difficult. Because managers can often manipulate both the numerator (earnings) and the denominator (investment), the resulting ROI figure can be meaningless. Advertising, maintenance, and research efforts can be reduced. Mergers can be undertaken that will do more for this year's earnings (and next year's paycheck) than for the division's or corporation's future profits. (Research of 55 firms that engaged in major acquisitions revealed that even though the firms performed poorly after the acquisition, top management still received significant increases in

COMPANY SPOTLIGHT

MAYTAG Corporation

Evaluation of Maytag Performance After the Hoover Acquisition

When Maytag Corporation purchased Hoover for its international appliance business, its debt soared to $923 million from $134 million just nine months earlier. Maytag's total outstanding shares swelled to 105 million from 75 million during the same time period. Interest payments leaped to $70 million in 1989 from $20 million the year before.

The corporation no longer had the best profit margin in the industry. Return on equity had been over 25% before the Magic Chef merger in 1986, peaked at over 30% in 1988, and was nearly halved to 18.3% in 1989 after the Hoover acquisition. By 1991 Maytag was earning just 8% on equity. 1992 marked the first time since the 1920s when the annual report showed a net loss. The stock price had dropped from $26.50 per share in 1988 to $13 in 1993—far lower than the $20 per share one takeover investor had concluded that Maytag's assets were worth. Some analysts were wondering if the corporation might soon be forced to sell Hoover or have no choice but to sell out to a competitor by the end of the decade.

compensation!)[7] Expensive retooling and plant modernization can be delayed as long as a manager can manipulate figures on production defects and absenteeism.

Why Is Goal Displacement a Problem?

Monitoring and measuring of performance (if not carefully done) can actually result in a decline in overall corporate performance. **Goal displacement** is the confusion of means with ends and occurs when activities originally intended to help managers attain corporate objectives become ends in themselves—or are adapted to meet ends other than those for which they were intended. Two types of goal displacement are behavior substitution and suboptimization.

What Is Behavior Substitution?

Behavior substitution refers to a phenomenon that occurs when people substitute activities that do not lead to goal accomplishment for activities that do lead to goal accomplishment because the wrong activities are being rewarded. Managers, like most people, tend to focus more of their attention on those behaviors that are clearly measurable than on those that are not. Employees often receive little to no reward for engaging in hard-to-measure activities such as cooperation and initiative. However, easy-to-measure activities might have little to no relationship to the desired good performance. Rational people, nevertheless, will tend to work for those rewards that the system has to offer. Therefore, people tend to substitute behaviors that are recognized and rewarded for those behaviors that are ignored, without regard to their contribution to goal accomplishment. A U.S. Navy quip sums up this situation: "What you inspect is what you get." If the evaluation and control system of an auto plant rewards the meeting of quantitative goals and pays only lip service to qualitative goals, consumers can expect to get a very large number of very poorly built cars! The law governing the effect of measurement on behavior seems to be that *quantifiable measures drive out nonquantifiable measures.*

What Is Suboptimization?

Suboptimization refers to the phenomenon that occurs when a unit optimizes its goal accomplishment to the detriment of the organization as a whole. The emphasis in large corporations on developing separate responsibility centers can create some problems for the corporation as a whole. To the extent that a division or functional unit views itself as a separate entity, it might refuse to cooperate with other units or divisions in the same corporation if cooperation could in some way negatively affect its performance evaluation. The competition between divisions to achieve a high ROI can result in one division's refusal to share its new technology or work-process improvements. One division's attempt to optimize the accomplishment of its goals can cause other divisions to fall behind and thus negatively affect overall corporate performance. One common example of this type of suboptimization occurs when a marketing department approves an early shipment date to a customer as a means of getting an order and forces the manufacturing department into overtime production for this one order. Production costs are raised, which reduces the manufacturing department's overall efficiency. The end result might be that, although marketing achieves its sales goal, the corporation as a whole fails to achieve its expected profitability.

9.5   Guidelines for Proper Control

In designing a control system, top management should remember that *controls should follow strategy.* Unless controls ensure the use of the proper strategy to achieve objectives, dysfunctional side effects are likely to completely undermine the implementation of the objectives. The following guidelines are recommended:

1. **Controls should involve only the minimum amount of information needed to give a reliable picture of events.** Too many controls create confusion. Focus on the *critical success factors*: the 20% of the factors that determine 80% of the results.
2. **Controls should monitor only meaningful activities and results,** regardless of measurement difficulty. If cooperation between divisions is important to corporate performance, some form of qualitative or quantitative measure should be established to monitor cooperation.
3. **Controls should be timely.** Corrective action must be taken before it is too late. Steering controls, controls that monitor or measure the factors influencing performance, should be stressed so that advance notice of problems is given.

4. **Controls should be long-term and short-term.** If only short-term measures are emphasized, a short-term managerial orientation is likely.
5. **Controls should pinpoint exceptions.** Only those activities or results that fall outside a predetermined tolerance range should call for action.
6. **Controls should be used to reward meeting or exceeding standards rather than to punish failure to meet standards.** Heavy punishment of failure typically results in goal displacement. Managers will "fudge" reports and lobby for lower standards.

To the extent that the culture complements and reinforces the strategic orientation of the firm, there is less need for an extensive formal control system. In their book *In Search of Excellence*, Peters and Waterman state that "the stronger the culture and the more it was directed toward the marketplace, the less need was there for policy manuals, organization charts, or detailed procedures and rules. In these companies, people way down the line know what they are supposed to do in most situations because the handful of guiding values is crystal clear."[8]

9.6 Strategic Incentive Management

To ensure congruence between the needs of the corporation as a whole and the needs of the employees as individuals, management and the board of directors should develop an incentive program that rewards desired performance. Incentive plans should be linked in some way to corporate and divisional strategy. For example, a survey of 600 business units indicates that the pay mix associated with a growth strategy emphasizes bonuses and other incentives over salary and benefits, whereas the pay mix associated with a stability strategy has the reverse emphasis.[9]

The following three approaches are tailored to help match measurements and rewards with explicit strategic objectives and timeframes.[10]

1. **Weighted-factor method:** This method is particularly appropriate for measuring and rewarding the performance of top SBU managers and group-level executives when performance factors and their importance vary from one SBU to another. The measurements that one corporation uses might contain the following variations: the performance of high-growth SBUs measured in terms of market share, sales growth, designated future payoff, and progress on several future-oriented strategic projects; the performance of low-growth SBUs, in contrast, measured in terms of ROI and cash generation; and the performance of medium-growth SBUs measured for a combination of these factors. (See Table 9.3.)
2. **Long-term evaluation method:** This method compensates managers for achieving objectives set over a multiyear period. An executive is promised some company stock or "performance units" (convertible into money) in amounts to be based on long-term performance. An executive committee, for example, might set a particular objective in terms of growth in earnings per share during a five-year period. Awards would be contingent on the corporation's meeting that objective within the designated time. Any executive who

<table>
<tr><td>TABLE 9.3</td><td colspan="2">Weighted-Factor Approach to Strategic Incentive Management</td></tr>
</table>

Strategic Business Unit Category	Factor	Weight
High Growth	Return on assets	10%
	Cash flow	0%
	Strategic-funds programs (developmental expenses)	45%
	Market-share increase	45%
		100%
Medium Growth	Return on assets	25%
	Cash flow	25%
	Strategic-funds programs (developmental expenses)	25%
	Market-share increase	25%
		100%
Low Growth	Return on assets	50%
	Cash flow	50%
	Strategic-funds programs (developmental expenses)	0%
	Market-share increase	0%
		100%

Source: Reprinted by permission of the publisher from "The Performance Measurement and Reward System: Critical to Strategic Management," by Paul J. Stonich, from *Organizational Dynamics* (Winter 1984), p. 51. Copyright © 1984 by American Management Association, New York. All rights reserved.

leaves the corporation before the objective is met receives nothing. The typical emphasis on stock price makes this approach more applicable to top management than to business unit managers.

3. **Strategic-funds method:** This method encourages executives to look at developmental expenses as being different from those expenses required for current operations. The accounting statement for a corporate unit enters strategic funds as a separate entry below the current ROI. It is therefore possible to distinguish between those expense dollars consumed in the generation of current revenues and those invested in the future of the business. Therefore, the manager can be evaluated on both a short- and a long-term basis and has an incentive to invest strategic funds in the future. (See Table 9.4.)

An effective way to achieve the desired strategic results through a reward system is to combine the three approaches.

1. Segregate strategic funds from short-term funds, as is done in the strategic-funds method.
2. Develop a weighted-factor chart for each SBU.
3. Measure performance on three bases: the pretax profit indicated by the strategic-funds approach, the weighted factors, and the long-term evaluation of SBU and corporate performance.

General Electric and Westinghouse are two firms using a version of these measures.

TABLE 9.4	Strategic-Funds Approach to an SBU's Profit-and-Loss Statement	
	Sales	$12,300,000
	Cost of sales	6,900,000
	Gross margin	$5,400,000
	General and administrative expenses	−3,700,000
	Operating profit (return on sales)	$1,700,000
	Strategic funds (development expenses)	−1,000,000
	Pretax profit	$700,000

Source: Reprinted by permission of the publisher from "The Performance Measurement and Reward System: Critical to Strategic Management," by Paul J. Stonich, from *Organizational Dynamics* (Winter 1984), p. 51. Copyright © 1984 by American Management Association, New York. All rights reserved.

In Conclusion . . .

Seitz Corporation of Torrington, Connecticut, was a family-owned company that grew from a garage-based tool shop into a major supplier of the gears and bearings that circulate paper in copiers and dot matrix printers. By the mid 1980s, however, laser and ink jet printers were starting to replace dot matrix printers. Seitz was forced to lay off all but 80 employees as sales dropped significantly. Facing greater losses, management embarked on a major overhaul using benchmarking. It first identified firms and activities to study and then adopted several of the practices that it had examined. Among those incorporated were techniques to reduce new-product to market cycle time and just-in-time manufacturing. Cycle time was reduced from about nine weeks to three weeks. The use of just-in-time cut inventories, thus increasing floor space by 30%. With these and other improvements, Seitz's annual revenue reached a record $21 million in 1992 and employment climbed back to 190 people. Seitz's management group agreed that benchmarking had been key in implementing its turnaround strategy.[11]

Discussion Questions

1. Is Figure 9.1 a realistic model of the evaluation and control process?
2. What are some examples of behavior controls? Output controls?
3. Is EVA an improvement over ROI, ROE, or EPS?
4. How much faith can a manager place in a transfer price as a substitute for a market price in measuring a profit center's performance?
5. Is the evaluation and control process appropriate for a corporation that emphasizes creativity? Are control and creativity compatible?

Key Terms

evaluation and control process
performance
steering controls
behavior controls
output controls
return on investment
earnings per share
return on equity
shareholder value
economic value added
management audits

responsibility centers
transfer price
benchmarking
goal displacement
behavior substitution
suboptimization
critical success factors
weighted-factor method
long-term evaluation method
strategic-funds method

⑩

Suggestions for Case Analysis

An analysis of a corporation's strategic management calls for a comprehensive view of the organization. The case method of analysis provides the opportunity to move from a narrow, specialized view that emphasizes technical skills to a broader, less precise analysis of the overall corporation that emphasizes conceptual skills. Concentrating on strategic management processes forces you to develop a better understanding of the political, social, and economic environment of business, and to appreciate the interactions of the functional specialties required for corporate success.

10.1 The Case Method

The analysis and discussion of case problems has been the most popular method of teaching strategy and policy for many years. Cases present actual business situations and enable you to examine both successful and unsuccessful corporations. In case analysis, you might be asked to critically analyze a situation in which a manager had to make a decision of long-term corporate importance. This approach gives you a feel for what it is like to be faced with making and implementing strategic decisions.

10.2 Frameworks for Case Analysis

There is no one best way to analyze or present a case report. Each instructor has personal preferences for format and approach. Nevertheless, we suggest an approach for both written and oral reports in **Appendix 10.A**, which provides a systematic method for successfully attacking a case.

Case discussion focuses on critical analysis and logical development of thought. A solution is satisfactory if it resolves important problems and is likely to be implemented successfully. How the corporation actually dealt with the case problems has no real bearing on the analysis because management might have analyzed its problems incorrectly or implemented a series of flawed solutions.

The presentation of a case analysis can be organized on the basis of several frameworks. One framework is *SWOT Analysis,* followed by a discussion of strategic alternatives and a recommendation. Another is the *strategic audit* as shown in **Appendix 10.C.** Regardless of the framework chosen, be especially careful to include a complete analysis of key environmental variables, especially industry trends, the competition, and international developments.

10.3 ▶ Library Research

You should undertake outside research into the environmental setting of the case. Find out the date when the case situation occurred and then screen the business periodicals for that time period. Use the computerized company and industry information services such as COMPUSTAT, Compact Disclosure, and CD/International, which are available on CD-ROM or on-line at the library. On the World Wide Web, Hoover's On Line Corporate Directory (http://www.hoovers.com) provides access to corporate reports.

This background will give you an appreciation for the situation as the participants in the case experienced it. A company's annual report and 10-K form from that year can be very helpful. An understanding of the economy during that period will help you avoid making a serious error in your analysis—for example, suggesting a sale of stock when the stock market is at an all-time low or taking on more debt when the prime interest rate is over 15%. Information on the industry will provide insights on its competitive activities. Some resources available for research into the economy and a corporation's industry are suggested in **Appendix 10.B.**

10.4 ▶ Financial Analysis: A Place to Begin

Ratio analysis is the calculating of ratios from data in a company's financial statements. It is done to identify possible financial strengths or weaknesses. Thus it is a valuable part of SWOT analysis. A review of key financial ratios can help you assess the company's overall situation and pinpoint some problem areas. Ratios control for firm size and enable you to compare a company's ratios with industry averages. Table 10.1 lists some of the most important financial ratios: (1) **liquidity ratios,** (2) **profitability ratios,** (3) **activity ratios,** and (4) **leverage ratios.**

How Are Financial Statements Analyzed?

In your analysis do not simply make an exhibit including all the ratios but select and discuss only those ratios that have an impact on the company's problems. For instance, accounts receivable and inventory may provide a source of funds. If

TABLE
10.1

Financial Ratio Analysis

	Formula	How Expressed	Meaning
1. Liquidity Ratios			
Current ratio	$\dfrac{\text{Current assets}}{\text{Current liabilities}}$	Decimal	A short-term indicator of the company's ability to pay its short-term liabilities from short-term assets; how much of current assets are available to cover each dollar of current liabilities.
Quick (acid test) ratio	$\dfrac{\text{Current assets} - \text{Inventory}}{\text{Current liabilities}}$	Decimal	Measures the company's ability to pay off its short-term obligations from current assets, excluding inventories.
Inventory to net working capital	$\dfrac{\text{Inventory}}{\text{Current assets} - \text{Current liabilities}}$	Decimal	A measure of inventory balance; measures the extent to which the cushion of excess current assets over current liabilities may be threatened by unfavorable changes in inventory.
Cash ratio	$\dfrac{\text{Cash} + \text{Cash equivalents}}{\text{Current liabilities}}$	Decimal	Measures the extent to which the company's capital is in cash or cash equivalents; shows how much of the current obligations can be paid from cash or near-cash assets.
2. Profitability Ratios			
Net profit margin	$\dfrac{\text{Net profit after taxes}}{\text{Net sales}}$	Percentage	Shows how much after-tax profits are generated by each dollar of sales.
Gross profit margin	$\dfrac{\text{Sales} - \text{Cost of goods sold}}{\text{Net sales}}$	Percentage	Indicates the total margin available to cover other expenses beyond cost of goods sold, and still yield a profit.
Return on investment (ROI)	$\dfrac{\text{Net profit after taxes}}{\text{Total assets}}$	Percentage	Measures the rate of return on the total assets utilized in the company; a measure of management's efficiency, it shows the return on all the assets under its control regardless of source of financing.
Return on equity (ROE)	$\dfrac{\text{Net profit after taxes}}{\text{Shareholders' equity}}$	Percentage	Measures the rate of return on the book value of shareholders' total investment in the company.

(*continued*)

TABLE 10.1

Financial Ratio Analysis *(continued)*

	Formula	How Expressed	Meaning
Earnings per share (EPS)	$\dfrac{\text{Net profit after taxes } - \text{ Preferred stock dividends}}{\text{Average number of common shares}}$	Dollars per share	Shows the after-tax earnings generated for each share of common stock.

3. Activity Ratios

	Formula	How Expressed	Meaning
Inventory turnover	$\dfrac{\text{Net sales}}{\text{Inventory}}$	Decimal	Measures the number of times that average inventory of finished goods was turned over or sold during a period of time, usually a year.
Days of inventory	$\dfrac{\text{Inventory}}{\text{Cost of goods sold} \div 365}$	Days	Measures the number of one day's worth of inventory that a company has on hand at any given time.
Net working capital turnover	$\dfrac{\text{Net sales}}{\text{Net working capital}}$	Decimal	Measures how effectively the net working capital is used to generate sales.
Asset turnover	$\dfrac{\text{Sales}}{\text{Total assets}}$	Decimal	Measures the utilization of all the company's assets; measures how many sales are generated by each dollar of assets.
Fixed asset turnover	$\dfrac{\text{Sales}}{\text{Fixed assets}}$	Decimal	Measures the utilization of the company's fixed assets (i.e., plant and equipment); measures how many sales are generated by each dollar of fixed assets.
Average collection period	$\dfrac{\text{Accounts receivable}}{\text{Sales for year} \div 365}$	Days	Indicates the average length of time in days that a company must wait to collect a sale after making it; may be compared to the credit terms offered by the company to its customers.
Accounts receivable turnover	$\dfrac{\text{Annual credit sales}}{\text{Accounts receivable}}$	Decimal	Indicates the number of times that accounts receivable are cycled during the period (usually a year).
Accounts payable period	$\dfrac{\text{Accounts payable}}{\text{Purchases for year} \div 365}$	Days	Indicates the average length of time in days that the company takes to pay its credit purchases.
Days of cash	$\dfrac{\text{Cash}}{\text{Net sales for year} \div 365}$	Days	Indicates the number of days of cash on hand, at present sales levels.

(continued)

TABLE 10.1   **Financial Ratio Analysis** *(continued)*

	Formula	How Expressed	Meaning
4. Leverage Ratios			
Debt to asset ratio	$\dfrac{\text{Total debt}}{\text{Total assets}}$	Percentage	Measures the extent to which borrowed funds have been used to finance the company's assets.
Debt to equity ratio	$\dfrac{\text{Total debt}}{\text{Shareholders' equity}}$	Percentage	Measures the funds provided by creditors versus the funds provided by owners.
Long-term debt to capital structure	$\dfrac{\text{Long-term debt}}{\text{Shareholders' equity}}$	Percentage	Measures the long-term component of capital structure.
Times interest earned	$\dfrac{\text{Profit before taxes} + \text{Interest charges}}{\text{Interest charges}}$	Decimal	Indicates the ability of the company to meet its annual interest costs.
Coverage of fixed charges	$\dfrac{\text{Profit before taxes} + \text{Interest charges} + \text{Lease charges}}{\text{Interest charges} + \text{Lease obligations}}$	Decimal	A measure of the company's ability to meet all of its fixed-charge obligations.
Current liabilities to equity	$\dfrac{\text{Current liabilities}}{\text{Shareholders' equity}}$	Percentage	Measures the short-term financing portion versus that provided by owners.
5. Other Ratios			
Price/earnings ratio	$\dfrac{\text{Market price per share}}{\text{Earnings per share}}$	Decimal	Shows the current market's evaluation of a stock, based on its earnings; shows how much the investor is willing to pay for each dollar of earnings.
Divided payout ratio	$\dfrac{\text{Annual dividends per share}}{\text{Annual earnings per share}}$	Percentage	Indicates the percentage of profit that is paid out as dividends.
Dividend yield on common stock	$\dfrac{\text{Annual dividends per share}}{\text{Current market price per share}}$	Percentage	Indicates the dividend rate of return to common shareholders at the current market price.

Note: In using ratios for analysis, calculate ratios for the corporation and compare them to the average and quartile ratios for the particular industry. Refer to Standard and Poor's and Robert Morris Associates for average industry data. For an in-depth discussion of ratios and their use, refer to a financial management text such as E. F. Brigham, *Essentials of Managerial Finance*, 10th ed. (Chicago: Dryden, 1993), pp. 48–68. Special thanks to Dr. Moustafa H. Abdelsamad, Dean, Business School, Texas A&M University, Corpus Christi, Texas, for his definitions of these ratios.

receivables and inventories are double the industry average, reducing them may provide needed cash. In this situation, the case report should include not only sources of funds, but also the number of dollars freed for use. Compare these ratios with industry averages to discover if the company is out of line with others in the industry.

A typical financial analysis of a firm would include a study of the operating statements for five or so years, including a trend analysis of sales, profits, earnings per share, debt-to-equity ratio, return on investment, and so on, plus a ratio study comparing the firm under study with industry standards. To begin, scrutinize historical income statements and balance sheets. These two basic statements provide most of the data needed for analysis. Statements of cash flow may also be useful. Compare the statements over time if a series of statements is available. Calculate changes that occur in individual categories from year to year and the cumulative total change. Determine the change as a percentage as well as an absolute amount. You may also need to adjust for inflation if that was a significant factor. Examination of this information may reveal developing trends. Compare trends in one category with trends in related categories. For example, an increase in sales of 15% over three years may appear to be satisfactory until you note an increase of 20% in the cost of goods sold during the same period. The outcome of this comparison might suggest that further investigation into the manufacturing process is necessary.

What Are Common-Size Statements?

Common-size statements are income statements and balance sheets in which the dollar figures have been converted into percentages. For the income statement, net sales represent 100%: calculate the percentage of each category so that the categories sum to the net sales percentage (100%). For the balance sheet, give the total assets a value of 100% and calculate other asset and liability categories as percentages of the total assets. (Individual asset and liability items, such as accounts receivable and accounts payable, can also be calculated as a percentage of net sales.)

When you convert statements to this form, it is relatively easy to note the percentage that each category represents of the total. Look for trends in specific items, such as cost of goods sold, when compared to the company's historical figures. To get a proper picture, however, compare these data with industry data, if available, to see if fluctuations merely reflect industrywide trends. If a firm's trends are generally in line with those of the rest of the industry, the likelihood of problems is less than if the firm's trends are worse than industry averages. These statements are especially helpful in developing scenarios and pro forma statements because they provide a series of historical relationships (for example, cost of goods sold to sales, interest to sales, and inventories as a percentage of assets).

How Are the Z-value and Index of Sustainable Growth Used?

If the corporation being studied appears to be in poor financial condition, use *Altman's Bankruptcy Formula* to calculate its Z-value. The **Z-value** formula

combines five ratios by weighting them according to their importance to a corporation's financial strength. The formula is:

$$Z = 1.2x_1 + 1.4x_2 + 3.3x_3 + 0.6x_4 + 1.0x_5$$

where:

x_1 = Working capital/Total assets (%)
x_2 = Retained earnings/Total assets (%)
x_3 = Earnings before interest and taxes/Total assets (%)
x_4 = Market value of equity/Total liabilities (%)
x_5 = Sales/Total assets (number of times)

Scores below 1.81 indicate significant credit problems, whereas scores above 3.0
indicate a healthy firm. Scores between 1.81 and 3.0 indicate question marks.[1]

The **index of sustainable growth** is useful to learn if a company embarking on
a growth strategy will need to take on debt to fund this growth. The index indicates how much of the growth rate of sales can be sustained by internally generated funds. The formula is:

$$g^* = [P(1 - D)\,(1 + L)] / [T - P\,(1 - D)\,(1 + L)]$$

where:

P = (Net profit before tax/Net sales) * 100
D = Target dividends/Profit after tax
L = Total liabilities/Net worth
T = (Total assets/Net sales) * 100

If the planned growth rate calls for a growth rate higher than its g^*, external capital will be needed to fund the growth unless management is able to find efficiencies, decrease dividends, increase the debt/equity ratio, or reduce assets by renting
or leasing arrangements.[2]

Takeover artists and leveraged buyout (LBO) specialists look at a corporation's financial statements for **operating cash flow**: the amount of money a company generates before the cost of financing and taxes. This is the company's net
income plus depreciation plus depletion, amortization, interest expense, and income tax expense. LBO specialists take on as much debt as the company's operating cash flow can support. Although operating cash flow is a broad measure of a
company's funds, some takeover artists look at a much narrower **free cash flow**:
the amount of money a new owner can take out of the firm without harming the
business. This is net income plus depreciation, depletion, and amortization less
capital expenditures and dividends.[3]

How Should Inflation, Interest Rates, and GDP Be Used?

If you are analyzing a company over many years, you may want to adjust sales and
net income for inflation to arrive at "true" financial performance in constant dollars. **Constant dollars** are dollars adjusted for inflation to make them comparable

over various years. One way to adjust for inflation is to use the Consumer Price Index (CPI), as shown in Table 10.2. Dividing sales and net income by the CPI factor for that year changes the figures to 1982–1984 constant dollars.

Another helpful analytical aid is **prime interest rate (PIR)**, the rate of interest banks charge on their lowest risk loans. To better assess strategic decisions, note the level of the prime interest rate at the time of the case. (See Table 10.2.) A decision to borrow money to build a new plant would have been a good one in 1992, but less practical in 1989.

In preparing a scenario for your pro forma financial statements, you may want to use the **Gross Domestic Product (GDP)** from Table 10.2. GDP is used worldwide and measures the total output of goods and services within a country's borders. The previous U.S. measure was Gross National Product (GNP), which covered production by a country's workers wherever they were in the world.

TABLE 10.2

U.S. Economic Indicators: Gross Domestic Product (GDP), in Billions of Dollars; Consumer Price Index for All Items (CPI), 1982–1984 = 1.0; Prime Interest Rate (PIR), percent

Year	GDP	CPI	PIR
1980	2,708.0	.824	15.27%
1981	3,030.6	.909	18.87
1982	3,149.6	.965	14.86
1983	3,405.0	.996	10.79
1984	3,777.2	1.039	12.04
1985	4,038.7	1.076	9.93
1986	4,268.6	1.096	8.33
1987	4,539.9	1.136	8.21
1988	4,900.4	1.183	9.32
1989	5,250.8	1.240	10.87
1990	5,546.1	1.307	10.01
1991	5,722.9	1.362	8.46
1992	6,038.5	1.403	6.25
1993	6,327.6	1.445	6.00
1994	6,931.4	1.482	7.14
1995	7,247.7	1.536	8.70

Sources:

1. Gross Domestic Product from *Survey of Current Business* (March, 1996), Vol. 76, No. 3, Table 1.1, p. 7.

2. Consumer Price Index from U.S. Department of Commerce, *1992 Statistical Abstract of the United States,* 112th edition, Chart no. 738, p. 469; U.S. Bureau of Labor Statistics, *Monthly Labor Review* (January/February, 1996), Chart no. 31, p. 116.

3. Prime Interest Rates from D. S. Benton, "Banking and Financial Information," Table 1-2, p. 3, in *Thorndike Encyclopedia of Banking and Financial Tables,* 3rd ed., 1996 Yearbook (Boston: Warren, Gorham and Lamont, 1996).

10.5 ▶ Using the Strategic Audit in Case Analysis

Appendix 10.C is an example of a strategic audit proposed for use not only in strategic decision making, but also as a framework for the analysis of complex business policy cases. The questions in the audit parallel the eight steps depicted in Figure 1.2, the strategic decision making process. The **strategic audit** provides a checklist of questions, by area or issue, that enables you to make a systematic analysis of various corporate activities. It is extremely useful as a diagnostic tool to pinpoint problem areas and to highlight strengths and weaknesses. It is not an all-inclusive list, but it presents many of the critical questions that need to be addressed in the strategic analysis of any business corporation. Some questions or even some areas might be inappropriate for a particular case; in other cases, the questions may be insufficient for a complete analysis. However, each question in a particular area of the strategic audit can be broken down into an additional series of subquestions. It is up to you to develop these subquestions when they are needed.

You may also find the audit helpful in organizing a case for written or oral presentation and in seeing that all areas have been considered. The strategic audit can thus maximize your efficiency, both in analyzing why a certain area is creating problems for a corporation and in considering solutions to the problems.

In Conclusion . . .

Case study is one of the best ways to understand and remember the strategic management process. By applying the concepts and techniques you have learned to cases, you will be able to remember them long past the time when you have forgotten other memorized bits of information. The use of cases to examine actual situations brings alive the field of strategic management and helps build your analytic and decision making skills.

Discussion Questions

1. Why should you begin a case analysis with a financial analysis? When are other approaches appropriate?
2. What are common-size financial statements? What is their value to case analysis? How are they calculated?
3. When should you go to the library to gather information outside the case?

Key Terms

ratio analysis
common-size statements
Z-value
index of sustainable growth
operating cash flow
free cash flow

Consumer Price Index
constant dollars
prime interest rate
Gross Domestic Product
strategic audit

Appendix 10.A:
Suggested Techniques for
Case Analysis and Presentation

A. Case Analysis

1. Read the case to get an overview of the nature of the corporation and its environment. Note the date on which the case was written so that you can put it into proper context.
2. Read the case a second time, and give it a detailed examination according to the strategic audit (see **Appendix 10.C**) or some other framework of analysis. Regardless of the framework used, you should end up with a list of the salient issues and problems in the case. Perform a financial analysis.
3. Undertake outside research, when appropriate, to uncover economic and industrial information. **Appendix 10.B** suggests possible sources for outside research. These data should provide the environmental setting for the corporation. Conduct an in-depth analysis of the industry. Analyze the important *competitors*. Consider the bargaining power of both *suppliers* and *buyers* that might affect the firm's situation. Consider also the possible threats of *new entrants* in the industry and the likelihood of new or different products or services that might *substitute* for the company's present ones. Consider *other stakeholders* who might affect strategic decision making in the industry.
4. Compile facts and evidence to support selected issues and problems. Develop a framework or outline to organize the analysis. Consider using one of the following methods of organization:
   a) The strategic decision making process or the strategic audit.
   b) The key individual(s) in the case.
   c) The corporation's functional areas: production, management, finance, marketing, and R&D.
   d) SWOT analysis.

5. Clearly identify and state the central problem(s) as supported by the information in the case. Use the SWOT format to sum up the *strategic factors* facing the corporation: Strengths and Weaknesses of the company; Opportunities and Threats in the environment. Use the External (**EFAS**) and Internal (**IFAS**) Factor Analysis Summary matrixes as well as the Strategic Factor Analysis Summary (**SFAS**) Matrix. (**See Table 3.2 in Chapter 3 for EFAS Matrix, Table 4.2 in Chapter 4 for IFAS Matrix, and Figure 5.1 in Chapter 5 for SFAS Matrix.**)

6. Develop a logical series of mutually exclusive alternatives that evolve from the analysis to resolve the problem(s) or issue(s) in the case. One of the alternatives should be to continue the company's current strategy. Develop at least two other strategy alternatives. However, don't present three alternatives and then recommend that all three be adopted. That's one alternative presented in three parts!

7. Evaluate each of the alternatives in light of the company's environment (both external and internal), mission, objectives, strategies, and policies. Discuss pros and cons. For each alternative, consider both the possible obstacles to its implementation and its financial implications.

8. Make recommendations assuming that action must be taken regardless of whether or not needed information is available. The individuals in the case may have had the same or even less information than is given in the case.

   a) Base your recommendations on a total analysis of the case.

   b) Provide the evidence gathered earlier in **Step A4** to justify suggested changes.

   c) List the recommendations in order of priority.

   d) Show clearly how your recommendations deal with each of the *strategic factors* that were mentioned earlier in **Step A5**. How do they build on corporate *Strengths* to take advantage of environmental *Opportunities*? How do they deal with environmental *Threats* and corporate *Weaknesses*?

   e) Explain how each recommendation will be implemented. How will the plan(s) deal with anticipated resistance?

   f) Suggest feedback and control systems to ensure that the recommendations are carried out as planned and to give advance warning of needed adjustments.

B. Written Report

1. Use the outline from **Step A4** to write the first draft of the case analysis. Follow **Steps A5** through **A8**.

   a) Don't rehash the case material; rather, supply the salient evidence and data to support your analysis and recommendation.

   b) Develop exhibits on financial ratios and other data, such as strategic factors summary, for inclusion in your report. The exhibits should provide meaningful information. Reference key elements of an exhibit in the text of the written analysis. If you include a ratio analysis as an exhibit, explain the implications of the ratios in the text and cite the critical ones in your analysis.

2. Review your written case analysis for content and grammar. Compare the outline (**Step A4**) with the final product. Make sure you've presented sufficient data or evidence to support your problem analysis and recommendations. If the final product requires rewriting, do so. Keep in mind that the written report is going to be judged not only on what is said, but also on the manner in which it is said. *Style, grammar, and spelling are just as important as the content in a written case analysis!*

3. If your written report requires pro forma statements, you may wish to develop a scenario for each year in your forecast. A well-constructed *corporate scenario* helps improve the accuracy of your forecast. (**See Chapter 6 for corporate scenario construction.**)

C. Oral Presentation by Teams

1. The team should first decide on a framework or outline for analysis, as mentioned in **Step A4**. Although teams often divide the analysis work, each team member should follow **Steps A5** through **A8** to develop a preliminary analysis of the entire case and share it with team members.

2. The team should combine member input into one consolidated team analysis, including SWOT analysis, alternatives, and recommendation(s). Obtain agreement on the strategic factors and the best alternative(s) to support.

3. Divide further development and presentation of the case analysis and recommendation(s). Agree on responsibilities for the preparation of visual aids and handouts. As in written reports, scenarios and pro forma financial statements should support any recommendation.

4. Modify the team outline, if necessary, and have one or two rehearsals of the presentation. If exhibits are used, make sure to allow sufficient time to explain them. Check to ensure that any visual aids can be easily seen from the back of the room. Critique one another's presentations and make the necessary modifications to the analysis. Again, *style, grammar, and delivery are just as important in an oral presentation as is content!*

5. Begin your presentation by handing out a copy of the agenda specifying not only the topics to be covered, but also who will deal with each topic area. Introduce yourselves. Dress appropriately. If a presenter misses a key fact during the class presentation, deal with it in the summary speech.

6. Encourage questions from both the instructor and classmates. Begin the questioning period by calling on someone you consider a friend who can be expected to ask a question you can easily field to get you off to a good start. You may want to have one person act as a moderator who refers questions to the appropriate team member.

Appendix 10.B:
Resources for Case Library Research

A. Company Information

1. Annual Reports.
2. *Moody's Manuals on Investment* (a listing of companies within certain industries that contains a brief history and a five-year financial statement of each company).
3. Securities and Exchange Commission Annual *Report Form 10-K* (annually) and *Report Form 10-Q* (quarterly).
4. Standard and Poor's *Register of Corporations, Directors, and Executives.*
5. Value Line *Investment Survey.*
6. *Findex: The Directory of Market Research Reports, Studies and Surveys* (a listing by Find/SVP of over 11,000 studies conducted by leading research firms).
7. COMPUSTAT, *Compact Disclosure, CD/International,* and *Hoover's Online Corporate Directory* (computerized operating and financial information on thousands of publicly held corporations).

B. Economic Information

1. Regional statistics and local forecasts from large banks.
2. *Business Cycle Development* (Department of Commerce).
3. Chase Econometric Associates' publications.
4. U.S. Census Bureau publications on population, transportation, and housing.
5. *Current Business Reports* (U.S. Department of Commerce).
6. *Economic Indicators* (U.S. Joint Economic Committee).
7. *Economic Report of the President to Congress.*
8. *Long-Term Economic Growth* (U.S. Department of Commerce).

9. *Monthly Labor Review* (U.S. Department of Labor).
10. *Monthly Bulletin of Statistics* (United Nations).
11. *Statistical Abstract of the United States* (U.S. Department of Commerce).
12. *Statistical Yearbook* (United Nations).
13. *Survey of Current Business* (U.S. Department of Commerce).
14. *U.S. Industrial Outlook* (U.S. Department of Defense).
15. *World Trade Annual* (United Nations).
16. *Overseas Business Reports* (by country, published by U.S. Department of Commerce).

C. Industry Information

1. Analyses of companies and industries by investment brokerage firms.
2. *Business Week* (provides weekly economic and business information, and quarterly profit and sales rankings of corporations).
3. *Fortune* (each April publishes listings of financial information on corporations within certain industries).
4. *Industry Survey* (published quarterly by Standard and Poor's Corporation).
5. *Industry Week* (late March/early April issue provides information on 14 industry groups).
6. *Forbes* (mid-January issue provides performance data on firms in various industries).
7. *Inc.* (May and December issues give information on small companies).

D. Directory and Index Information on Companies and Industries

1. *Business Periodical Index* (on computer in many libraries).
2. *Directory of National Trade Associations*.
3. *Encyclopedia of Associations*.
4. Funk and Scott *Index of Corporations and Industries*.
5. Thomas's *Register of American Manufacturers*.
6. *Wall Street Journal Index*.

E. Ratio Analysis Information

1. *Almanac of Business and Industrial Financial Ratios* (Prentice Hall).
2. *Annual Statement Studies* (Robert Morris Associates).
3. *Dun's Review* (Dun and Bradstreet; published annually in September–December issues).
4. *Industry Norms and Key Business Ratios* (Dun and Bradstreet).

Appendix 10.C:
Strategic Audit of a Corporation

I. Current Situation

A. Performance
See Section 9.2 on pages 164–166.

How is the corporation performing in terms of return on investment, overall market share, profitability trends, earnings per share, etc.?

B. Strategic Posture
See Section 1.3 on pages 6–9.

What are the corporation's current mission, objectives, strategies, and policies?

1. Are they clearly stated or are they merely implied from performance?
2. **Mission:** What business(es) is the corporation in? Why?
3. **Objectives:** What are the corporate, business, and functional objectives? Are they consistent with each other, with the mission, and with the internal and external environments?
4. **Strategies:** What strategy or mix of strategies is the corporation following? Are they consistent with each other, with the mission and objectives, and with the internal and external environments?
5. **Policies:** What are they? Are they consistent with each other; with the mission, objectives, and strategies; and with the internal and external environments?
6. Do the current mission, objectives, strategies, and policies reflect the corporation's international operations?

Source: T. L. Wheelen and J. D. Hunger, "Strategic Audit of a Corporation." Copyright © 1982 by Wheelen and Hunger Associates. Reprinted by permission. Revised 1988, 1991, 1994, and 1996.

II. Strategic Managers

A. Board of Directors   See Section 2.1 on pages 19–25.

1. Who are they? Are they internal or external?
2. Do they own significant shares of stock?
3. Is the stock privately held or publicly traded?
4. What do they contribute to the corporation in terms of knowledge, skills, background, and connections? If the corporation has international operations, do board members have international experience?
5. How long have they served on the board?
6. What is their level of involvement in strategic management? (See **Figure 2.1 on page 21.**) Do they merely rubber-stamp top management's proposals or do they actively participate and suggest future directions?

B. Top Management   See Sections 2.2 and 2.3 on pages 25–31.

1. What person or group constitutes top management?
2. What are top management's chief characteristics in terms of knowledge, skills, background, and style? If the corporation has international operations, does top management have international experience?
3. Has top management been responsible for the corporation's performance over the past few years?
4. Has it established a systematic approach to the formulation, implementation, and evaluation and control of strategic management?
5. What is its level of involvement in the strategic management process?
6. How well does top management interact with lower level management and with the board of directors?
7. Are strategic decisions made in a socially responsible manner?
8. Is top management sufficiently skilled to cope with likely future challenges?

III. External Environment: Opportunities and Threats (S.W.<u>O</u>.T.)

A. Societal Environment   See Section 3.1 on pages 35–40.

1. What general environmental factors among the *sociocultural*, *economic*, *political-legal*, and *technological* forces are currently affecting both the corporation and the industries in which it competes? Which present current or future threats? Opportunities?

B. Task Environment/Industry Analysis   See Section 3.2 on pages 40–50.

1. What forces drive industry competition?
   a. threat of new entrants
   b. bargaining power of buyers
   c. threat of substitute products or services
   d. bargaining power of suppliers
   e. rivalry among competing firms
   f. relative power of unions, governments, special interest groups, etc.
2. What key factors in the immediate environment (that is, *customers, competitors, suppliers, creditors, labor unions, governments, trade associations, interest groups, local communities,* and *stockholders*) are currently affecting the corporation? Which present current or future threats? Opportunities?

C. Summary of External Factors

Which of these forces and factors are the most important to the corporation and to the industries in which it competes at the present time? Which will be important in the future? (See EFAS Matrix in Table 3.2 on page 78.)

IV. Internal Environment: Strengths and Weaknesses (S.W.O.T.)

A. Corporate Structure   See Sections 4.2 and 7.4 on pages 60–61 and 133–136.

1. How is the corporation structured at present?
   a. Is the decision-making authority centralized around one group or decentralized to many groups or units?
   b. Is it organized on the basis of functions, projects, geography, or some combination of these?
2. Is the structure clearly understood by everyone in the corporation?
3. Is the present structure consistent with current corporate objectives, strategies, policies, and programs?
4. In what ways does this structure compare with those of similar corporations?

B. Corporate Culture   See Section 4.2 on page 62.

1. Is there a well-defined or emerging culture composed of shared beliefs, expectations, and values?
2. Is the culture consistent with the current objectives, strategies, policies, and programs?

3. What is the culture's position on important issues facing the corporation (that is, on productivity, quality of performance, adaptability to changing conditions)?

4. Is the culture compatible with the employees' diversity of backgrounds?

C. Corporate Resources

1. Marketing — See Section 4.2 on pages 63–64.

a. What are the corporation's current marketing objectives, strategies, policies, and programs?
  i) Are they clearly stated, or merely implied from performance and/or budgets?
  ii) Are they consistent with the corporation's mission, objectives, strategies, policies, and with internal and external environments?
b. How well is the corporation performing in terms of analysis of market position and marketing mix (that is, product, price, place, and promotion)? **See Table 4.1 on page 64.**
  i) What trends emerge from this analysis?
  ii) What impact have these trends had on past performance and how will they probably affect future performance?
  iii) Does this analysis support the corporation's past and pending strategic decisions?
  iv) Does marketing provide the company with a competitive advantage?
c. How well does this corporation's marketing performance compare with those of similar corporations?
d. Are marketing managers using accepted marketing concepts and techniques to evaluate and improve product performance? (Consider *product life cycle, market segmentation, market research,* and *product portfolios.*)
e. What is the role of the marketing manager in the strategic management process?

2. Finance — See Sections 4.2 and 10.4 on pages 64–65 and 179–185.

a. What are the corporation's current financial objectives, strategies, policies, and programs?
  i) Are they clearly stated or merely implied from performance and/or budgets?
  ii) Are they consistent with the corporation's mission, objectives, strategies, policies, and with internal and external environments?
b. How well is the corporation performing in terms of financial analysis? (Consider *liquidity ratios, profitability ratios, activity ratios, leverage ratios, capitalization structure,* and *constant dollars.*)

       i) What trends emerge from this analysis?

       ii) Are there any significant differences when statements are calculated in constant versus reported dollars?

       iii) What impact have these trends had on past performance and how will they probably affect future performance?

       iv) Does this analysis support the corporation's past and pending strategic decisions?

       v) Does finance provide the company with a competitive advantage?

    c. How well does this corporation's financial performance compare with that of similar corporations?

    d. Are financial managers using accepted financial concepts and techniques to evaluate and improve current corporate and divisional performance? (Consider *financial leverage*, *capital budgeting*, and *ratio analysis*.)

    e. What is the role of the financial manager in the strategic management process?

3. Research and Development (R&D)   See Section 4.2 on pages 66–67.

    a. What are the corporation's current R&D objectives, strategies, policies, and programs?

       i) Are they clearly stated or are they implied from performance and/or budgets?

       ii) Are they consistent with the corporation's mission, objectives, strategies, policies, and with internal and external environments?

       iii) What is the role of technology in corporate performance?

       iv) Is the mix of basic, applied, and engineering research appropriate given the corporate mission and strategies?

       v) Does R&D provide the company with a competitive advantage?

    b. What return is the corporation receiving from its investment in R&D?

    c. Is the corporation technologically competent?

    d. What role does technological discontinuity play in the company's products?

    e. How well does the corporation's investment in R&D compare with the investments of similar corporations?

    f. What is the role of the R&D manager in the strategic management process?

4. Operations (Manufacturing/Service)   See Section 4.2 on pages 67–70.

    a. What are the corporation's current manufacturing/service objectives, strategies, policies, and programs?

       i) Are they clearly stated or are they merely implied from performance and/or budgets?

       ii) Are they consistent with the corporation's mission, objectives, strategies, policies, and with internal and external environments?

b. What is the type and extent of operations capabilities of the corporation?

i) If product oriented, consider plant facilities, type of manufacturing system (*continuous mass production*, *intermittent job shop*, or *flexible manufacturing*), age and type of equipment, degree and role of automation and/or robots, plant capacities and utilization, productivity ratings, and availability and type of transportation.

ii) If service oriented, consider service facilities (e.g., hospital, theater, or school buildings), type of operations systems (continuous service over time to same clientele or intermittent service over time to varied clientele), age and type of supporting equipment, degree and role of automation and/or use of mass communication devices (e.g., diagnostic machinery, videotape machines), facility capacities and utilization rates, efficiency ratings of professional/service personnel, and availability and type of transportation to bring service staff and clientele together.

c. Are manufacturing or service facilities vulnerable to natural disasters, local or national strikes, reduction or limitation of resources from suppliers, substantial cost increases of materials, or nationalization by governments?

d. Is operating leverage being used successfully with an appropriate mix of people and machines, in manufacturing firms, or of support staff to professionals, in service firms?

e. How well does the corporation perform relative to the competition? Consider costs per unit of labor, material, and overhead; downtime; inventory control management and/or scheduling of service staff; production ratings; facility utilization percentages; and number of clients successfully treated by category (if service firm), or percentage of orders shipped on time (if product firm).

i) What trends emerge from this analysis?

ii) What impact have these trends had on past performance and how will they probably affect future performance?

iii) Does this analysis support the corporation's past and pending strategic decisions?

iv) Does operations provide the company with a competitive advantage?

f. Are operations managers using appropriate concepts and techniques to evaluate and improve current performance? Consider cost systems, quality control and reliability systems, inventory control management, personnel scheduling, learning curves, safety programs, and engineering programs that can improve efficiency of manufacturing or of service.

g. What is the role of the operations manager in the strategic management process?

5. Human Resources Management (HRM)   See Section 4.2 on pages 70–72.

a. What are the corporation's current HRM objectives, strategies, policies, and programs?

    i) Are they clearly stated or are they merely implied from performance and/or budgets?

    ii) Are they consistent with the corporation's mission, objectives, strategies, policies, and with internal and external environments?

b. How well is the corporation's HRM performing in terms of improving the fit between the individual employee and the job? Consider turnover, grievances, strikes, layoffs, employee training, and quality of work life.

    i) What trends emerge from this analysis?

    ii) What impact have these trends had on past performance and how will they probably affect future performance?

    iii) Does this analysis support the corporation's past and pending strategic decisions?

    iv) Does HRM provide the company with a competitive advantage?

c. How does this corporation's HRM performance compare with that of similar corporations?

d. Are HRM managers using appropriate concepts and techniques to evaluate and improve corporate performance? Consider the *job analysis program, performance appraisal system, up-to-date job descriptions, training and development programs, attitude surveys, job design programs,* and *quality of relationship with unions.*

e. How well is the company managing the diversity of its work force?

f. What is the role of the HRM manager in the strategic management process?

6. Information Systems (IS)   See Section 4.2 on page 72.

a. What are the corporation's current IS objectives, strategies, policies, and programs?

    i) Are they clearly stated or are they merely implied from performance and/or budgets?

    ii) Are they consistent with the corporation's mission, objectives, strategies, policies, and with internal and external environments?

b. How well is the corporation's IS performing in terms of providing a useful database, automating routine clerical operations, assisting managers in making routine decisions, and providing information necessary for strategic decisions?

    i) What trends emerge from this analysis?

    ii) What impact have these trends had on past performance and how will they probably affect future performance?

    iii) Does this analysis support the corporation's past and pending strategic decisions?

    iv) Does IS provide the company with a competitive advantage?

c. How does this corporation's IS performance and stage of development compare with that of similar corporations?

d. Are IS managers using appropriate concepts and techniques to evaluate and improve corporate performance? Do they know how to build and manage a complex database, conduct system analyses, and implement interactive decision-support systems?

e. What is the role of the IS manager in the strategic management process?

D. Summary of Internal Factors

Which of these factors and resources are the most important at the present time? Which will be important in the future? (**See IFAS Matrix in Table 4.2 on page 74.**)

V. Analysis of Strategic Factors (SWOT)   See Sections 5.1 and 5.2 on pages 76–81.

A. What are the most important internal and external factors (**Strengths, Weaknesses, Opportunities, Threats**) that strongly affect the corporation's present and future performance? List eight to ten **strategic factors**. (**See IFAS Matrix in Figure 5.1 on page 79.**)

B. Are the current mission and objectives appropriate in light of the key strategic factors and problems?

1. Should the mission and objectives be changed? If so, how?

2. If changed, what will the effects on the firm be?

VI. Strategic Alternatives and Recommended Strategy   See Sections 5.3, 6.1, and 6.2 on pages 81–98 and 101–114.

A. Strategic Alternatives

1. Can the current or revised objectives be met by the simple, more careful implementing of those strategies presently in use (for example, fine tuning the strategies)?

2. What are the major feasible alternative strategies available to this corporation? What are the pros and cons of each? Can corporate scenarios be developed and agreed upon?

a. Consider *stability, growth,* and *retrenchment* as corporate strategies. (See Section 5.3 on pages 81–98.)

b. Consider *cost leadership* and *differentiation* as business/competitive strategies. (See Section 6.1 on pages 101–109.)

c. Consider any functional strategic alternatives that might be needed to reinforce an important corporate or business strategic alternative. (See Section 6.2 on pages 109–114.

B. Recommended Strategy

1. Specify which of the strategic alternatives you are recommending for the corporate, business, and functional levels of the corporation. Do you recommend different business or functional strategies for different units of the corporation?
2. Justify your recommendation in terms of its ability to resolve both long- and short-term problems and effectively deal with the strategic factors.
3. What **policies** should be developed or revised to guide effective implementation? (See Section 6.5 on page 121.)

VII. Implementation   See Chapters 7 and 8.

A. What kinds of **programs** (for example, restructuring the corporation or instituting TQM) should be developed to implement the recommended strategy?

1. Who should develop these programs?
2. Who should be in charge of these programs?

B. Are the programs financially feasible? Can pro forma **budgets** be developed and agreed upon? Are priorities and timetables appropriate to individual programs?

C. Will new standard operating **procedures** need to be developed?

VIII. Evaluation and Control   See Chapter 9.

A. Is the current information system capable of providing sufficient feedback on implementation activities and performance?

1. Can performance results be pinpointed by area, unit, project, or function?
2. Is the information timely?

B. Are adequate control measures to ensure conformance with the recommended strategic plan in place?

1. Are appropriate standards and measures being used?
2. Are reward systems capable of recognizing and rewarding good performance?

Chapter 1

1. T. L. O'Brien, "Beleaguered Schwinn Seeks Partner to Regain Its Luster," *Wall Street Journal* (May 20, 1992), p. B2.
2. S. D. Atchison, "Pump, Pump, Pump at Schwinn," *Business Week* (August 23, 1993), p. 79.
3. B. Lancaster, "American Hospital's Marketing Program Places Company Atop a Troubled Industry," *Wall Street Journal* (August 24, 1984), p. 19.
4. F. W. Gluck, S. P. Kaufman, and A. S. Walleck, "The Four Phases of Strategic Management," *Journal of Business Strategy* (Winter 1982), pp. 9–21.
5. K. G. Smith, and C. M. Grimm, "Environmental Variation, Strategic Change and Firm Performance: A Study of Railroad Deregulation," *Strategic Management Journal* (July–August 1987), pp. 363–376.
6. H. Mintzberg, "Planning on the Left Side and Managing on the Right," *Harvard Business Review* (July–August 1976), p. 56.
7. D. J. Hickson, R. J. Butler, D. Cray, G. R. Mallory, and D. C. Wilson, *Top Decisions: Strategic Decision-Making in Organizations* (San Francisco: Jossey-Bass, 1986), pp. 26–42.
8. H. Mintzberg, "Strategy-Making in Three Modes," *California Management Review* (Winter 1973), pp. 44–53.
9. J. B. Quinn, *Strategies for Change: Logical Incrementalism* (Homewood, Ill.: Irwin, 1980), p. 58.
10. F. A. Maljers, "Strategic Planning and Intuition at Unilever," *Long Range Planning* (April 1990), p. 63.
11. Atchison, "Pump, Pump, Pump at Schwinn," p. 79.

Chapter 2

1. J. A. Kidney, *Eastman Kodak Company* (December 5, 1995).
2. J. H. Dobrzynski, "These Board Members Aren't IBM-Compatible," *Business Week* (August 2, 1992), p. 23.
3. A. Demb, and F. F. Neubauer, "The Corporate Board: Confronting the Paradoxes," *Long Range Planning* (June 1992), p. 13.
4. W. Q. Judge, Jr., and C. P. Zeithaml, "Institutional and Strategic Choice Perspectives on Board Involvement in the Strategic Decision Process," *Academy of Management Journal* (October 1992), pp. 766–794.
5. R. M. Ferry, *Board of Directors Twentieth Annual Study: 1993* (New York: Korn/Ferry International, 1993), pp. 1–2.
6. J. A. C. Baum, and C. Oliver, "Institutional Linkages and Organizational Mortality," *Administrative Science Quarterly* (June 1991), pp. 187–218.
7. P. L. Rechner, and D. R. Dalton, "CEO Duality and Organizational Performance: A Longitudinal Analysis," *Strategic Management Journal* (February 1991), pp. 155–160; P. L. Rechner, and D. R. Dalton, "The Link Between Financial Performance and Board Leadership Structure," *Handbook of Business Strategy, 1992/93 Yearbook*, edited by H. E. Glass and M. A. Hovde (Boston: Warren, Gorham, and Lamont, 1992), pp. 20.1–20.7.
8. H. Mintzberg, *The Nature of Managerial Work* (New York: HarperCollins, 1973), pp. 54–94.
9. N. Tichy, and R. Charan, "Speed, Simplicity, Self-Confidence: An Interview with Jack Welch," *Harvard Business Review* (September–October 1989), p. 113.
10. M. Friedman, "The Social Responsibility of Business Is to Increase Its Profits," *New York Times Magazine* (September 13, 1970), pp. 30, 126–127; and *Capitalism and Freedom* (Chicago: University of Chicago Press, 1963), p. 133.
11. A. B. Carroll, "A Three-Dimensional Conceptual Model of Corporate Performance," *Academy of Management Review* (October 1979), pp. 497–505.
12. P. Rechner, and K. Roth, "Social Responsibility and Financial Performance: A Structural Equation Methodology," *International Journal of Management* (December 1990), pp. 382–391; K. E. Aupperle, A. B. Carroll, and J. D. Hatfield, "An Empirical Examination of the Relationship Between Corporate Social Responsibility and Profitability," *Academy of Management Journal* (June 1985), p. 459.
13. K. Anderson, "The Purpose at the Heart of Management," *Harvard Business Review* (May–June 1992), pp. 52–62.

Chapter 3

1. L. M. Grossman, "Families Have Changed But Tupperware Keeps Holding Its Parties,"

Wall Street Journal (July 21, 1992), pp. A1, A13.

2. J. B. Thomas, S. M. Clark, and D. A. Gioia, "Strategic Sensemaking and Organizational Performance: Linkages Among Scanning, Interpretation, Action, and Outcomes," *Academy of Management Journal* (April 1993), pp. 239–270.

3. M. Charlier, "U.S. Ski Resorts Stress Family Values," *Wall Street Journal* (November 20, 1992), p. B1.

4. M. Mallory, and S. Anderson, "Waking Up to a Major Market," *Business Week* (March 23, 1992), pp. 70–73.

5. D. A. Szymanski, "Six Trends That Will Drive Businesses in the 90s," *Tampa* (Fl) *Tribune* (November 5, 1990), pp. 10D–11D.

6. K. Ohmae, "The Triad World View," *Journal of Business Strategy* (Spring 1987), pp. 8–19.

7. M. E. Porter, *Competitive Strategy* (New York: Free Press, 1980), p. 3.

8. This summary of the forces driving competitive strategy is taken from Porter, *Competitive Strategy*, pp. 7–29.

9. Ibid., p. 23.

10. M. E. Porter, "Changing Patterns of International Competition," *California Management Review* (Winter 1986), pp. 9–40.

11. K. J. Hatten, and M. L. Hatten, "Strategic Groups, Asymmetrical Mobility Barriers, and Contestability," *Strategic Management Journal* (July–August 1987), p. 329.

12. R. E. Miles, and C. C. Snow, *Organizational Strategy, Structure, and Process* (New York: McGraw-Hill, 1978).

13. R. T. Pascale, "Perspective on Strategy: The Real Story Behind Honda's Success," *California Management Review* (Spring 1981), p. 70.

14. J. P. Herring, "Scientific and Technical Intelligence: The Key to R & D," *Journal of Business Strategy* (May–June 1993), pp. 10–12; J. P. Herring, "Business Intelligence in Japan and Sweden: Lessons for the U.S.," *Journal of Business Strategy* (March–April 1992), pp. 44–49.

15. H. E. Klein, and R. E. Linneman, "Environmental Assessment: An International Study of Corporate Practices," *Journal of Business Strategy* (Summer 1984), p. 72.

16. This process of scenario development is adapted from M. E. Porter, *Competitive Advantage* (New York: Free Press, 1985), pp. 448–470.

17. Taken from B. Marsh, "Merchants Mobilize to Battle Wal-Mart in a Small Community," *Wall Street Journal* (June 5, 1991), pp. A1, A4; L. Pasquarella, "Study: Wal-Mart Has Varied Effects on Towns," *The* (Ames, Ia) *Daily Tribune* (March 1, 1993), p. C13.

Chapter 4

1. L. Ingrassia, "Gillette Holds Its Edge by Endlessly Searching for a Better Shave," *Wall Street Journal* (December 10, 1992), pp. A1, A6.

2. R. M. Grant, "The Resource-Based Theory of Competitive Advantage: Implications for Strategy Formulation." *California Management Review* (Spring 1991), pp. 114–135.

3. D. M. Rousseau, "Assessing Organizational Culture: The Case for Multiple Methods," in *Organizational Climate and Culture*, edited by B. Schneider (San Francisco: Jossey-Bass, 1990), pp. 153–192. Quotes are taken from pp. 181–182.

4. L. Smircich, "Concepts of Culture and Organizational Analysis," *Administrative Science Quarterly* (September 1983), pp. 345–346.

5. P. Pascarella, "Are You Investing in the Wrong Technology?" *Industry Week* (July 25, 1983), p. 37.

6. Ibid., p. 38.

7. J. S. Lublin, "Trying to Increase Worker Productivity, More Employees Alter Management Style," *Wall Street Journal* (February 13, 1992), p. B1.

8. A. Versteeg, "Self-Directed Work Teams Yield Long-Term Benefits," *Journal of Business Strategy* (November–December 1990), pp. 9–12.

9. D. Milbank, "Unions' Woes Suggest How the Labor Force in U.S. Is Shifting," *Wall Street Journal* (May 5, 1992), p. A1, A4; G. Koretz, "Why Unions Thrive Abroad—But Wither in the U.S." *Business Week* (September 10, 1990), p. 26.

10. J. G. Sifonis, "Mining for Gold in Your Information Systems," *Directors and Boards* (Summer 1989), p. 23.

Chapter 5

1. R. D. Hof, "Hewlett-Packard Digs Deep for a Digital Future," *Business Week* (October 18, 1993), pp. 72–75.
2. W. H. Newman, "Shaping the Master Strategy of Your Firm," *California Management Review*, Vol. 9, No. 3 (1967), pp. 77–88.
3. K. Kelly, "Henry Schacht," *The 1993 Business Week 1000* (1993), p. 80.
4. J. B. White, and C. Chandler, "Pressed by All Sides, Hard-Driving Toyota Trims Back Its Goals," *Wall Street Journal* (May 19, 1992), p. A1.
5. L. Armstrong, "Packard Bell Discovers a Bon Ami," *Business Week* (July 5, 1993), pp. 103–106.
6. J. B. Treece, "U.S. Parts Makers Just Won't Say 'Uncle,'" *Business Week* (August 10, 1987), pp. 76–77.
7. D. K. Sinha, "Strategic Planning in the Fortune 500," in *Handbook of Business Strategy, 1991/92 Yearbook*, edited by H. E. Glass and M. A. Hovde (Boston: Warren, Gorham & Lamont, 1991), p. 9.6.
8. B. Hedley, "Strategy and the Business Portfolio," *Long Range Planning* (February 1977), p. 9.
9. R. G. Hamermesh, *Making Strategy Work* (New York: John Wiley & Sons, 1986), p. 14. For a more complete list of characteristics, see McNamee, "Competitive Analysis," pp. 102–103.
10. J. J. Curran, "Companies That Rob the Future," *Fortune* (July 4, 1988), p. 84.

Chapter 6

1. M. E. Porter, *Competitive Strategy* (New York: The Free Press, 1980), pp. 34–41 as revised in M. E. Porter, *The Competitive Advantage of Nations* (New York: The Free Press, 1990), pp. 37–40.
2. Porter, *Competitive Strategy*, p. 35.
3. R. E. Caves, and P. Ghemawat, "Identifying Mobility Barriers," *Strategic Management Journal* (January 1992), pp. 1–12.
4. Summarized from various articles by L. Fahey in *The Strategic Management Reader*, edited by L. Fahey (Englewood Cliffs, N.J.: Prentice Hall, 1989), pp. 178–205.

5. This information on defensive tactics is summarized from M. E. Porter, *Competitive Advantage* (New York: Free Press, 1985), pp. 482–512.
6. J. B. Quinn, "The Intelligent Enterprise: A New Paradigm," *Academy of Management Executive* (November 1992), pp. 48–63.
7. W. Redmond, "The Strategic Pricing of Innovative Products," in *Handbook of Business Strategy, 1992/1993 Yearbook*, edited by H. E. Glass and M. A. Hovde (Boston: Warren, Gorham & Lamont, 1992), pp. 16.1–16.13.
8. R. H. Hayes, and S. C. Wheelwright, *Restoring Our Competitive Edge: Competing Through Manufacturing* (New York: John Wiley and Sons, 1984).
9. M. Cadden, and B. Laird, "Rising Market for Temps," *USA Today* (May 8, 1995), p. B1.
10. B. Dumaine, "Who Needs a Boss?" *Fortune* (May 7, 1990), pp. 52–60.
11. D. K. Sinha, "Strategic Planning in the Fortune 500," in *Handbook of Business Strategy, 1991/92 Yearbook*, edited by H. E. Glass and M. A. Hovde (Boston: Warren, Gorham & Lamont, 1991), pp. 9.6–9.8.
12. R. A. Cosier, and C. R. Schwenk, "Agreement and Thinking Alike: Ingredients for Poor Decisions," *Academy of Management Executive* (February 1990), p. 69.
13. S. Poe, "To Compete with Giants, Choose Your Niche," *Nation's Business* (July 1992), p. 6.

Chapter 7

1. L. D. Alexander, "Strategy Implementation: Nature of the Problem," in *International Review of Strategic Management*, Vol. 2, No. 1, edited by D. E. Hussey (New York: John Wiley & Sons, 1991), pp. 73–113.
2. A. D. Chandler, *Strategy and Structure* (Cambridge, Mass.: MIT Press, 1962).
3. A. P. Sloan, Jr., *My Years with General Motors* (Garden City, N.Y.: Doubleday, 1964).
4. A. K. Gupta, "SBU Strategies, Corporate-SBU Relations, and SBU Effectiveness in Strategy Implementation," *Academy of Management Journal* (September 1987), pp. 477–500.

5. L. E. Greiner, "Evolution and Revolution as Organizations Grow," *Harvard Business Review* (July–August 1972), pp. 37–46.

6. M. Leontiades, "A Diagnostic Framework for Planning," *Strategic Management Journal* (January–March 1983), p. 14.

7. L. G. Hrebiniak, and W. F. Joyce, *Implementing Strategy* (New York: Macmillan, 1984), pp. 85–86.

8. Summarized from M. Hammer, "Reengineering Work: Don't Automate, Obliterate," *Harvard Business Review* (July–August 1990), pp. 104–112.

9. T. A. Stewart, "Reengineering: The Hot New Managing Tool," *Fortune* (August 23, 1993), pp. 41–42.

10. J. R. Hackman, and G. R. Oldham, *Work Redesign* (Reading, Mass.: Addison-Wesley, 1980), pp. 135–141.

11. J. Hoerr, "Sharpening Minds for a Competitive Edge," *Business Week* (December 17, 1990), pp. 72–78.

12. K. Deveny, "Man Walked on the Moon but Man Can't Make Enough Devil's Food Cookie Cakes," *Wall Street Journal* (September 28, 1993), pp. B1, B12.

Chapter 8

1. J. Magidson, and A. E. Polcha, "Creating Market Economies within Organizations: A Conference on 'Internal Markets'," *Planning Review* (January–February 1992), p. 39.

2. J. Hoerr, "Sharpening Minds for a Competitive Edge," *Business Week* (December 17, 1990), pp. 72–78.

3. R. Henkoff, "Companies That Train Best," *Fortune* (March 22, 1993), pp. 62–75.

4. M. Smith, and M. C. White, "Strategy, CEO Specialization, and Succession," *Administrative Science Quarterly* (June 1987), pp. 263–280.

5. R. F. Vancil, *Passing the Baton* (Boston: Harvard Business School Press, 1987).

6. P. Lorange, and D. Murphy, "Bringing Human Resources into Strategic Planning: System Design Characteristics," in *Strategic Human Resource Management*, edited by C. J. Fombrun, N. M. Tichy, and M. A. Devanna (New York: John Wiley & Sons, 1984), pp. 281–283.

7. R. A. Pitts, "Strategies and Structures for Diversification," *Academy of Management Journal* (June 1977), pp. 197–208.

8. B. O'Reilly, "Is Your Company Asking Too Much?" *Fortune* (March 12, 1990), p. 41.

9. R. L. Tung, *The New Expatriates* (Cambridge, Mass.: Ballinger, 1988); J. S. Black, M. Mendenhall, and G. Oddou, "Toward a Comprehensive Model of International Adjustment: An Integration of Multiple Theoretical Perspectives," *Academy of Management Review* (April 1991), pp. 291–317.

10. G. G. Gordon, "The Relationship of Corporate Culture to Industry Sector and Corporate Performance," in *Gaining Control of the Corporate Culture*, edited by R. H. Kilmann, M. J. Saxton, R. Serpa, and Associates (San Francisco: Jossey-Bass, 1985), p. 123.

11. A. R. Malekzadeh, and A. Nahavandi, "Making Mergers Work by Managing Cultures," *Journal of Business Strategy* (May–June 1990), pp. 53–57; A. Nahavandi, and A. R. Malekzadeh, "Acculturation in Mergers and Acquisitions," *Academy of Management Review* (January 1988), pp. 79–90.

12. R. J. Schonberger, "Total Quality Management Cuts a Broad Swath—Through Manufacturing and Beyond," *Organizational Dynamics* (Spring 1992), pp. 16–28.

13. G. Hofstede, *Cultures and Organizations: Software of the Mind* (London: McGraw-Hill, 1991); G. Hofstede, and M. H. Bond, "The Confucius Connection: From Cultural Roots to Economic Growth," *Organizational Dynamics* (Spring 1988), pp. 5–21.

14. Hofstede and Bond, "The Confucius Connection," p. 20.

15. M. Baechler, "Tom Peters Ruined My Life," *Wall Street Journal* (October 25, 1993), p. A18.

Chapter 9

1. P. B. Carroll, "The Failures of Central Planning—at IBM," *Wall Street Journal* (January 28, 1993), p. A14.

2. S. Tully, "The Real Key to Creating Wealth," *Fortune* (September 20, 1993), p. 38.

3. J. S. Lublin, "Corporate Chiefs Polish Their Relations with Directors," *Wall Street Journal* (October 15, 1993), p. B1.

4. H. Rothman, "You Need Not Be Big to Benchmark," *Nation's Business* (December 1992), p. 64.

5. G. Fuchsberg, "Here's Help in Finding Corporate Role Models," *Wall Street Journal* (June 1, 1993), p. B1.

6. R. M. Hodgetts, and M. S. Wortman, *Administrative Policy*, 2nd ed. (New York: John Wiley & Sons, 1980), p. 128.

7. D. R. Schmidt, and K. L. Fowler, "Post-Acquisition Financial Performance and Executive Compensation," *Strategic Management Journal* (November–December 1990), pp. 559–569.

8. T. J. Peters, and R. H. Waterman, *In Search of Excellence* (New York: HarperCollins, 1982), pp. 75–76.

9. D. B. Balkin, and L. R. Gomez-Mejia, "Matching Compensation and Organizational Strategies," *Strategic Management Journal* (February 1990), pp. 153–169.

10. P. J. Stonich, "The Performance Measurement and Reward System: Critical to Strategic Management," *Organizational Dynamics* (Winter 1984), pp. 45–57.

11. Rothman, "You Need Not Be Big to Benchmark," p. 64.

Chapter 10

1. M. S. Fridson, *Financial Statement Analysis* (New York: John Wiley & Sons, 1991), pp. 192–194.

2. D. H. Bangs, *Managing by the Numbers* (Dover, N.H.: Upstart Publications, 1992), pp. 106–107.

3. J. M. Laderman, "Earnings, Schmernings—Look at the Cash," *Business Week* (July 24, 1989), pp. 56–57.